A PRACTICAL GUIDE TO THE

CONSERVATION AND CARE OF COLLECTIONS

A PRACTICAL GUIDE TO THE

CONSERVATION AND CARE OF COLLECTIONS

EDITED BY

DAVID GILROY AND IAN GODFREY

Western Australian museum

Disclaimer

The Western Australian Museum does not accept any responsibility for the use of materials and methods described herein. The information is advisory only and use of the materials and methods is solely at the risk of the user.

The National Library of Australia
Cataloguing-in-Publication entry:

Conservation and care of collections

Includes index.
ISBN 0 7307 1215 X.

1. Museum conservation methods. I. Gilroy, David.
II. Godfrey, Ian. III. Western Australian Museum.

069.53

Edited by David Gilroy and Ian Godfrey

Published and printed by the Western Australian Museum
Francis Street, Perth, Western Australia 6000

Photography by Jon Carpenter and David Gilroy
unless otherwise acknowledged

Cover designed by Robyn Mundy Design
Cover and colour pages printed by Frank Daniels Pty. Ltd.
158 Wellington Street, Perth, Western Australia
Cover photographs by members of the Materials Conservation Department

FOREWORD

The aim of compiling *A Practical Guide to the Conservation and Care of Collections* is to provide a basis for an holistic approach to the care and conservation of movable cultural material held in small museums, National Trust houses, historical societies and private collections. The layout and content is designed with these client groups in mind. As such, it is not intended to be the definitive conservation manual. The publication is concerned specifically with the objects and images found in the targeted collections and does not attempt to comment on or categorise heritage sites or buildings.

Information has been presented on a range of levels suitable to both institutions and individuals.

The chapter layouts are designed to provide a breadth of information for collectors. For example, a brief historical background is included in the introduction to each material type. Such information, used in conjunction with details concerning agents of decay, possible treatments and correct storage and display conditions, should ensure that appropriate conservation management strategies are adopted.

There is a deliberate concentration on material types as opposed to types of objects. In this way we hope to broaden the understanding of approaches to conservation rather than merely deal with object-specific treatments. An example of this approach can be seen in the chapter on wood where an understanding of the nature of the material is primary and the treatment of furniture as a specific object is secondary.

Although the emphasis of this book is on preventive conservation, hands-on treatments will be necessary for some materials. For this reason specific treatment regimes are described. Caution should be exercised in applying these treatments and professional assistance is recommended in most cases.

The Department of Materials Conservation of the Western Australian Museum has had a commitment to an outreach program since its inception. This publication is an extension of the program, and in conjunction with continued cooperation between conservation professionals and collectors in all areas, should provide a sound basis for the care of our widely scattered cultural heritage.

The editors wish to thank all of the contributors and pay respect to previous employees whose work helped establish the reputation of this department. Special thanks must go to departmental registrar Lucy Burrow for her help in preparing this publication, particularly the graphics.

David Gilroy
Ian Godfrey

DEPARTMENT OF MATERIALS CONSERVATION
WESTERN AUSTRALIAN MUSEUM

CONTENTS

		Page
Foreword		v
Preventive conservation	D. Gilroy and I.M. Godfrey	1
Mould and insect attack in collections	I.M. Godfrey and N. King Smith	11
General points on artefact treatments	D. Gilroy and I.M. Godfrey	19
Leather	I.M. Godfrey	23
Textiles	N. King Smith	33
Ivory, bone and related materials	I.M. Godfrey	47
Wood	S.R. Garcia. I.M. Godfrey and S. Lussier	53
Paper and books	U. Broeze-Hoernemann	61
Photographs	D. Gilroy	73
Paintings	D. Gilroy and I.M. Godfrey	83
Ceramics	C. Corvaia	87
Glass	C. Corvaia	95
Stone	C. Corvaia and I.M. Godfrey	103
Metals	S.R. Garcia, D. Gilroy and I.D. MacLeod	113
Modern organic materials	I.M. Godfrey	127
Ethnographic material	D. Gilroy and C. Harley	131
Wet materials	J. Carpenter, I.M. Godfrey, I.D. MacLeod and V.L. Richards	135
Case studies	S.R. Garcia, D. Gilroy and U. Broeze-Hoernemann	149
Appendices		159
Glossary		177
Index		179

Ulrike Broeze-Hoernemann
Conservator
Paper & Textiles

Lucy Burrow
Registrations Officer

Jon Carpenter
Conservator
Archaeological Metals

Carmela Corvaia
Objects Conservator

Richard Garcia
Technology Conservator

David Gilroy
Conservator
Environment & Objects

Dr Ian Godfrey
Curator of Conservation

Nikki King Smith
Conservator
Textiles, Ethnographic
and Boats

Dr Ian MacLeod
Head of Department

Vicki Richards
Research Officer

PREVENTIVE CONSERVATION

INTRODUCTION

The simplest and most inexpensive way to look after an object or collection is to prevent it suffering deterioration in the first place. Whether an object is in a home or in a museum, the same causes of deterioration apply. A metal artefact in a garden shed will suffer more damage than it would if stored in a box inside a house. Similarly a painting on display in a home or gallery may deteriorate more if placed into a less favourable museum storage environment. There is no point in spending time and materials to treat an object if it is returned to the same storage conditions which led to the original deterioration.

Information presented in this section concentrates on the environmental factors which cause deterioration in materials. Other obvious dangers to collections include fire, flooding and theft. Although these factors also must be considered by those in charge of a collection they are not covered in detail in this book.

It is important to know from what materials an object is made and their susceptibility to the various causes of decay. This information is useful in determining where and how it should be stored or displayed.

Different climatic zones have their own distinct problems. High humidity in the tropics or salt-laden air in coastal regions are typical examples which should be given extra consideration.

Thorough preventive practices should be established and regular inspections are essential if the best conditions for a collection are to be maintained. It is important, for example, not to take food or drink into display or storage areas. Spillages have the potential to not only damage objects but also to attract potentially damaging pests. Smoking also is not recommended in these areas because of fire and smoke damage risks.

Another important issue is the level of access to artefacts. Materials used daily for educational purposes should be copies or non-essential artefacts because constant handling will cause deterioration through either breakage or general wear and tear.

To reduce the risk of cross contamination in storage and/or display areas, any new material coming into a collection should be isolated initially, inspected and if necessary, cleaned. Treatment of pests also should be arranged if infestations are found.

The most significant environmental factors which contribute to the degradation of objects are listed below:

- light;
- temperature;
- relative humidity (RH);
- air contamination;
- biological pests; and
- dust.

Many of these factors are interrelated and cannot be considered separately. Bright sunlight, for example, will cause photochemical damage to light-sensitive material, increased temperature and decreased relative humidity.

Each of these agents of deterioration will be discussed in turn in the following sections. Guidelines are given regarding the types of conditions that will enhance the longevity of materials. As most collections are made up of an assortment of objects and material types no one set of conditions will be suitable for all objects. Where a choice has to be made, conditions should be tailored to minimise damage to the most sensitive of the objects.

LIGHT

Principles

Light is an energy form capable of damaging organic materials such as textiles, watercolour paintings, dyed materials, coloured leather, biological specimens and colour photographs.

The human eye can detect only those wavelengths of light that make up the visible spectrum (rainbow colours). Unseen components of light, such as ultraviolet (UV) and infra-red (IR) light, also can affect particular material types severely (see Figure 1).

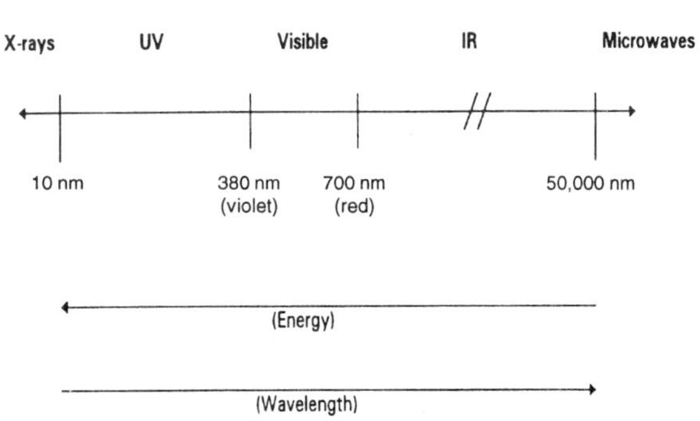

Figure 1: Preventive conservation - light region of the electromagnetic spectrum

Ultraviolet (UV) radiation
(10-380 nanometres)

As wavelengths below 300 nanometres (nm) do not penetrate the earth's atmosphere and glass cuts out UV light with wavelengths of less than 320 nm, the UV band of concern is 320-380 nm. This shortwave, invisible UV radiation is highly energetic and is most likely to cause photochemical deterioration. There is a high proportion of UV radiation in daylight and a significant amount also is emitted by fluorescent tubes.

Visible light
(380-760 nm)

Visible light affects an object in two important ways - it can lead to its deterioration and it can affect the way an observer perceives it.

Deterioration is caused not only by high energy light at the blue end of the spectrum but also by heat produced by the lower energy red light. The brighter the light the greater the rate at which damage will occur.

If colour-corrected light is not used for viewing, a colour shift human eyes cannot perceive may occur. Examples of this include the apparent change in colour when red meat is removed from the specially lit butcher's display (metamerism) into the ordinary light of the store and the yellow tinge imparted to objects by a dimmed incandescent globe.

Fluorescent tubes, on the other hand, are an excellent source of accurate colour-rendering light. Unfortunately this same light is capable of causing significant damage to objects.

Infra-red (IR) radiation
(760 nm upwards)

IR radiation can cause objects to heat up and accelerate chemical deterioration processes. It also is capable of producing changes in relative humidity. Under reduced relative humidity objects can become brittle, while under increased relative humidity metals will corrode. Such changes in relative humidity would correspond to the IR source being turned on and off respectively.

Light measurement

The human eye responds well to green-yellow light but less so to the blue and red ends of the spectrum. Both UV and IR radiation are invisible to the human eye. Light meters, cameras and lux meters have been designed to measure visible light in the same way that the eye perceives it.

The brightness, or intensity of light, is measured in units called lumens. One lumen every square metre is equivalent to one lux. When measuring light intensity the meter must face the direction of the light source.

UV radiation, measured as a proportion of visible light, has units of microwatts per lumen (μW/lumen).

Usually IR radiation is not measured, with its effect most easily detected by monitoring associated temperature changes.

The brightness of visible light can be measured easily using a camera or light meter, but measuring UV light requires a special - and expensive - monitor. To avoid this expenditure, it is best to be aware of the approximate levels of UV radiation generated by various sources.

Examples of illumination (visible light) levels:	**Lux**
Daylight, fluorescent lights in an office or laboratory	600-1500
Daylight coming in through a window	35,000
Direct sunlight	up to 136,000

Examples of UV from various sources:	**μW/lumen**
Fluorescent (low UV)	33
Fluorescent lights (general)	80-250
Tungsten globe	60-80
Direct sun	400
Light overcast sky	800
Blue sky	1600

Measuring light levels with a camera

A 35 millimetre camera with a built-in meter can be used to obtain approximate light levels. This method is described in Appendix 1.

Light-induced deterioration

Light has many effects, the most noticeable of which are colour changes induced in objects. For instance the bleaching of ivory, the fading of pigments, dyes and inks and the discolouration of wood, varnishes and lacquers are all due to exposure to light.

Different materials react to light in different ways; some materials fade while others darken. For instance some types of wood yellow, others bleach and some turn grey when exposed to light. A more subtle effect can be observed in colour photographs where there may be a colour shift when one of the more light-sensitive dyes is affected by light.

In addition to inducing colour changes in objects, exposure to light is also responsible for weakening fibres in textiles and paper.

Light has the potential to damage organic materials whether they are in pure form or make up part of a composite object. Natural organic materials such as wood, fibres and biological specimens are all vulnerable, as are modern polymeric materials (plastics) and even metal objects which contain an organic component (paint, lacquer or inlay). The inlaid ivory handle of a hand gun, for instance, would be susceptible to light damage.

For composite objects the most sensitive component must be considered when planning for display and/or storage. The relative sensitivities of different materials may be gauged by comparing the recommended maximum lighting levels for these materials (see below). The most sensitive objects should be exposed to lower light levels to minimise photochemical damage.

Reciprocity rule

The same amount of damage will be produced by strong light in a short time as will be done by a weaker light in a long time. For example, 500 lux exposure for 10 hours will cause an equivalent amount of deterioration as 50 lux exposure for 100 hours.

Recommended maximum light levels

These values are set so the item can be viewed with a minimum of damage.

50 lux	Textiles, costumes, watercolours, tapestries, prints and drawings, manuscripts, miniatures, distemper in frescoes, wallpapers, gouache, dyed leather, most natural exhibits, botanical specimens, fur and feathers.
200 lux	Oil and tempera paintings, undyed leather, horn, bone, ivory and oriental lacquer.
300 lux	Stone, metal, glass, ceramic, jewellery, enamel and wood.
75 μW/lumen	This is the maximum UV level recommended for all material types.

Controlling light levels

Light levels may be controlled by using some or all of the following strategies:

- exclude all daylight;
- place the most light-sensitive objects furthest from light sources;
- use low UV light sources;
- use UV filters over light sources or in display cabinets;
- alternate sensitive materials between display and low-light storage;
- use copies for display; and
- use automatic light switching.

Ideally, all daylight should be excluded from storage and display areas. This would have two beneficial effects. Firstly, it would reduce light levels significantly and secondly, it would allow the intensity of interior light and the amount of UV exposure to be controlled. This control may be achieved by using appropriate artificial lighting sources such as low UV fluorescent lights and arrangements such as reflected rather than direct lighting. Whatever the light sources and arrangements, the end result must be conditions that meet the required specifications for the illuminated objects. Options to eliminate daylight include the use of blinds, shutters, curtains and even paint. If external light cannot be eliminated completely then windows should be treated with UV-absorbing films and tints.

As the intensity of light is reduced with distance from the light source the most light-sensitive objects always should be placed furthest from them. The same result may be achieved by bouncing light off a reflecting surface to create a diffuse effect. The intensity of the light is reduced as the path length of the light from the source to the object is increased, some of the incident light is absorbed and some is scattered by the reflecting surface. This is an excellent way of not only reducing light intensity but also of creating interesting lighting effects.

Options to reduce the impact of UV radiation on objects include the use of low UV fluorescent tubes, installation of UV-absorbing perspex covers over light sources and/or the use of UV-absorbing perspex in display case construction.

Light exposure also can be reduced by adopting appropriate management strategies. Material that is particularly light-sensitive may be alternated between display and storage. To cut light exposure by half in an historic house, for example, only open half of the rooms for six months of the year and the other half for the following six months. Similarly, if a diary or register is displayed open then rotate the pages exposed.

Another alternative is to use lights that are activated when someone enters the collection area room and which remain on for a limited period (automatic light switching).

Note that the importance of an object as well as its sensitivity to light damage must be considered carefully before remedial measures are taken. Occasionally, maximum light levels do not show artefact details adequately. This problem may arise when general light levels are too high, making the artefact, at 50 or 200 lux, relatively dark. This situation may be overcome by decreasing general light levels in the vicinity of the artefact.

If the light on an artefact must be increased above recommended levels then display time should be reduced proportionately. For example, if the recommended light level is 50 lux and the actual level is 150 lux then the object should be on display for only three months per year and kept in dark storage for the other nine months.

If appropriate environmental conditions cannot be established then particularly sensitive or significant photographs, prints and similar objects should be copied. The copy may then be put on display and original safely stored.

In balancing light for a display it is necessary to consider the colour temperature of the light source so that good colour rendering is obtained. As there are a wide variety of light sources available consultation with manufacturers and suppliers is recommended.

RELATIVE HUMIDITY AND TEMPERATURE

Principles

The relative humidity (RH) of the air is an indication of how much water vapour is in the air at a particular temperature compared with how much water vapour the air could hold at that temperature. It is expressed as a percentage and can be defined as follows:

$$\text{RH} = \frac{\text{amount of water in a given amount of air}}{\text{max. amount of water the air can hold at that temperature}} \times \frac{100}{1}$$

Air at 100 per cent relative humidity is holding the maximum amount of water possible at that particular temperature and is said to be saturated. Saturated air at 10 degrees Celsius holds about 10 grams per cubic metre of moisture; at 20°C about 17 g/m^3 and at 30°C more than 30 g/m^3. The relative humidity is a measure of the percentage saturation of the air. Therefore, air at 50% relative humidity, regardless of temperature, is holding half of its total water capacity.

In essence, cold air cannot hold as much water vapour as warm air. In a closed environment, such as a display case, there will be a fixed amount of water vapour, referred to as the absolute humidity. If the temperature inside the case falls then the relative humidity will rise; if the temperature rises the relative humidity will fall. Such changes in relative humidity could be caused by direct sunlight or by spotlights.

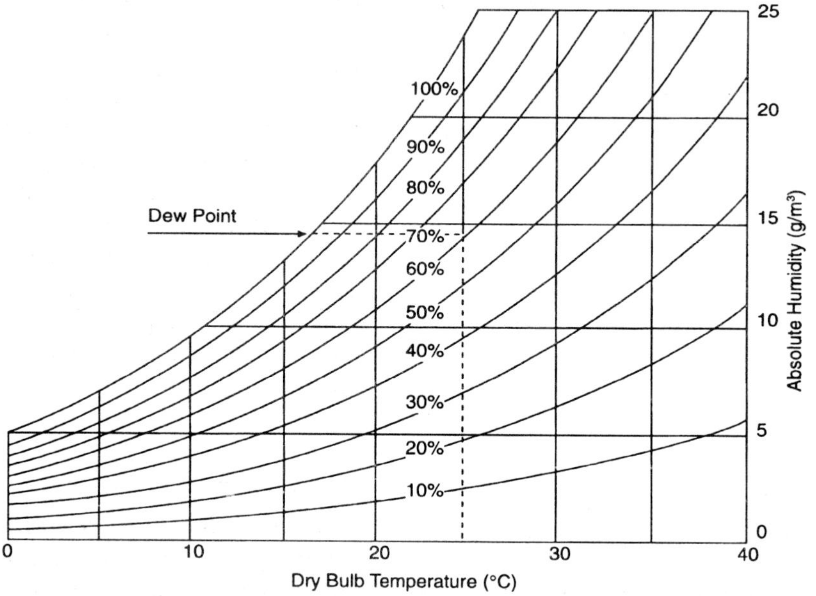

Figure 2: Preventive conservation - hygrometric chart (adapted from Thomson, 1986)

The hygrometric chart above (see Figure 2) illustrates that a relative humidity of 60% in a display case kept at 25°C will rise to about 80% relative humidity if the temperature falls to 20°C. Dew point will be reached if the temperature falls to about 16°C. Condensation will then occur.

For many years the recommended ideal temperature and relative humidity conditions for museum collections were given as 20°C and 55% respectively . These conditions are difficult to maintain unless expensive airconditioning systems are used and may not be possible or even desirable in certain areas. For instance, in the tropics where the average yearly relative humidity is about 65%, it is better to have this as the optimum level whereas in an arid region it may be better to aim for a relative humidity range of 45-50%. This not only saves on energy costs but also means that material which is conditioned to the ambient relative humidity will not be damaged by change.

Two recent studies have re-examined the conditions considered suitable for storage and display of objects (Michalski 1993, Erhardt and Mecklenburg 1994). Findings from these studies suggest that although certain material types benefit from storage in strictly controlled conditions, most mixed materials in sound order only need be maintained in an environment with a relative humidity range of 40-70%. A relative humidity range of ± 5% is suggested for sensitive objects (Michalski 1993).

The humidity tolerances of some commonly encountered materials, their dimensional responses and susceptibilities to mould are provided in Appendix 2. We have opted for a slightly more conservative approach to relative humidity levels, recommending a range of 45-65% for most materials. For objects containing more than one material type, the relative humidity level of the storage environment should reflect the recommended conditions for the most sensitive component.

Measurement

Relative humidity may be measured by using any of the following devices:

- sling psychrometer;
- thermohygrograph;
- hair hygrometer;
- calibrated electronic devices which provide a digital readout of temperature and RH; and
- data loggers linked to relative humidity sensors

The simplest and most inexpensive instrument for measuring relative humidity is the **sling psychrometer.** This device also is known simply as the 'sling' or as a whirling hygrometer. It consists of two matched thermometers mounted side-by-side, one of which has a fabric sleeve covering it. The end of this sleeve is inserted into a reservoir which is filled with distilled water. When the thermometers are swung around the water in the sleeve of the wet bulb evaporates, making it cooler than the dry bulb. The amount of evaporation, and therefore cooling, depends on the amount of moisture present in the air - the drier the air the greater the level of cooling and vice versa. The difference in the temperatures of the thermometers indicates how dry or humid the air is; the greater the difference the lower the ambient relative humidity, the smaller the difference the higher the relative humidity. A standard hygrometric chart, which displays a series of wet and dry bulb temperature differences and corresponding dry bulb temperatures, is then used to give an accurate measure of the relative humidity.

The sling is used to calibrate almost all other types of hygrometers. Coupled with a **thermohygrograph** (seven-day or one-month), an accurate day-to-day or hour-to-hour record of temperature and humidity can be obtained all year round.

Electronic instruments are also available which record changes in temperature and relative humidity. While these devices are expensive they do have certain advantages. For example, they may be placed relatively unobtrusively in display cases or in small storage areas in which a thermohygrograph either would not be appropriate or would not fit.

Other relative humidity sensors, linked to data loggers, can be programmed to record temperature and relative humidity conditions at regular intervals over periods of many months. These sensors are very small and by operating continuously over the different seasons, allow useful profiles of storage and display conditions to be established.

This information may be used to see how well the building buffers the external ambient conditions and also to see how well a display case further buffers the gallery environment. If the temperature is steady then the relative humidity within a display case will remain constant.

Relative humidity and temperature effects

The main impacts of temperature (unless it is so extreme as to freeze or melt objects) within the museum environment are on relative humidity and the rate of chemical deterioration of objects. A 10°C rise in temperature approximately doubles the rate at which chemical reactions proceed.

After light, relative humidity is the most significant factor to be considered in climate control. Constant relative humidity above 65% can cause mould growth and increase corrosion whereas a relative humidity below 45% can cause sensitive materials such as paper and textiles to become brittle.

It is important not only to control relative humidity but also to minimise fluctuations. Large and rapid changes in relative humidity, caused by sudden temperature variations, can have significant effects on materials. A sudden drop in temperature in a display case for example, may result in the dew point being reached. The subsequent condensation will accelerate metal corrosion and encourage biological attack on organic materials.

Materials such as paper, wood, textiles, bone and ivory expand and contract as they absorb and release water in response to changes in relative humidity. Rapid fluctuations can lead to cracking and warping of these materials and also cause bonded materials to separate. Paint, for instance, may craze or peel from wooden surfaces and paper glued to a backing board may buckle.

Controlling relative humidity and temperature

Relative humidity and temperature control strategies include the use of:

- the buffering effects of buildings and storage media;
- moisture-absorbing desiccants (silica gel and zeolites);
- natural moisture-absorbing materials such as wood, paper and textiles;
- refrigerant dehumidifiers; and
- thorough and well-planned building maintenance.

Fluctuations in temperature and humidity are caused by daily and seasonal fluctuations in the local weather. Even without airconditioning, the insulating effect of a building ensures temperature and relative humidity variations inside a building are generally smaller than those outside.

Cupboards, boxes and display cases are secondary insulating barriers, which provide an additional buffer, helping to stabilise conditions even more.

The climate within a showcase or cabinet can be controlled if material particularly sensitive to humidity is to be stored or displayed. If the relative humidity is too high (above 65%) then it may be necessary to use some form of desiccant within the display case to absorb excess water vapour. Self-indicating silica gel can be used for this purpose. It is important that any silica gel used in display cases is conditioned to the desired relative humidity. This process is best left in the hands of conservators as there is a risk of too much moisture being absorbed, resulting in desiccation of vulnerable objects.

Zeolite pellets may be of use in climatic areas in which the endemic relative humidity is naturally high (Australian Library and Information Association 1989). A Japanese researcher has developed a treated natural zeolite pellet capable of absorbing and releasing large amounts of water vapour. The pellets have been combined with Japanese paper with the resultant material being produced as a sheet or a paper-covered honeycomb board filled with pellets. Incorporating these materials in storage and display cabinets should allow relative humidity conditions to be controlled.

An alternative way of controlling relative humidity is to use other materials that absorb moisture, such as treated wood, paper and textiles, in the cabinet or display case with the moisture-sensitive artefacts. These materials will reduce relative humidity fluctuations by taking up or releasing moisture as conditions change. In this way the artefact is subjected to smaller relative humidity variations. Materials used must be compatible with the moisture-sensitive object. It would not be appropriate, for instance, to store a lead object in an oak box or to use buffered acid-free tissue paper with leather objects.

The Japanese traditionally have used this type of approach to deal with the naturally humid climatic conditions which exist in their country. Objects are stored in wooden chests in wooden buildings to take advantage of the natural moisture-absorbing and releasing properties of wood. In this way the box contents are buffered against both the naturally high relative humidity and against any changes in external conditions. This approach would not be suitable for all material types, especially those sensitive to the acidic vapours given off by wood. With the right choice of wood (for example, hoop pine) and wrapping of artefacts in acid-free tissue, this approach may allow some of the problems associated with endemically high relative humidity conditions to be overcome.

Alternatively, if passive methods such as those outlined above are not sufficient, this problem may be tackled by lowering the relative humidity of the storage or display area itself. This can be achieved by employing a refrigerant dehumidifier to remove excess moisture. As mould formation is encouraged by conditions of high relative humidity, warm temperatures and stagnant air, it may be necessary to employ a combination of dehumidification, air circulation and temperature control.

Refrigerated air coolers can remove moisture from a building or room by condensing it outside.

It is important to prevent extreme conditions of temperature and relative humidity developing. Usually such extremes are very localised and often only affect a few objects. For example, localised heating and consequent low relative humidity may be caused by direct sunlight falling on an object, by having spotlights positioned too close or by having radiators or heaters adjacent to an object.

A common cause of high humidity is leakage of rainwater through the roof or walls. It is wise not to store objects against external walls as damp and localised extremes of both temperature and relative humidity are likely. Common sense and adequate building maintenance should minimise such problems.

BIOLOGICAL PESTS

Although a chapter in this book is devoted entirely to biological pests a few of the major points are discussed briefly in this section.

Biological pests include moulds, bacteria, insects and other small animals such as mice, rats and birds. All of these organisms are capable of causing severe damage to objects in a collection.

Problems can be minimised by adopting appropriate housekeeping practices and ensuring that the building in which objects are housed is well maintained. Some of the practical ways in which this can be achieved include:

- blocking ceiling space access to nesting birds, possums and other animals;
- controlling populations of mice, rats and insects;
- keeping food sources away from objects; and
- controlling the environmental conditions so that mould growth is not encouraged (keep relative humidity below 65%).

Note that trapping rodents is preferable to poisoning them. Trapping allows the rodent's body to be disposed of appropriately, while poisoning means the body usually ends up as a source of food for some other pest.

POLLUTANTS

Pollutants may emanate from:

- the materials associated with a collection;
- the objects in the collection themselves; and
- the surrounding air.

Storage and display materials

The most common sources of pollutants in storage areas are the materials used to store and/or display objects. Materials which are known to release harmful vapours at room temperature (Padfield *et al* 1982) include:

- wood (particularly hardwood);
- protein-based glues (except photographic gelatin);
- cellulose nitrate and cellulose diacetate;
- polyvinyl chloride and polyvinyl alcohol;
- polyurethane; and
- some dyes which contain labile sulfur.

Materials which are considered to be 'safe' (Padfield *et al* 1982) include:

- metals;
- ceramics;
- inorganic pigments;
- polyethylene;
- acrylic polymers (solutions rather than emulsions);
- glass;
- polycarbonates;
- polystyrene;
- polyester fibres; and
- cotton and linen.

Materials such as chipboard, wood, certain polymers and paints all can contribute to the deterioration of objects in a collection. Chipboard and wood products can give off formaldehyde and organic acids respectively, promoting corrosion of nearby metal objects.

Objects in contact with certain polymer storage files may become contaminated as plasticisers migrate from these polymers. Artefacts stored in polyvinyl chloride are particularly at risk owing to the release of corrosive hydrogen chloride from this polymer.

The placement of objects in freshly painted cupboards also is not recommended as the solvent fumes from the drying paint may affect the organic components (glues, resins, plastics, lacquers, and the like) of some objects. It is recommended that a newly painted surface be allowed to cure for three months before use.

Artefacts

Alternatively, the objects themselves may prove to be the source of contamination as they degrade.

Cellulose nitrate movie films, for example, not only release acidic, oxidising gases but also pose a fire risk as they deteriorate. These materials must be stored in their own well-ventilated and preferably fire-proof area.

Air pollutants

Air pollutants may arise from vehicle emissions, industrial activity or decaying organic matter. These pollutants, which include dust, oxides of nitrogen and sulfur, hydrogen sulfide and airborne salt, are likely to lead to increased corrosion of metals and degradation of organic materials.

Preventive measures

The significance of any air pollution problem will be determined largely by the particular collection environment and its location, be it in an industrial, tropical, coastal or desert site. Each particular environment will have its own set of problems.

Preventive measures include the use of:

- archival quality storage and display materials; and
- filtered airconditioning.

Use enamelled metal cabinets or shelves in preference to wood or chipboard for storage and display.

If wood or chipboard are used then they should be sealed with an epoxy or water-based polyurethane varnish and left to cure for about three months before use. This will allow volatile additives to vent before objects are exposed to these materials.

Alternatively, chipboard which is to be used in a display case or similar, may be given a coating of urea (400g in one litre of water). This will help to prevent any excess formaldehyde from being released from the wood. Then coat the wood with a water-based polyurethane or paint it with an oil-based primer and top-coat. Leave the chipboard for about 3 months to allow the volatile materials to vent.

Boxes should be constructed from acid-free materials and objects wrapped in acid-free tissue (where appropriate).

Activated charcoal cloth can be incorporated as a liner in storage and display areas. This cloth absorbs harmful vapours thereby protecting the artefacts. Although expensive, charcoal cloth can last up to ten years, depending on the level of pollution.

Larger institutions should have filtered airconditioning (as per museum specifications) while smaller collections and the private collector can alleviate some of these problems by using archival storage and display materials which act as buffers against these agents of decay.

Note that if airconditioning is used to maintain objects in the best possible conditions, then it should be run for 24 hours a day. If the airconditioning is turned off overnight the environment inside the building will tend towards external values. In winter, a lowering of temperature will result in an increase in relative humidity. When the airconditioning plant is turned on in the morning there will be a rapid increase in temperature accompanied by a rapid decrease in relative humidity. These rapid changes in relative humidity should be avoided. It is obviously better to use passive controls to minimise fluctuations in environmental conditions.

DUST

Dust causes damage to objects by:

- physical abrasion;
- attracting moisture; and
- attracting biological pests such as insects, mould and bacteria.

Dust promotes both chemical and biological attack on objects.

Regular cleaning and building maintenance should minimise this problem.

STORAGE AND DISPLAY

The aim of storage, whether in a large museum or in a private home, is to ensure that objects are protected against the agents of decay - dust, pests, pollutants, changes in temperature and relative humidity, and exposure to light.

Poorly designed, built or maintained **buildings** will produce environmental problems. The most common problem is the entry of water into the building with resultant high humidity levels. Typical causes of water entry are:

- leaking roofs, walls or windows, permitting entry of water;
- porous walls and/or ineffective damp courses which allow entry of ground water. This problem is most pronounced in basements, cellars, and buildings affected by rising damp;
- poor positioning of gardens and garden watering systems causing sections of the building to be frequently wet. This problem is aggravated if the building is constructed from porous materials such as sandstone or limestone; and

- poor ventilation of kitchen and bathroom areas, allowing water vapour to enter storage or display areas.

Extremely low humidity generally is associated with heating, caused either by sunlight entering through windows or poor placement of radiators and heaters. These factors have been discussed previously.

While private collectors probably will not have the luxury of having access to a **holding area**, it is strongly recommended that collecting institutions such as museums and historical societies set aside such an area. This area is used for temporary storage, while objects slowly acclimatise to their new surroundings or await inspection.

Acclimatisation is particularly important for objects that have been moved from one climatic zone to another. For instance, wooden artefacts that were stable in the higher relative humidity surroundings of the tropics will lose moisture if moved to the drier southern regions. Slow acclimatisation is necessary to minimise drying stresses. This may be achieved by sealing the artefact in clear plastic. Over time the bag should be perforated to allow for slow exchange of moisture with the surroundings. The number and size of the perforations can be increased slowly as the object progressively loses moisture.

Similarly, artefacts from a dry climate also have to be buffered if transferred to a wetter zone. Great care must be taken when acclimatising objects as no hard-and-fast rules apply. The length of time before an object can be exposed safely to a new environment will depend on a number of factors, including the difference in the climatic conditions of the areas involved, the condition, material type (for example, wood, leather, textile) and the size of the object. Periods of acclimatisation of up to one year are not unusual.

While artefacts are acclimatising to a new environment, take advantage of the time to check for the presence of insects and other pests. If biological pests are detected then action can be taken to eradicate them before they have the opportunity to contaminate other objects in a collection.

The overall condition of the artefacts and the presence of dust and grime also should be noted. If this dirt is not an essential part of an object's history then it should be removed before the object comes into contact with other parts of the collection.

Objects can be thought to be in a state of storage whatever their location. While on display, artefacts are in a visually accessible form of storage and objects grouped together in a time capsule are simply in another more specialised form of storage. In the latter case great care must be taken with packing and control of the climate if deterioration processes are to be minimised (see the chapter, Case Studies: Time Capsules).

Different material and artefact types have specific requirements for safe storage. These requirements are described in later chapters.

HANDLING

Specific guidelines are given in later chapters for handling particular materials, but the importance of care and common sense cannot be overemphasised. A few general principles relating to handling and moving artefacts are described below.

- Cleanliness is very important. Wash hands thoroughly and wear disposable, well-fitting gloves (white cotton or vinyl).
- Avoid unnecessary handling.
- Assess the weight and condition of the object to be handled.
- Handle only one object at a time.
- Remove all loose parts (for example, lids and drawers) to reduce the chance of breakages.
- Do not assume that handles are strong enough to support the weight of an object. Pick up all objects by their strongest points.
- Use flat supports to carry objects that are fragile or unable to support their own weight.
- Use a trolley or similar device to move heavy objects. Do not drag or push them across a surface.
- Provide protection against temperature and relative humidity changes for objects being transported to an area in which different environmental conditions may be encountered (see Packing below).

PACKING

Factors to be considered before packing and moving an object include:

- fragility and condition - is the object strong enough to withstand transportation stresses;
- size, weight and value of the object;
- mode of transportation;
- type and material of the container to be used; and
- type of packing materials.

Assume the degree of care during transportation may not be ideal and pack accordingly.

Containers may be made of either cardboard or wood, depending on the nature of the object to be transported. These materials provide some degree of protection against both shock and environmental changes.

The size of the container should be such that the object and its packing fits snugly, but not too tightly, inside the container. In this way internal movement is restricted and the risk of damage is reduced.

Materials used in packing should:

- be resistant to shock;
- provide a buffer against changes in environmental conditions (temperature and relative humidity);
- not settle to the bottom of the container following packing;
- be chemically inert; and
- be easily distinguishable from the packed object.

Suitable packing materials include bubble wrap, foam core and ethafoam. Do not use polystyrene beads or other loose packing materials prone to settling.

Depending on the nature of the object it should be wrapped in materials such as acid-free tissue or unbleached lined, followed by two layers of bubble wrap. Line the walls of the container with polyethylene or mylar sheeting to provide both water resistance and protection from any harmful vapours that may emanate from the container itself.

BIBLIOGRAPHY

Australian Library and Information Association, 1989, Fumigation, *Conservation of Library Materials*, Newsletter No. 5, p. 3.

Bachmann, K., (Ed.), 1992, *Conservation Concerns: A Guide for Collectors and Curators*, Smithsonian Institute Press, Washington.

Erhardt, D. and Mecklenburg, M., 1994, Relative humidity re-examined, in *Preventive Conservation: Practice, Theory and Research*, Preprints of the Contributions to the Ottawa Congress, September, 1994, IIC, pp. 32-38.

Michalski, S., 1993, Relative humidity: a discussion of correct/incorrect values, in *Preprints, ICOM Committee for Conservation 10th Triennial Meeting*, Washington DC, pp. 624-629.

Museums Australia Inc. (NSW), 1994, *Museum Methods: A Practical Manual for Managing Small Museums*, Museums Australia Inc. (NSW).

Padfield, T., Erhardt, D. and Hopwood, W.R., 1982, Trouble in store, in *Science and Technology in the Service of Conservation*, Preprints of the Contributions to the Washington Congress, 3-9 September, 1982, Eds N.S. Brommelle and G. Thomson, IIC, London, pp. 24-27.

Powerhouse Museum, 1994, *Caring for Heritage Objects*, Powerhouse Museum Research Series No. 3, Sydney.

Thomson, G., 1986, *The Museum Environment*, 2nd Edition, Butterworths, London.

MOULD AND INSECT ATTACK IN COLLECTIONS

INTRODUCTION

Although mould and insect attack are treated separately in this section it is important that pest control is dealt with in a coordinated fashion. Pest management should be a routine part of the operations associated with a collection - not a series of responses to crises.

Strang (1993) recommends conducting a survey to assess the existing situation before any attempt is made to implement a pest management regime. This survey should consider the following factors:

- the building and its location;
- portable fittings and hardware; and
- procedures and people.

These factors should be examined to determine their impact on pests. Is the building well sealed? Do storage cabinets restrict the entry of pests? Do staff eat and keep foodstuffs well away from collection areas? These are some of the questions that should be considered in the initial survey.

Having assessed the existing situation, Strang recommends designing and implementing pest management activities which will minimise the risks posed to collections by pests. These activities should be centred around 'five stages of control':

- avoid;
- block;
- detect;
- respond; and
- recover.

This sort of approach to pest control is often called 'integrated pest management'. Integrated pest management involves:

- preventive measures;
- monitoring of collection areas;
- treatment of artefacts;
- treatment of infestations; and
- review and assessment of procedures.

Preventive measures

Key pest preventive measures include:

- excluding pests by using screens and seals, and ensure that additions to a collection are not infested;
- control of relative humidity, temperature and air circulation to prevent mould formation;
- not allowing food, drink or plant material (fresh or dried) in collection areas;
- thoroughly cleaning all areas associated with a collection (vacuuming is recommended). This includes storage areas, display areas, tea rooms and the area immediately outside the collection; and
- applying appropriate pesticides to the external perimeters of buildings and on skirting boards (see Appendix 3).

Monitoring collection areas

Collection areas should be monitored by:

- regularly inspecting for insect frass, cocoons, silk webbings and any other signs of pest activity; and
- using commercially available sticky traps to identify insect activity and type.

Treatment of artefacts

Ways to treat artefacts to prevent or control pest infestations include:

- bagging and removing any affected artefacts from the storage and display areas; and
- freezing or fumigating artefacts, using inert gases, low oxygen or chemical techniques.

Treatment of infestations

If an area of the collection is infested by pests, then:

- after isolating the affected artefacts, clean the area (vacuuming is recommended); and
- apply pesticides if pest activity continues.

Review and assessment of procedures

Management of pest infestations should be assessed against existing procedures to determine their effectiveness. The following steps should be taken following an outbreak:

- document the outbreak. Record details concerning the artefacts affected, the extent of damage incurred, when the infestation occurred and the nature of the infestation (for example, type of insect attack);
- determine the circumstances that led to the infestation; and
- decide what actions can be taken to prevent similar problems in the future.

Note that the cycle does not end with the treatment of an object. In fact it begins again. There is no point in eradicating pests if reinfestation is likely. Follow treatment with remedial action and careful monitoring so that the chances of pests returning are reduced.

If in any doubt, consult a conservator who will be able to provide you with the latest information on control and treatment techniques.

MOULD

Most people have seen mould growths on old bread, cheese, jam, damp wood or leather. This mould growth, usually appearing as a fine, fluffy mass, is referred to as the 'fungal colony'.

When conditions are favourable to mould growth (that is, high humidity) the appearance of the colony changes. The older parts take on a different colour and fruiting structures appear. These fruiting structures, which contain the individual reproductive bodies called spores, are usually only visible with a microscope. The fruiting structures stand up above the mass of the colony so that the spores may be discharged into the atmosphere and carried by air currents to suitable growth surfaces.

Under such conditions spores absorb water, enlarge rapidly and branch repeatedly, forming a new colony. When the colony is established and large enough, fruiting structures appear, spores are produced and the cycle is repeated.

If the environment is suitable, mould will form on organic materials (dead plant and animal matter). Provided there is sufficient moisture available, either in the material or in the environment, fungi will feed on leather, cotton, wool, bone, paper, wood, bark, fur and rawhide. Fungi are also capable of growing on metal and stone surfaces, particularly those with a coat of dust or organic debris. Some species even grow on creosote-treated wood while others can incorporate poisonous, chlorine-containing compounds into their diets.

Examples of undesirable effects of fungal infestation include the complete destruction of wooden and paper materials, staining of paper-based objects and attack on photographic gelatin.

Fungi can tolerate temperatures as low as minus 10°C and as high as 110°C. Fungi are affected more by relative humidity levels than by temperature. A few species can survive below 60 per cent relative humidity but the majority require a relative humidity of at least 70% to survive and reproduce. Should the relative humidity drop below 60%, fungal bodies normally die. The spores released at such adverse times will lie dormant until suitable conditions for growth are again available.

Preventing mould growth

Preventing contamination by fungal spores within any building is practically impossible. It is possible, however, to control conditions for storage and display so that it is very difficult for spores to germinate. This can be done by controlling the relative humidity. Methods used to control relative humidity have been described previously (see the chapter, Preventive Conservation).

If the relative humidity is maintained at a sufficiently low level spores cannot germinate. A relative humidity of between 50 and 60% is considered safe. Too low a value (that is, below 45%), while stopping mould formation, can damage susceptible materials such as leather or silk.

As mould growth is encouraged under stagnant conditions, it is also important to maintain adequate ventilation in storage and display areas.

Although complete elimination of the sources of fungal spores is not possible, surface contamination of objects can be reduced by:

- storing objects in dustproof containers;
- covering objects temporarily removed from containers; and
- vacuuming objects gently, prior to storage or display.

It is more efficient to control collection conditions and prevent mould growth, rather than have to treat objects contaminated by active colonies.

Material on display

Provided the temperature does not vary greatly, individual display cases can act as buffer zones within a collection, helping to maintain humidity at a reasonably constant level. High relative humidity periods may occur sporadically (average relative humidity below 65% but with occasional spells with high relative humidity) or endemically (average relative humidity above 65%). Different methods are needed to control display case humidity under these conditions.

Sporadically high relative humidity

Occasional periods of high relative humidity can usually be controlled by using a well-sealed display case as a buffer against the ambient conditions. If this is not successful it may be necessary to use a dehydrating agent, such as self-indicating silica gel, to absorb the excess moisture. A change in colour from blue to pink indicates that the silica gel is saturated with moisture and needs to be changed. A disadvantage of using silica gel is the large quantity required to achieve and maintain a reduced relative humidity. For transporting objects, or for short periods of high relative humidity, one kilogram of silica gel is needed for each cubic metre of space. If the problem is endemic then 20 kg/m^3 is necessary (Thomson 1986).

Endemically high relative humidity

The options for controlling prolonged periods of high relative humidity are to use silica gel (20 kg/m^3) in a well-sealed display case or to improve the ventilation so that mould growth is not possible. Although the use of air curtains and fans greatly improve conditions in tropical regions these may have to be combined with the use of silica gel if mould growth continues to be a problem.

TREATMENT OF MOULD

Mould must be killed before it is removed from an object. If living mould is physically removed from artefacts there is a danger of spreading live spores to other objects, not to mention the associated health risks of such a practice.

Two basic types of treatments are available, persistent and non-persistent. Non-persistent methods treat the infestation, killing the mould, but give no protection against further outbreaks. Persistent treatments give some long-term resistance to the treated materials, but have a greater risk of causing future damage to the materials through adverse chemical reactions.

Non-persistent treatments of mould are just short-term solutions. Fumigation and other treatments will have little effect unless something is done about the conditions that led to the development of mould in the first place. Implementing passive environmental controls, effective housekeeping techniques and building maintenance will be of much greater benefit in the long term.

There are a variety of methods for treating mould-affected objects. In recent years there has been a move away from purely chemical treatments towards the use of less toxic and potentially less damaging methods.

Freezing treatment

Freezing of artefacts is an example of a non-chemical approach to mould treatment. Details of the technique outlined below are based on a method described by Dodd (1991).

Freezing has the potential to kill germinating spores and associated hyphae (fine fibrous strands), but may not be effective against dry spores (Florian 1994). Controlling environmental storage conditions following freezing treatment is critical to avoid activating dormant spores.

If mould attack has occurred already, then the affected object, its storage area and any materials in contact with the object should be treated by one of the methods described below. Steps involved in the treatment of mould attack include:

- isolation of all affected material to stop further contamination;
- treatment of affected materials and storage areas;
- determination of the cause of the mould outbreak; and
- rectification of any problems which may have contributed to mould formation.

Isolation

The steps involved in the isolation of mould-affected objects are summarised below:

- place affected objects in plastic bags and remove them from the collection;
- if the mould outbreak is due to wetting of an object then allow it to dry out partly, acclimatise to a relative humidity of 50-60% and then wrap it in acid-free tissue;
- place the object in a polyethylene bag and remove most of the air from the bag. Carry out this procedure in a well-ventilated area and wear a mask to reduce the risk of inhaling fungal spores; and
- seal the bag (heat seal if possible).

Treatment of affected materials

To ensure treatment of mould-affected materials is effective and that the risk to the artefacts is minimised, follow these steps:

- seal the objects in polyethylene bags and place them in a freezer for at least four days at minus 20°C or below. Pack objects in the freezer so that the drop in temperature is as rapid as possible for all objects;
- allow objects to thaw slowly (in a refrigerator) and then warm to ambient conditions before unsealing; and
- carefully vacuum objects in a well-ventilated area to remove dead hyphae and spores. Correct vacuum cleaning techniques are described elsewhere (see the chapter, Textiles).

Unless access to industrial freezers is possible, there are limitations on the size of the object that can be treated in this fashion. Take care not to freeze artefacts likely to suffer damage during the freezing process. Objects that should **not** be frozen include the following (Berkouwer 1994):

- desiccated or seriously degraded objects;
- objects which contain a variety of materials, especially layers; and
- materials which have a high natural water content.

Such objects may not be able to withstand the fluctuations in relative humidity due to temperature changes and any ensuing dimensional changes. Examples of such materials include furniture with veneered, inlaid or gilded surfaces, resinous materials, some plastics and painted textiles and certain mixed media artefacts that contain adhesives (Berkouwer 1994).

Many textiles, most paper-based objects, leather artefacts and natural history specimens may be frozen to eradicate mould and insects.

Treatment of previous storage and display areas

If possible, storage and display equipment should be dried at elevated temperatures. Spores cannot survive three to four hours of temperatures greater than 36°C. While this is desirable, it may not be possible for large storage racks, or indeed may damage the equipment.

Swab the equipment with alcohol as a further precaution against re-contamination (unless the material may be damaged by alcohol application). This should be done in a well-ventilated area.

Determining cause of the outbreak

All possible causes of mould growths should be examined and maintenance organised if a leaking roof, overflowing gutter or similar building problem contributed to increased relative humidity in the collection area.

Implement relative humidity control strategies if the mould outbreak was the result of adverse weather conditions (see the chapter, Preventive Conservation).

Chemical fumigation

For some mould-affected objects, freezing or low oxygen methods may not be available options (see the section, Insect attack, for details). In some instances, a small amount of residual pesticide or chemical treatment may be needed to prevent a further outbreak.

Consult a conservator to obtain the most recent information on chemical techniques. In many cases chemical treatments are damaging to objects and great care is needed. It is preferable to avoid chemical intervention if possible.

Use commercial pest control agencies to deal with heavy infestations of either fungi or insects. Again, consult a conservator prior to such intervention to minimise risks to artefacts.

Safety equipment

When removing dead fungal matter, wear suitable safety gear such as a dust mask or respirator.

Put on protective gloves and goggles when handling methylated spirits and other potentially dangerous chemicals.

INSECT ATTACK

The most common insects encountered in museums or private collections include the:

- case bearing clothes moth;
- webbing clothes moth;
- hide beetle;
- carpet beetle;
- furniture beetle;
- silverfish;
- cockroach; and
- termite.

Details of the life cycles and identification of these pests are given in Appendix 4.

The insects mentioned above can contaminate, damage or even completely destroy artefacts contained in ethnographic, natural science, archaeological and historic collections. Unless the attack has been in progress for considerable time, most of the damage is detectable only by close inspection.

Depending on the species, insects will feed on organic materials composed of either proteins or cellulose. Objects made up of materials such as wool, fur, leather, paper, wood, feathers, hair and plant specimens are particularly susceptible to attack. Occasionally some insects will attack non-food materials during certain stages of their life cycle.

Preventive measures

The first step in the control of biological pests is the adoption of preventive measures to minimise infestations. Although no building will ever be insect-proof, steps can be taken to reduce potential problems. Non-chemical strategies to minimise insect problems have been reviewed by Pearson (1993). Some recommended strategies include:

- thoroughly inspecting objects to be incorporated into a collection. If necessary, quarantine objects by storing them in polyethylene bags and checking for any signs of activity after two months. If in doubt, assume that pests are present;

- keeping garden and household rubbish away from buildings and disposing of it as soon as possible;
- ensuring food and food preparation areas are away from collection and display areas;
- keeping doors and windows closed. Fit screens and draft excluders to doors, windows, vents and drains;
- sealing spaces around pipes and ducts with caulking compounds (both interior and exterior). Repair cracks and other possible entry points;
- cleaning drains and gutters regularly;
- thorough housekeeping (regular vacuum cleaning rather than just dusting) is essential as dirt and debris provide food and shelter for pests and create damaging microenvironments; and
- using storage units and display cases as secondary barriers to insect intrusion. These should be well sealed (gaskets) to prevent insect entry to collected objects.

Low temperature storage also will assist in the control of insect pests. Below 5°C breeding cycles are interrupted and insect development reduced, while temperatures between 5 and 10°C effectively prevent large increases in insect numbers (Pinniger 1989).

Chemical treatments are a useful adjunct to the range of preventive measures described above.

Applying chemicals to the exterior of a building, skirting boards and display surfaces particularly susceptible to insect attack (dioramas, for instance) will assist in minimising damage to collections.

In choosing a particular insecticide, a balance has to be found between the effects of the chemical on insects and its impact on the environment (such as, residual nature, toxicity), the artefacts in the collection and the people who may come into contact with it. A summary of commonly used pesticides, their characteristics and known effects on materials is provided in Appendix 3.

If correctly applied, pyrethrins, organophosphorous and carbamate-based pesticides all can be used on buildings and internal structures with minimum risk to artefacts housed there.

Very few adverse reactions have been observed from using pyrethrins near artefacts. These materials may be either natural or synthetic, persistent or non-persistent. They generally have a low toxicity towards humans and are characterised by their ability to rapidly knock down insects. Synthetic pyrethrins (for example, permethrin) have been prepared to overcome the lack of persistence of the naturally occurring compounds. However, the increased persistence of permethrin is accompanied by an increased toxicity to humans. Other synthetic pyrethrins, such as bioresmethrin and phenothrin, are less toxic than natural pyrethrins and consequently are suitable for space treatments.

Organophosphorous insecticides, which include chlorpyrifos, dichlorvos, diazinon and malathion, are usually highly toxic. They have a moderate residual activity and among other effects on materials, most compounds stain red carpets.

Carbamates, like the organophosphorous insecticides, have a moderate residual activity and effective knockdown ability. They are found often in commercially available household products. Carbamate-based insecticides include carbaryl, bendiocarb and propoxur.

Desiccant dusts, usually made up of diatomaceous earth or silica, are non-poisonous and extremely effective for use under cupboards, in cracks and in other secluded areas. They remain active for long periods and can be obtained with pyrethrin additives which enhance their knockdown capability.

Monitoring collection areas

Regularly and carefully inspect collection areas. Observe objects in the collection, storage and display units and secluded areas (cracks, crevices, under furniture) in which either insects or signs of activity may be present. Use a torch to inspect secluded places. Indications of potential problems include:

- sightings of insects (adult, pupal or larval forms);
- frass (wood dust and faecal debris), remnants of cocoons, webs, skins, and the like; and
- exit holes in wood, damage to materials in the collection.

Sticky traps are commercially available and may be used to provide evidence of both the presence and the type of insects in a collection, long before they are noticed by visual inspections. If sticky traps are used, keep records of the dates, positions of placement and insects detected.

As some sticky traps incorporate pheromones (insect sex attractants), they provide an early warning system that will allow action to be taken before collections are damaged. Of course, this will only be the case if traps are inspected regularly.

Use insect traps and visual inspections in a complementary fashion - the visual sighting of larval casts should be followed up by placing sticky traps in that area and the capture of insects by a sticky trap should be followed by a careful inspection of the collection area.

If it appears that insects are active the next steps are to determine the nature and extent of the infestation. Any material that would aid in the identification of pests should be collected - frass and obviously insects (at any stage of their life cycle) are diagnostic. Sticky traps are useful in this process.

Place live insects, especially larval forms, in a glass jar containing methylated spirits so their shape and size can be maintained before identification by experts.

To determine if an infestation is new or old, objects (for example, textiles) should be isolated and sealed in polyethylene bags or placed on a contrasting background (wooden objects). Regular inspections in the following months will allow new frass or other signs of activity to be noted.

When placing objects in polyethylene bags, take care to ensure that unfavourable microenvironments do not form within the bag.

At this stage two concurrent activities take place. Artefacts that have been infested by insects must be treated and the extent and source of the infestation must be determined and eradicated. The latter activity may involve treatment of the object, the storage and display area, the building itself or a combination of these. Each of these aspects of overall pest management will be dealt with in turn.

Treatment of artefacts

There has been a very strong move away from the use of chemicals to treat insect infestations with much research being directed towards the development of techniques based on the use of either freezing or low oxygen environments. These approaches, if correctly used, have the potential to treat infestations without any risk of artefact contamination. Despite this trend, there is still a place in an overall management program for chemical treatments whether they are used in treatments of infested objects or purely in a prophylactic mode.

Freezing techniques

Freezing techniques may be used for many organic materials but are not suitable for all artefact types. Artefacts which contain resin, for example, should not be frozen.

Steps in the freezing process and details of materials for which freezing is not appropriate are outlined in the section on Treatment of mould.

Although it has been recommended that a double freezing method be used if temperatures of only minus 18 to minus 20°C are used for pest control (Berkouwer 1994), the procedure described in this text has been successfully used for many years. It is very effective against Australian insects, killing eggs, larvae and adults.

A temperature of minus 20°C is convenient because it is the temperature at which most household chest freezers operate. Freezing is the cheapest, easiest and most convenient form of insect treatment. Check with a conservator if there is doubt about the suitability of an artefact for this type of treatment.

Low oxygen atmospheres

Killing insects using oxygen-depleted atmospheres is a useful, non-contaminating alternative for objects that cannot be treated by freezing. Low oxygen atmospheres can be produced by flushing a storage system with either nitrogen or carbon dioxide or by using an oxygen scavenger to remove oxygen from a closed system.

Carbon dioxide is more effective than nitrogen but is not as chemically inert. There is the possibility of interaction between carbon dioxide and objects to produce carbonic acids and/or carbonates, which are potentially damaging.

There have been numerous studies carried out to determine optimum treatment times for particular insect pests but at this time no hard-and-fast rules have been developed. Some general principles do apply. Shorter exposure times will be effective if higher temperatures, lower relative humidities and lower oxygen concentrations are used. To be most effective against insect pests the oxygen concentration must be kept below 1%.

The method of lowering the oxygen concentration will be determined by the size of the object to be treated and by the availability and cost of appropriate equipment and expertise.

Methods which may be used to treat infested objects include:

- flushing a bag with an inert gas until the oxygen concentration is less than 0.1% and then adjusting the gas flow to maintain the low oxygen level;
- flushing a bag as described above and sealing it after an appropriate amount of an oxygen scavenger has been added; and
- adding a calculated number of satchels of oxygen scavenger to a bag and sealing it.

These three methods have been described in detail by Daniel *et al* (1993) with additional information on the properties and use of oxygen scavengers, Ageless, being provided by Grattan and Gilberg (1994) and Gilberg and Roach (1993).

In all cases the bags into which the artefacts are placed must have a very low gas permeability. Suitable bags for use with oxygen scavengers include those made from polychlorofluoroethylene ('Aclar') and polyvinylidene chloride ('Cryovac').

The first two oxygen-depletion methods, which are best suited for the treatment of large objects, should be left in the hands of professionals. Specialised equipment is needed and careful control must be exercised over the relative humidity of the gas used to flush the system to avoid desiccation of sensitive objects.

The third method is well suited to the treatment of small objects, in particular those with a volume of less than about 100 litres. The oxygen scavenger, Ageless Z-2000, which is capable of absorbing 2000 millilitres of oxygen from 10 litres of air is recommended for museum objects. An indicator, Ageless Eye, should be incorporated in the treatment bag. This product indicates when the oxygen level has increased beyond 0.5%. Steps involved in the treatment of small objects include:

- buy or make bags using a heat sealer and appropriate barrier film (see above). The latter option is recommended as bags can be tailored to particular objects. Unfortunately both bags and barrier film are quite expensive; and
- calculate the approximate volume of oxygen in the bag, using the dimensions of the bag, the approximate volume of the object and the concentration of oxygen (O_2) in the air.

Volume O_2 = (bag volume - object volume) x 0.2

- place the objects and enough packets of Ageless Z-2000 in the prepared bag. As the Ageless packets become hot when the scavenger reacts with oxygen they must **not** come into contact with the objects;
- seal the bag. If possible, evacuate the bag before sealing, using a vacuum cleaner operating in reverse. This will extend the life of the Ageless scavenger significantly but take care to ensure that objects are not crushed;
- store the bags at 30°C for about three weeks. If the objects are left at room temperature treatment should continue for at least three months; and
- following treatment remove the objects from the bags, discard the Ageless packets, inspect and carefully vacuum the objects. The bags may be reused.

Chemical treatments

Factors to be considered when choosing chemical insecticides include:

- toxicity to the insect;
- toxicity to people;
- effects on objects;
- environmental effects; and
- cost.

The area of chemical control of insects is highly specialised. Insecticides act in a variety of ways - as stomach poisons, by interrupting developmental stages or by contact - and they may be applied in many different forms - as dusts, emulsions, oil concentrates, gases and impregnated resin strips. The active ingredients of pesticides also vary.

Insect growth regulators are persistent chemicals which may be used in storage and display areas. They do not rapidly knock down insects; instead, they act by upsetting the balance of hormones needed to control growth and development of insects. In this way breeding cycles are interrupted and control is exerted over developing insect populations.

While there is merit in the application of residual pesticides to a building and its internal structures, the treatment of artefacts should be based on the application of non-residual chemicals followed by appropriate remedial action to prevent reinfestation. As many chemicals react with artefact materials, choose carefully insecticides for use near collections.

The availability of portable fumigation 'bubbles' increases the flexibility of larger organisations when treatment of objects becomes necessary. Bubbles of varying sizes are available and are particularly well suited to the treatment of wooden objects affected by borers.

Information about particular chemical treatments is provided in Appendix 3.

Review and assessment of procedures

It is important not just to 'clean up' after a pest problem. Assess the situation so similar problems do not occur in the future. Prepare an action plan outlining the steps to be taken to minimise future risks. Re-examine all factors which affect pest management to identify and take remedial action against any deficiencies in the control mechanisms.

BIBLIOGRAPHY

Australian Library and Information Association, 1989, *Conservation of Library Materials*, Newsletter No. 5, pp. 1-4.

Berkouwer, M., 1994, Freezing to eradicate insect pests in textiles at Brodsworth Hall, *The Conservator*, No. 18, pp. 15-22.

Daniel, V., Maekawa, S., Preusser, F.D. and Hanlon, G., 1993, Nitrogen fumigation: a viable alternative, in *Preprints, ICOM Committee for Conservation 10th Triennial Meeting*, Washington DC, pp. 863-867.

Dodd, W., 1991, Freezing as part of an integrated pest management system: Review after seven years maintaining a textile collection, *AICCM National Newsletter*, pp. 12-13.

Florian, M.-L. E., 1994, Conidial fungi (mould, mildew) biology: A basis for logical prevention, eradication and treatment for museum and archival collections, *Leather Conservation News*, vol. 10, pp. 1-29.

Gilberg, M and Roach, A., 1993, The effects of low oxygen atmospheres on the powderpost beetle, *Studies in Conservation*, vol. 38, pp. 128-132.

Grattan, D.W. and Gilberg, M., 1994, Ageless oxygen absorber: chemical and physical properties, *Studies in Conservation*, vol. 39, pp. 210-214.

Pearson, C., 1993, Building out pests, *AICCM Bulletin*, vol. 19, pp. 41-55.

Pinniger, D., 1989, *Insect Pests in Museums*, Institute of Archaeology Publications, London.

Strang, T., 1993, *Museum Pest Management*, Student Course Notes, Copyright 1992, Canadian Conservation Institute, Ottawa, Canada.

Thomson, G., 1986, *The Museum Environment*, 2nd Edition, Butterworths, London.

GENERAL POINTS ON ARTEFACT TREATMENTS

This chapter has been adapted from a previous Western Australian Museum publication (1981).

Before beginning any treatment of an artefact, consider these four factors:

- the history of the artefact;
- the materials present;
- how the artefact is constructed; and
- the condition of the artefact.

Knowledge of an artefact's history is important to prevent the removal of material that may provide information about its past. Before attempting to remove a stain from a textile, for example, assess the nature and significance of the stain. Does the stain pose a risk to the textile itself? Does it provide information about past usage of the textile?

If some form of treatment is necessary, examine the artefact thoroughly to determine the material type, mode of construction and its condition. If there is any doubt about either the type of treatment or the possible effect of a particular treatment, consult a conservator.

Only treat objects if the intervention is necessary. Usually intervention is warranted only if the object is likely to continue to deteriorate if not treated. Keep conservation treatments to the minimum necessary for stabilisation of the object.

The methods described in the following chapters are for artefacts constructed of one material type that are reasonably sound.

Composite objects, made up of different materials, are often difficult to treat. In some cases the components can be separated and treated individually. If this path is taken, exercise great care as reassembly may be difficult following treatment.

If an object is fragile, badly deteriorated or very valuable, seek advice from a conservator before attempting any treatment.

If possible, try treatments on scrap or spare pieces of material to gain experience and to observe the effect of the treatment on the material itself. If no extra material is available, attempt the treatment on an inconspicuous part of the object itself. Only apply treatment to the whole object after this has been done.

Note that if an object needs conservation treatment its environment should be examined as carefully as the object itself. There is no point in treating an object and then returning it to the environment that may have contributed to its deterioration in the first place.

Conservation or restoration?

With every object to be treated, make a decision whether to conserve or restore it. **Conservation** is the minimum treatment needed to stabilise the object and to prevent it suffering further damage. **Restoration** involves conservation treatment plus the repair or replacement of missing or damaged sections.

Restoration, although often carried out to enhance the aesthetic value of objects, is really only necessary when replacement of missing parts will help stabilise and protect the object from further damage.

With all restoration work it is essential to know exactly how the original object was constructed. This may involve much research as the key to ethical restoration is the quality of the evidence that is available. Useful evidence may arise from:

- the symmetry of an object;
- the presence of patterns or lines of continuation;
- old photographs; and
- scientific examinations of the object, which may reveal old paint fragments, paint layers, and the like.

Do not carry out any restoration unless there is definitive evidence of what should be reinstated or replaced.

Conservators are governed by a Code of Ethics prepared by the Australian Institute for the Conservation of Cultural Material Inc (AICCM). It is recommended that anyone contemplating restoration work use this code as a guide. With regard to restoration, section 16 of the Code states:

> *Restoration and reconstruction are means of re-establishing the cultural values of cultural material. If undertaken, they shall be: without fraudulent intention, to the minimum extent necessary, and fully documented. The conservator shall use techniques which affect the object least, and materials which can be most easily and completely removed without hazard to any original part. The presence and extent of restoration or reconstruction must be detectable, though they need not be conspicuous.*

In theory, nothing original should be taken away, but in practice (and often for the greater good) material from the centre of an object is sometimes removed to make way for dowels or other jointing methods that do not distort the surface.

Restoration techniques are beyond the scope of this book and are dealt with only briefly.

Documentation

Whenever an object is treated it is essential to keep a detailed, permanent record of the treatment. This record should include details of the:

- condition of the object before the work was done;
- treatment carried out; and
- condition of the object following treatment.

The aim of the record is to provide as much information as possible about the object. Include photographs, drawings and written descriptions of the object where relevant. In many cases a sketch and written description will provide more information than a photograph.

Also add to the record any known history of the object, dimensions, the size of cracks (if any), missing parts, colours, component materials, treatment chemicals and procedures and so on.

Basic chemical information

Many of the treatments described in this book involve the use of chemicals. Take the following precautions when mixing and handling these substances, especially acids:

- always wear rubber gloves and protective glasses;
- work in a well-ventilated area; and
- when mixing and diluting chemicals, always add the measured quantity of the chemical to the water, never the reverse. This is especially important with acids and alkalis.

Preparing solutions

Chemicals come in both solid and liquid forms. Citric acid, for example, is a solid whereas concentrated hydrochloric acid is a liquid. When solids are involved in a formulation the composition is usually expressed in parts by weight of solid, whereas liquid formulations are expressed in parts by volume.

For most of the formulations mentioned in this book kitchen scales are accurate enough for weighing purposes and any convenient volume measure can be used.

A solution made up of a solid in water may be specified as the percentage weight of solid per weight of water (w/w) or, more usually, as the percentage weight of solid per volume of water (w/v). The two are almost equivalent as 1000 millilitres of water weighs about 1000 grams. Examples are given below.

citric acid (10%, w/w) = a solution in which 10 g of citric acid is dissolved in 100 g of water

citric acid (10%, w/v) = a solution in which 10 g of citric acid is dissolved in 100 ml of water

Solution strengths

Acids and alkalis - Concentrated acids and alkalis in liquid form are sold by specific gravity (SG) as they are not necessarily 100% strength.

Specific gravities of some commonly used solutions are listed below:

Sulfuric acid	1.84
Nitric acid	1.42
Hydrochloric acid	1.18
Ammonia	0.88

The convention adopted in preparing dilute solutions is to assume that the commercial chemical is 100% and to dilute it accordingly. For example:

10% sulfuric acid = 100 ml of sulfuric acid (SG 1.84) dissolved in 900 ml of distilled water

50% ammonia solution = equal volumes of ammonia (SG 0.88) and distilled water are mixed

The strength of a hydrogen peroxide solution is indicated by the number of volumes of oxygen gas produced by the decomposition of one volume of solution. It is available commercially as follows:

100 volumes = about 30% hydrogen peroxide

20 volumes = about 6% hydrogen peroxide

10 volumes = about 3% hydrogen peroxide

These solutions are supplied in amber coloured bottles. Store them in a cool place, protected from light (a refrigerator is ideal).

Mixing chemicals

Mix chemicals thoroughly in glass, stainless steel or enamel-coated containers. Do not use concrete water troughs, aluminium, copper or brass containers as the chemicals may damage them. Do not use polyethylene bowls as these may distort with the heat generated during mixing of certain chemicals.

Once the chemicals are mixed and cold, store them in glass or polyethylene containers. The majority of treatment solutions can be re-used a number of times. Discard the solutions when they are no longer effective and prepare fresh ones.

Disposal of chemicals

Local authorities restrict discharge of chemicals directly into a sewage system. Obtain copies of local by-laws and follow the regulations regarding chemical disposal.

Acid-alkali scale

All chemicals may be classified as being either acidic, neutral or alkaline. The pH value of a chemical gives an indication of its acidic or alkaline nature.

pH values range from 0 to 14. A neutral solution has a pH of 7 whereas an acidic solution has a pH less than 7. The more acidic a material the lower is its pH value. Alkaline solutions have pH values greater than 7. The more alkaline a solution, the higher its pH value.

The pH value of a solution may be determined in a number of ways. These range from the use of sophisticated equipment to impregnated papers that give characteristic colours in acidic or alkaline solutions. In the latter case, the colour of the paper after it has been dipped in the solution is compared with standard colour charts to determine approximate pH values. Colours range from red (acidic) through pale orange (neutral) to dark blue (alkaline).

Vinegar (acetic acid) and lemon juice (citric and tartaric acid) have low pH values and turn the paper red, whereas household soap and cleaning fluids usually have high pH values (alkaline) and turn the paper blue. Tap, distilled or rainwater should have a neutral pH value close to 7.

Usually pH measurements are used to determine whether all the chemicals have been removed by rinsing following the treatment of an object. Moisten pH paper with distilled water and place it on the clean object. Any traces of acid or alkali from the cleaning solution will show up as blue or red respectively. Repeat washing until the pH paper does not change colour.

BIBLIOGRAPHY

Department of Materials Conservation, Western Australian Museum, 1981, General points on artefact treatments, in *Conservation and Restoration for Small Museums*, 2nd Edition, Western Australian Museum, Perth, pp. 32-34.

LEATHER

INTRODUCTION

The skin of any animal can be used to make leather. The physical characteristics of a particular leather and its susceptibility to deterioration depend on the skin type and the treatment applied to it.

Long before genuine tanning processes were employed to prepare leather, raw hides and skins were subjected to a variety of procedures designed both to preserve and alter their properties. Examples of these procedures include working oil, grease and even brain substance into raw skins, softening hides by chewing (Eskimo) and exposing skins to smoke (Waterer 1972).

Animal skin products have been used for domestic purposes from ancient times until the present. The use of these materials has been documented in the early civilisations of Egypt, Assyria and Babylonia (2700-2500BC, Reed 1972).

By the year 1600BC, the Egyptians were processing into leather the hides and skins of the ox, calf, sheep, goat, lion, panther, gazelle, cheetah, antelope, leopard, camel and hippopotamus. Dehairing baths, alum tawing, vegetable and oil tannage, colouring and dyeing were all used depending on the requirements of the final product. Leather products of this period included document rolls, sandals, aprons, shields, saddles, boats, balls and thongs for bindings (Reed 1972).

Of major archaeological and historic interest are leathers derived from the more common animals, such as those of the cow, sheep, goat, pig and horse. Preparation of leather from the skins of marine animals and reptiles is a more recent development.

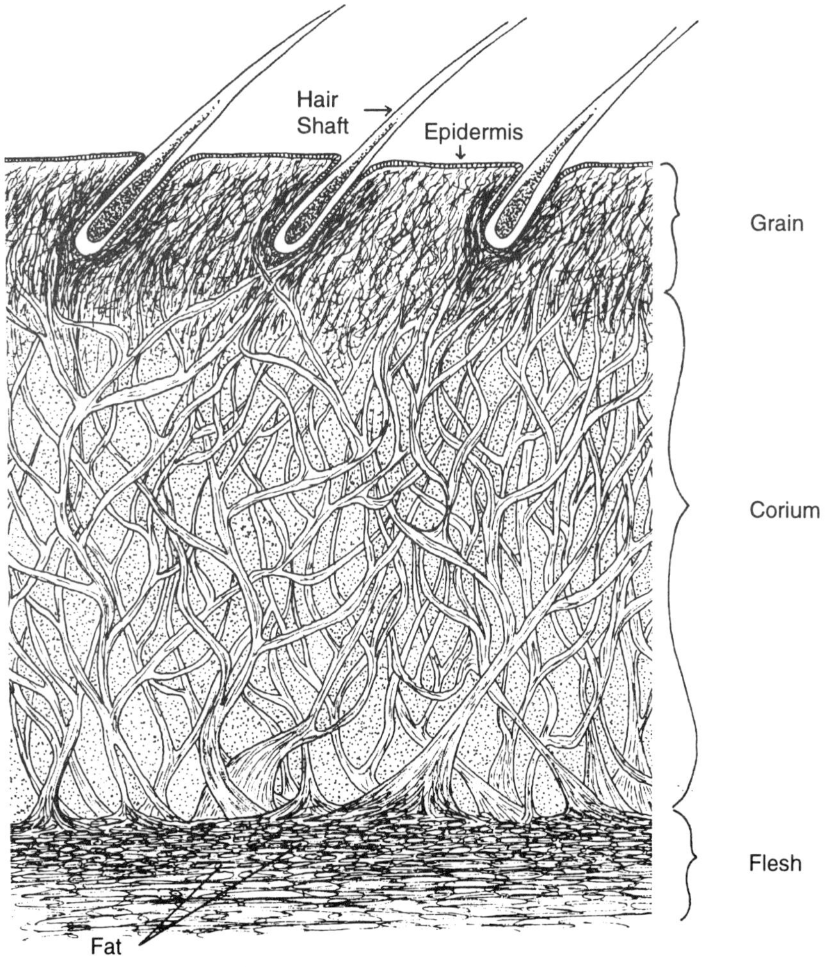

Figure 3: Leather – hide cross-section

Processing hides and skins

The nature of skin and its conversion into leather are described extremely well by Waterer (1972). The following summarises much of Waterer's descriptions.

Skin is a complex structure made up of hair, a protein-containing layer of collagen fibre bundles, sweat glands, fat and blood vessels (see Figure 3). The proteinaceous layer is a three-dimensional weave of collagen fibre bundles, which are large and loosely woven in the corium and fine and tightly packed in the protective grain layer.

The collagen molecule is made up of amino acids, linked by polypeptide bonds to form chains which combine in a helical fashion.

The processing of skins or hides may involve some or all of the following techniques:

- isolation of the corium (collagen layers);
- curing (dehydration by sun drying, dry or wet salting and pickling);
- tanning (vegetable, mineral or oil processing);
- dressing; and
- finishing.

During processing both the epidermal and the fatty layers of the skin are removed. Tanning processes are then used to stabilise the collagen fibre tissue. Details of some of these processes are outlined below.

Skin products include rawhide, parchment, semi-tanned leather and fully tanned leather.

Rawhide is the untanned skin of an animal which has had all of the flesh removed and been allowed to dry. It is not leather, having not been exposed to any tanning processes. It is usually a very rigid, tough material, used where these properties are essential. Despite its inherent toughness, rawhide is in many ways the least durable of the skin products because of its susceptibility to deterioration and moisture sensitivity. Some of its uses include the manufacture of suitcases, hammer heads, drum coverings, thongings and lashings.

Parchment is prepared by removing the flesh from the skin. The skin is dried under tension, by stretching on a frame. It is usually light coloured, opaque and smooth and takes ink and colours well. Modern parchments are considered inferior in their properties to medieval or ancient parchments because of the different processing methods and materials employed (Reed 1972).

Semi-tanned leather ('buckskin' or 'buff' leather) is produced by stretching the skin and rubbing into it an oil and fat emulsion (sometimes from the brain of the animal). The skin is manipulated until it is dry, soft and flexible; it is often smoked after this. When 'new', semi-tanned leather is soft, suede-like and extremely flexible. It is considered to be quite durable. Now oil 'tanned' leather is encountered most commonly in the form of 'chamois' or 'wash' leather. In earlier times it was used for purposes including clothing, pouches, gloves, saddle seats, and military uniforms and equipment.

Fully tanned leather is the end product of the tanning and finishing of cured skins. Either vegetable or mineral tanning processes are used to raise the shrinkage temperature of leather, to prevent bacterial decay and in the case of chrome tanning, to impart water resistance to the leather.

Vegetable tanning uses the tannins found in the bark, wood, leaves and fruits of particular plants to stabilise the collagen fibres. The colour of the leather before finishing ranges from pale to reddish brown, depending on the tanning agents used.

Mineral tanning refers to the use of metal salts to tan the leather. Salts that have been used include aluminium, chromium, zirconium and iron.

Originally a solution of alum and salt ('tawing') was used to produce a white leather, which could be dyed. Leather produced by tawing is not 'true leather' as the original raw skin can be regenerated by immersing it in warm water. Zirconium salts have been used to produce a washable white leather.

In the 1880s chrome salts were used to produce leathers which were hard-wearing, stable and water resistant. Chrome-tanned leather is characterised by a bluish colour in the middle of a cross-section of the skin. Chrome-tanned leathers cannot be embossed because of their resilience and open texture, making them unsuitable for some kinds of work, such as bookbinding.

Dressing leather involves incorporating materials such as fats and oils into it. The amount and type of fat incorporated into leather and the mechanical treatment of skins are both used at this stage to produce the desired properties. Sole leather, for example, is rolled and only lightly oiled to produce a hard, slightly pliable material, whereas harness leather has a mixture of oil and tallow worked into it to induce strength, flexibility and water resistance.

Finishing processes tend to affect the appearance of the leather, with little impact on other properties. Traditional finishing processes include staining, dyeing, graining, plating, boarding, enamelling (to produce 'patent' leather) and abrading (to produce a suede or velvet finish).

Today leathers are classified according to either the type of animal from which they were derived or the type of treatment to which they have been subjected. Smaller animals such as goats and sheep or the young of larger animals usually produce fine leathers.

Technically the term 'leather' only refers to skin products that have been fully tanned (vegetable or mineral tannages). The term will be used in this strict sense (unless specified otherwise) for the rest of this section.

DETERIORATION

Leather is composed of tanned collagen, moisture, oils and fat. Leather in good condition will have an acidity between pH 3 and pH 6, a water content between 12-20 per cent and a fat content in the range 2-10%. Within these limits equilibrium is maintained; outside them, deterioration accelerates.

If there is too much fat in the leather, water is repelled, resulting in the leather eventually becoming hard, brittle and inflexible. Once this occurs, it is difficult to return the leather to its original condition.

Leather is affected adversely by a range of environmental and biological agents, careless handling, and poor storage and display techniques. Some of these deterioration processes include:

- attack by moulds, bacteria, rats, termites and many kinds of insects. A combination of excessive lubrication and high relative humidity (above 65%) provides the right conditions for mould to develop on leather;
- drying out of leather and the development of hard, brittle and cracked leather due to excessive lubrication and low relative humidity (below 45%);
- corrosion of metals in contact with fatty materials incorporated in leather dressings. For example, a turquoise, waxy substance often forms on copper fastenings;
- attack on collagen molecules, and the subsequent breakdown of leather, which is catalysed by metal ions, copper (II) ions in particular. These metals may have been incorporated in the leather from water and other materials used in tanning, from dyes or by direct contact with metals as a result of manufacturing processes;
- the effects of light, which include attack on the polymeric collagen components themselves, fading of dyes incorporated in leather and interaction with atmospheric compounds to form harmful substances. Skin products that still have hair attached are susceptible to both insect attack and light-induced damage that may result in substantial hair loss;
- physical damage can be caused by too frequent or too vigorous cleaning, rough handling or storage of leather objects in conditions under which stresses and strains are induced in the object;
- the development of 'red rot' in vegetable tanned leather objects. Certain items of harness, military equipment, book bindings and upholstery are susceptible to this type of decay which is caused by atmospheric pollutants; and
- chemical and mechanical damage caused by dust. The sharp edges of minute particles are abrasive and can cause fibre damage if removed by methods other than suction. Dust also acts as a nucleation centre, attracting fungal spores and acting as a centre for condensation and subsequent chemical attack.

PREVENTIVE CONSERVATION

Environment

Display and store items made from leather, hide and skin in a clean, well-ventilated environment maintained at a maximum temperature of 25°C with a relative humidity in the 45-55% range.

Very dry conditions (less than 30% relative humidity) will cause loss of moisture and embrittlement while high humidity (greater than 65% relative humidity) encourages mould growth.

Parchment is very sensitive to relative humidity fluctuations and changes dimensions as it absorbs and releases moisture into its surroundings.

Protecting skin products in a storage or display cabinet will help to stabilise environmental fluctuations while also providing protection against dust and insect attack.

Keep light levels to a minimum, particularly for dyed leather (see below for recommended levels). Avoid exposing any leather to bright spotlights or direct sunlight as both of these can cause discolouration as well as desiccation.

Best light values for leather objects

Material	Total white light (lux)	Maximum UV light level (μwatts/Lumen)
Undyed leather	200	75
Dyed leather	50	50

More information on aspects of preventive conservation are provided in Raphael (1993).

Storage and display

To maintain leather in good condition a high standard of cleanliness is needed. Vacuum and dust storage areas regularly to minimise the likelihood of microbiological, insect or rodent attack.

Protect leather objects from dust (textile dust covers, acid-free boxes or acid-free tissue) and inspect them frequently, preferably every six months, to ensure mould or insect infestations are noted at an early stage. Note that acid-free materials must be unbuffered. Buffered acid-free materials are alkaline and are potentially damaging to the slightly acidic leather.

Support leather objects in their desired shape when in storage and on display so that they do not need reshaping as they age and harden.

Avoid sharp folds or creases in leather. Fill rounded items with unbuffered, acid-free tissue paper. Supports of other shapes can be made from chemically stable foams such as polyethylene or polypropylene. Store large or long leather pieces horizontally to avoid stressing them.

If three-dimensional objects are unable to support their own weight, support them internally. The form of the support will depend on the shape of the object and the weight of leather to be supported.

Fit leather clothing or large objects such as saddles on made-to-measure dummy mounts. Stable materials, such as the above-mentioned foams, linen, dacron and most metals, may be used in the manufacture of these supports.

Use painted metal storage cupboards and furniture to reduce the risk of acidic vapours from wood products coming into contact with skin materials. If wooden furniture is used then seal and line it with impermeable coatings (for example, clear polyurethane) or laminates.

Standard, conservation-quality mounting and framing is usually adequate to protect art or documents on parchment.

TREATMENTS

If leather materials are stored and displayed in the most suitable conditions possible, the need for potentially damaging treatments can be reduced or avoided.

Only attempt treatments that involve the use of detergents, stain removers and similar chemicals after consulting a conservator.

Cleaning leather

Any cleaning has the potential to damage leather and should not be considered an automatic option for leather objects.

There are situations, however, when cleaning is recommended. These include:

- objects that have been acquired recently. Before their addition to the collection such objects should be inspected and cleaned if necessary. This must be done to reduce the risk of contaminating the rest of the collection; and
- objects on display or in storage that are at risk due to surface contaminants.

Before cleaning any leather a number of factors should be addressed. These include:

- the type of leather;
- the type of surface;
- the nature of any contaminants; and
- exactly what is to be cleaned.

The last point needs to be considered carefully as dirt or other accretions accumulated during an object's historical usage must be viewed in a different light to that which has been deposited during its period in storage.

Surface deposits that may need to be removed by cleaning include:

- inorganic dirt, dust and salts;
- organic residues such as fatty or gummy spews; and
- mould.

To distinguish mould, spews and crystalline salts it may be necessary to examine the leather surface under a microscope.

The crystalline nature of **salts** would be clearly evident and the presence of **fungal hyphae** (fine fibrous strands) should allow these contaminants to be identified.

Gummy spews are formed when oils, fish oils in particular, breakdown. These resinous-looking substances are usually smelly and unpleasant to touch and handle.

Corrosion of copper alloy studs due to the excess fat in leather. Turquoise, waxy material is evidence of copper corrosion.

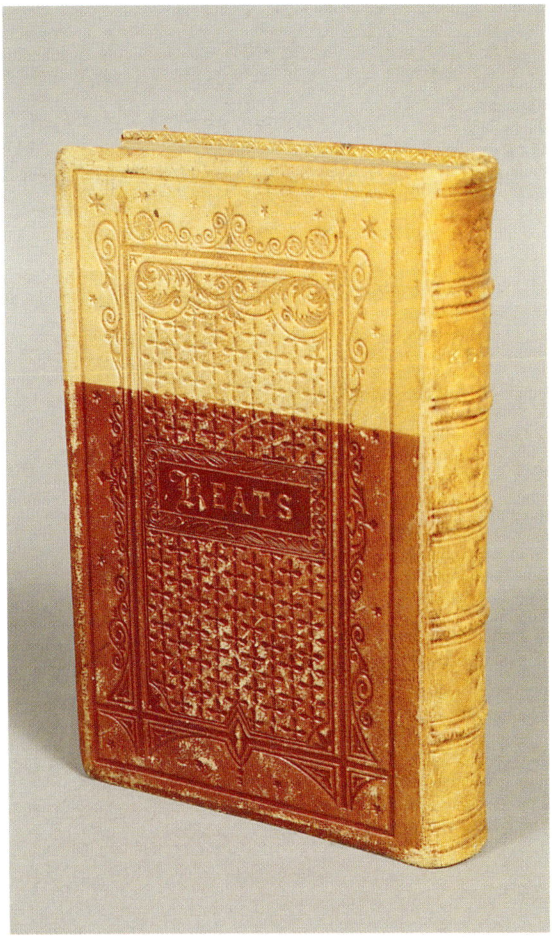

Leather bound book of Keats poems showing fading where exposed to daylight.

Indian knife and scabbard, showing embossing, dyeing and corrosion of the studs.

Fatty spews are greasy deposits that appear on the leather surface. They form when solid fats, or their breakdown products, migrate to the surface. Lubricants used to soften leather are often the source of these fatty materials.

If an object is in a fragile condition it may be better not to clean it to avoid further damage. Instead, try to protect the object against further soiling.

Cleaning techniques

If cleaning is necessary then the following mechanical and wet cleaning approaches may be used:

- vacuum cleaning;
- brushing with a soft brush;
- compressed air;
- granular erasers;
- scraping with a wooden spatula;
- petroleum-based solvents such as white spirit and hexane; and
- water-based cleaning - including the use of pure water, alcohol and water solutions, and emulsion cleaners.

Never wet the leather surface during cleaning as this increases the likelihood of the leather hardening when it dries. An additional risk associated with water-based cleaners is darkening of the leather surface. Avoid water-based cleaning methods unless the leather surface is relatively impervious to water.

Vacuum cleaning, with the nozzle just above the leather surface, is probably the safest cleaning method. It is particularly suited to cleaning dusty leather in good condition. Place a gauze screen on the end of the nozzle when cleaning. Check this periodically to make sure that pieces of the surface are not being removed.

Brushing with a soft squirrel hair or camel hair brush also may be used to remove surface dust. Note that even using a soft-bristled brush may not prevent damage to fragile objects. Dust is abrasive and pieces may be dislodged.

Gently applied **compressed air** may be appropriate for some objects. To prevent redeposition of dust, carry out this procedure either outside or in a fume cupboard. As with brushing, there is a danger of dislodging fragile pieces.

Granular erasers may be used to remove more stubborn dirt. Only apply this method to surfaces in good condition and only use approved erasers. This method is outlined below:

- use a household grater to grate an eraser finely (for example, Artgum 211 or Faber Castell). A plastic grater is preferred as the metal variety may rust or shed small metal particles;
- spread the grains over the leather and lightly rotate them with the palm of the hand or the flat of the fingers until the entire area has been covered; and
- remove the eraser crumbs with a vacuum cleaner. This is extremely important as the residues may affect texture, colour, pH and 'wettability' of the leather. In addition, as the crumbs age they harden and may cause physical damage to the leather.

Scraping, using a soft wooden spatula, may be used to remove thick surface deposits such as those occasionally formed by fatty spews. Only use this method to remove the bulk of the deposit and take particular care not to damage the leather surface. Solvents may be used to remove the residues left after scraping (see below).

Use a sponge, moistened slightly with **water,** to remove water-soluble dirt from leather objects in good condition and whose surface is protected by a water-resistant coating (wax, resin or similar). Identify the nature of the coating before carrying out this type of cleaning.

Use **petroleum-based solvents** such as white spirit or hexane, applied either as a poultice or with a sponge, to remove thin films of fatty or gummy spews. Test the solvents on an inconspicuous area of the object to ensure any surface finish is not affected.

Alcohol or alcohol and water solutions may be used to remove surface salts. A low water content is desirable to minimise damage to the leather. Also test the solution to ensure it has no detrimental effect on the leather surface.

An **emulsion cleaner**, whose ingredients and method of use are described below, is based on a formulation described in Fogle (1985). It has been used successfully to remove stubborn inorganic and organic dirt. As this formulation contains some water, test it before it is applied on a large scale.

non-ionic detergent (for example, Teric N9, Arkopal N090)	20 ml
carboxymethyl cellulose (CMC)	2 g
distilled water	1 L
X-4 solvent (hexane)	2 L

Prepare the cleaner in the following manner:

- vigorously mix the detergent, CMC and distilled water for several minutes;
- leave the mixture to stand overnight. This gives the CMC time to swell;

- add 150 ml of this solution to 1000 ml of X-4 solvent and shake vigorously until a creamy emulsion is formed; and
- the cleaning solution keeps indefinitely but should be shaken before use.

Before using the cleaner, test it on an inconspicuous area of the object to be cleaned to ensure it has no significant effect on either surface coatings or on the leather itself.

Rub the cleaner onto the surface with a clean cloth, rotating the cloth as it becomes soiled. If the object is very small or delicate, use cotton buds (or similar) to apply the cleaner.

Anecdotal evidence suggests that although **saddle soap** appears to have little detrimental effect on leather objects still in use, museum objects cleaned with this soap often seem to be in worse condition than untreated objects. Of major concern is the alkaline nature of the saddle soaps and the effect they can have on the leather (which is naturally acidic). Its use is not recommended for objects in storage or on display.

Biological infestation - mould and insects

Avoid using chemical reagents to treat biological infestations as there is the risk of damage or contamination of treated objects. Non-toxic methods of treatment are available.

Freezing, oxygen depletion and some chemical approaches are described earlier (see the chapter, Mould and Insect Attack in Collections). To be sure that the safest method is being employed to treat an object, contact a conservator before any treatment.

Mould

Aim to prevent mould growth by ensuring there is effective air circulation in storage areas and that relative humidity is kept below 65%.

Insects

Insects, including carpet beetles, spider beetles and cockroaches, will attack leather. Damage also may occur as a result of other insect types burrowing through leather in search of suitable foods such as the animal glue used in leather bindings or the wooden supports of upholstered furniture.

Preventing insect attack is preferable to treatment. Steps to minimise the risk of insect attack have been outlined earlier (see the chapter, Mould and Insect Attack in Collections).

Do **not** use methyl bromide as a fumigant for leather objects as it is damaging to leather.

Lubrication of leather

For most objects in a collection lubrication is probably **not** necessary. Take the following points into account before applying any lubricants to leather:

- for leather in storage, the main purpose of oils used in dressings is to prevent the leather from hardening if the relative humidity levels fluctuate widely. Environmental control of conditions is preferred to the application of dressings;
- the application of too much oil causes leather to repel moisture, a process that eventually produces a hard and brittle leather;
- too much applied oil also stains the surroundings and attracts dust and insects;
- excess lubricant encourages mould formation;
- some dressings darken leather and lead to increased stickiness;
- dressings do **not** provide protection against acidic pollutants;
- if reshaping only is required then often humidification alone will suffice (see below);
- dressings should not be used to 'feed' leather or to improve their appearance. If an improved appearance is desired and the object originally had a polished surface, apply a wax polish;
- never apply lubricants to objects containing untanned or semi-tanned materials; and
- lubrication of the leather covers of books is not recommended as the materials incorporated in the dressings make gluing repairs more difficult. There is also a tendency for these materials to migrate into the paper.

Note that as leathers age their ability to absorb fats and oils is reduced. The amount of fat and oil needed in archaeological and historic leathers (3-5%) is less than in their modern counterparts (10-12%). Pumping more of these materials into aged leather will only cause more problems.

To summarise, lubrication of leather is only necessary if:

- flexibility needs to be restored to an object;
- the storage or display environment fluctuates greatly, usually leading to an extremely dry or cracked object (due to shrinkage); and
- humidification alone is insufficient to induce enough flexibility for reshaping.

As most objects in collections rarely need to be flexible and hopefully will be stored in their desired shape and in relatively stable conditions, there should be little need for lubrication.

If flexibility is to be restored to hardened leather, rehumidify or 'condition' the leather before lubrication. Various procedures may be used (Calnan 1984). Some of these include:

- sponging the surface with an aqueous solution of an alcohol;
- covering the leather with damp sawdust (overnight). This approach can lead to problems as the sawdust is often difficult to remove; and
- placing the leather in a humidity chamber.

The lubricants, fats or oils, can then be added to leather using as the medium either:

- a water-based emulsion; or
- an organic solvent.

Vegetable oils are not used as frequently as fats because in the long term they are more prone to oxidation, a process accompanied by yellowing and hardening of the oil. Loss of lubricating properties follows.

Always test lubricants on an inconspicuous area before large-scale use and apply them to the grain surface (to minimise the risk of tide marks forming on this surface).

An **emulsion** (water-based) is the best vehicle for carrying the lubricant if tests show that:

- water does not discolour the surface; and
- the surface is permeable to water.

Applying oils in emulsion form increases the likelihood of oils remaining evenly distributed throughout the interior of the leather.

An emulsion formulation and method of application, as recommended in Fogle (1985), are described below:

lanolin	2 g
neats-foot oil	10 g
non-ionic detergent (Teric N9, Arkopal N090)	6 g
distilled water	100 ml

The emulsion may be prepared by:

- warming together (at about 60°C) the lanolin and the neats-foot oil until they melt;
- cooling the mixture to 20°C and then adding the detergent. Stir the mixture thoroughly and rapidly;
- slowly adding the distilled water (in small amounts) while stirring continuously; and
- observing the mixture for 10 minutes in a glass cylinder to see if it separates or remains stable

This mixture contains no preservatives and is best used soon after being prepared. Refrigeration will extend its life for a few months.

Paint the emulsion on the leather using a soft-bristled brush. If more than one coat is needed to achieve the desired flexibility allow the leather to dry before applying the next coat.

Use an **organic solvent-based dressing** if the leather is:

- fragile;
- darkened by water; or
- made impermeable to an emulsion by a wax or other coating.

As for the emulsion, a formulation and method of application of a solvent-based dressing are described in Fogle (1985).

lanolin	2 g
neats-foot oil	8 g
Shellsol T (aromatics-free White Spirit)	100 ml

Prepare the dressing by dissolving the lanolin and neats-foot oil in the Shellsol T.

Apply the dressing by painting the solution on the leather using a soft-bristled brush. Allow the leather to dry between coats if more than one coat is needed to induce the desired amount of flexibility.

Some commercial neats-foot oil products contain significant quantities of impurities, triglycerides in particular. Solid triglycerides will settle out on the surface of leather after dressing to form fatty spews. To remove these from neats-foot oil, refrigerate it and discard the solid upper layer. If possible purchase 'cold tested' neats-foot oil which has had the triglycerides removed.

If there is a surface finish that is impermeable to solvents it will resist penetration of oils and fats into the leather. In this situation it is better to rub an oil emulsion into the flesh side to encourage penetration.

A preparation such as **British Museum Leather Dressing** may be used to restore surface oil content if:

- dryness is only a surface condition; and
- the leather is very thin (for example, book covers, car seats).

This dressing, which should be applied sparingly, may be used with leather which incorporates metals. The beeswax in the composition leaves behind a thin film which will take a polish. A formulation is given below:

lanolin	200 g
cedar oil	30 ml
beeswax	15 g
X-4 solvent (or hexane)	300 ml

Prepare and apply the dressing as follows:

- mix the lanolin, cedar oil and beeswax together and melt by careful heating;
- rapidly pour the molten mixture into the cold X-4 solvent and allow it to cool with stirring;
- apply the dressing sparingly and rub it well into the leather with clean swabs; and
- after two days polish the leather with a soft cloth.

Note that a careful assessment should be made before any treatment is applied to the leather of a book cover. In most cases it is preferable to store books under the best possible conditions (see the chapter, Paper and Books).

For more information on the lubrication and dressing of leather refer to publications by Calnan (1984), Fogle (1985) and Tuck (1983).

Humidification

Humidification can be used to condition and reshape leather.

A simple humidity chamber can be prepared using polyethylene sheeting and tape. The object to be humidified is placed in the polyethylene 'tent', together with a jar containing water (50%) and alcohol (50%, methylated spirits or ethanol). The tent is sealed with tape. The alcohol inhibits the formation of mould in the high relative humidity environment created inside the tent. Monitor the set-up to prevent condensation formation.

Usually conditioning is carried out overnight whereas the time for reshaping varies considerably between objects. The time taken for softening to occur depends primarily on the leather thickness and the presence or otherwise of surface coatings.

As the leather softens it is able to be reshaped slowly. Remove the object from the chamber periodically and progressively **ease** it into the required shape. Usually it is necessary to use padding during this process to maintain the gradually changing shape. Non-buffered, acid-free tissue or polyethylene foam are suitable padding materials.

Treatment of attached metal fittings

Metals most commonly found associated with leather are iron and copper alloys. Fats present in leather enhance the corrosion of these materials. A turquoise-blue, waxy material which forms on copper fittings is usually the most visible sign of corrosion.

Due to the intimate contact between the metals and the leather, immersion in chemical baths is usually not an option for the removal of disfiguring corrosion products. Careful application of physical methods is recommended. In some instances treatment chemicals may be applied using bentonite paste (see the chapter, Metals).

Copper corrosion products may be treated in the following way:

- use a soft wooden spatula to remove the bulk of corrosion products;
- use cotton buds soaked in leather cleaner (see earlier) to remove any residues; and
- coat the fittings with either microcrystalline wax or renaissance wax to minimise further corrosion. A corrosion inhibitor, benzotriazole (5%), may be incorporated in the wax if additional protection is required.

Very careful abrasive methods are best to remove surface rust. Apply microcrystalline wax to the cleaned surfaces to provide protection against further corrosion.

Repair

The repair of tears and splits in leather is a specialised task. Advice from a conservator is strongly recommended.

Use a backing material to support any damaged areas. Materials that have been used include leather and woven and non-woven fabrics such as linen, Reemay and Cerex. Synthetic fabrics often are preferred for reinforcing fragile leather due to their dimensional stability, light weight and strength. Internally plasticised PVA emulsions or acrylic emulsions are suitable for bonding backing material to the flesh side (where accessible) of the damaged object.

Solvent-based adhesives are safest to use on moisture-sensitive materials made from rawhide and buckskin.

Details concerning all aspects of the conservation of leather upholstery are provided by Selm (1991).

SUMMARY

- If possible, identify the leather or types of leather used.
- Check for mould or insect attack and treat before adding to the collection.
- Maintain the temperature at 25°C or below and the relative humidity in the range 45-65%.

- Control light levels to below 200 lux and 75 μW/ lumen.
- Do not fold or crease leather material.
- Support shaped objects with inert foam material such as polyethylene, polypropylene or dacron.
- Store in acid-free boxes or use textile covers. These protect from dust and act as a buffer against changes in relative humidity.
- Consult a conservator if specific treatments are necessary.

BIBLIOGRAPHY

Calnan, C., 1984, The conservation of social history and industrial leather, in *Taken Into Care: The Conservation of Social and Industrial History Items*, Proceedings of the Joint UKIC/ AMSSEE meeting, United Kingdom Institute of Conservation, London.

Calnan, C., (Ed.), 1991, *Conservation of Leather in Transport Collections,* papers given at a UKIC conference, Restoration '91, United Kingdom Institute of Conservation, London.

Fogle, S., (Ed.), 1985, *Recent Advances in Leather Conservation*, The Foundation of the American Institute for Conservation of Historic and Artistic Works, Washington D.C.

Raphael, T.J., 1993, The care of leather and skin products: a curatorial guide, *Leather Conservation News,* vol. 9, pp. 1-15.

Reed, R., 1972, *Ancient Skins, Parchments and Leathers*, Seminar Press, London and New York.

Selm, R., 1991, The conservation of upholstery leather - an evaluation of materials and techniques, in *Conservation of Leather in Transport Collections*, papers given at a UKIC conference, Restoration '91, United Kingdom Institute of Conservation, London.

Tuck, D.H., 1983, *Oils and Lubricants Used on Leather*, The Leather Conservation Centre, Northampton.

Waterer, J.W., 1972, *A Guide to the Conservation and Restoration of Objects Made Wholly or in Part of Leather*, G. Bell & Sons, London.

TEXTILES

INTRODUCTION

Although the word textile literally means 'woven' and a 'woven fabric', it has come to encompass materials produced by knotting, knitting, lace making, braiding and felting. Methods used for preserving textiles are many and varied and depend on the nature of the textile material and its chemical and physical condition.

Although the longevity of textile materials is determined largely by how well they are looked after, the survival of ancient textiles is usually attributed to good fortune rather than to the application of particular treatments, or to careful management. Often fortuitous storage conditions, as a result of materials being forgotten, lost or buried, are responsible for their survival.

A qualified conservator is the best source of advice concerning the preservation of textile collections. As a first step, however, it is necessary to understand the materials themselves.

Fibre types

Until modern times all textiles were made from fibres drawn from natural sources such as animal fibres (wool and silk) and vegetable fibres (hemp, jute, flax and cotton). These natural fibres are either protein- (animal sources) or cellulose-based (plant sources). These materials have been used in textile manufacture for thousands of years, following the development of spinning and weaving technology.

In the early 19th century attempts were made to produce fibres in the laboratory. Initial attempts involving the dissolution and reforming of natural materials had only limited success. Despite this, some semi-synthetic fibres, such as casein (protein-based) and rayon (cellulose-based), have been produced commercially. Rayon is a generic term which covers a variety of fibres including cuprammonium rayon and viscose rayon. Fabrics derived from rayon are likely to be found as part of a textile collection while those derived from the less common casein are less likely to be encountered.

It was not until the 20th century and the development of the petrochemical industry, that materials other than those from natural sources were used to produce textiles on a large scale. Examples of fully synthetic fibres include polyesters ('terylene', 'dacron'), polyamides ('nylon') and acrylics ('acrilan', 'orlon'). Both polyesters and polyamides were developed in the 1940s.

To modify the properties of the individual constituents, blended fabrics have been developed. In these types of textiles two or more fibres are blended before they are spun into yarns. In combination, or union, textiles with individual yarns of one fibre type are interwoven with fibres of another type, again leading to the production of fabrics with modified properties. The addition of acrylic fibres to other fibre types, for example, leads to an increase in the softness and warmth of the resultant fabric.

Fibre identification

Different fibre types require different conservation treatments. For this reason the identification of textile fibre types is most important. Microscopic examination of representative fibres is the most conclusive method of identification. There are numerous texts available which describe the features which allow fibre types to be differentiated (Catling and Grayson 1982, The Textile Institute 1970).

As the features of degraded fibres may differ from those of corresponding undegraded fibres, take care when selecting fibres for identification. Careful sampling and examination are essential for accurate identifications.

In many cases the condition of a textile also can be determined during this examination and identification stage.

Woven textiles

To make a woven textile the fibres are prepared for the rigorous treatments involved in weaving. Fibres from a bulk supply are twisted to form a continuous thread. The resultant thread can be tightly or loosely spun, to produce materials of differing densities, in either 'S' or 'Z' twists. The thread can be twisted alongside other threads to be made more bulky and stronger.

The weaving process involves the use of a loom on which threads are laid down parallel to each other and held under tension. These threads, called the **warp**, run the entire length of the cloth being produced. Other thread then is interlaced between the threads of the warp in set patterns, alternating between travelling right and left through the warp. This interlacing thread, the **weft**, effectively creates the cloth.

Plain or tabby weave is the simplest weave with the structure consisting of a one over and a one under pattern for the warp and weft. This produces a uniform surface on both the front and the back of the cloth (see Figure 4a).

Twill weave is slightly more complex, involving a one over, two (or more) under structure in which each successive pass moves along one warp, creating a diagonal pattern (Figure 4b). Variations of this pattern include chevron, herringbone and diamond twills.

Satin weave, although similar in structure to that of twill, does not have the characteristic diagonal appearance that typifies twill. This weave is smooth on one surface and dull on the other (see Figure 4c).

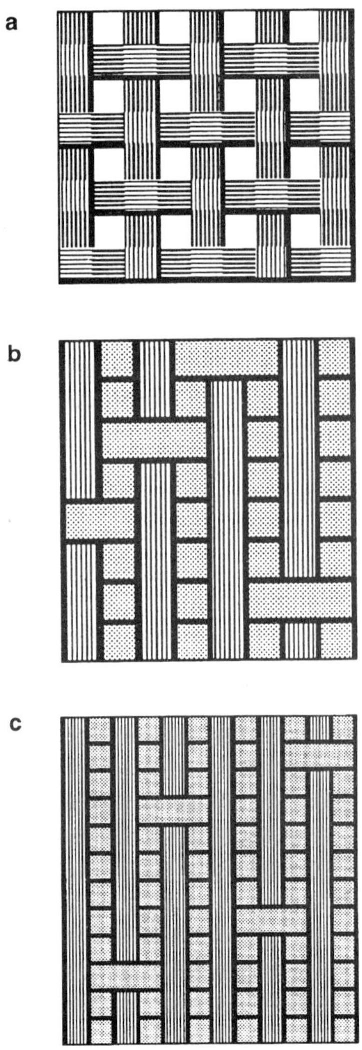

Figure 4: (a) Plain or tabby weave
(b) Twill weave - one over, three under
(c) Satin weave

Finishes

Often woven textiles are processed further before they are considered ready for use. Additional treatments may be aimed at improving appearance, texture, weight, flexibility, or ease of care. The most commonly applied treatments include dyeing, bleaching, mercerising, weighting, moth proofing, sizing and glazing. The majority of textiles in a collection will have had some sort of finish applied to them.

As the original treatment of a textile is an inherent part of the item, it must be taken into account before any treatment is embarked upon. Otherwise, ill-considered conservation treatments may change the character of the cloth irreversibly.

Dyes

Until the 19th century dyes were derived primarily from natural sources. Two of the best known natural dyes are indigo (from the indigo plant), and Tyrian purple (from molluscs).

Although some dyes have a natural affinity to fibres, most require the assistance of a mordant. The mordant, which is usually a metal salt, is applied to the fabric before dyeing to increase the attraction between the fibre and the dye. Mordants also are used to give the dyer a greater selection of colours. Madder dye, for example, gives a rust red colour when used with an alum mordant and a brown colour with an iron mordant. Mordant dyes are used on fibres or fabrics of wool, silk, nylon and cellulose.

Although natural dyes are not generally considered to be fast to light, actual colour fastness varies greatly, depending on both the fibre type and the method of application.

This section on weave structures, finishes and dyes was summarised from Landi (1985).

DETERIORATION

The principal agents of deterioration of textiles are:

- light;
- temperature and relative humidity;
- pollution;
- dust;
- insects; and
- mould.

Substances incorporated in finishing and manufacturing processes may contribute to textile degradation.

For instance, metal-based dyes and dye mordants can accelerate rotting of fibres, producing gaping holes in affected fabrics. For silks the weighting, which was introduced in the form of metal salts to increase the weight and make the silk crisper and more drapable, actively promotes the degradation of the fabric. There is little that can be done for these fabrics as even in stable conditions deterioration will continue.

Light

Light, in all of its forms, is damaging to textiles. Photochemical reactions initiated by light energy can lead to the deterioration of the principally organic material of which textiles are composed. Of particular importance is the UV band of light which supplies enough energy to break the molecular bonds found in textiles. Exposure to daylight is extremely damaging, particularly if the UV band has not been masked and the level of brightness is not diminished to the lowest practical level.

Duration of exposure to light is also crucial as the effects of light exposure are cumulative. Closely monitor and limit exposure times.

Heat generated from light sources is also a factor to be considered. Incandescent lighting is the most obvious source of this problem but fluorescent tubing will also cause heat build-up, especially if the light source is housed in a closed container (such as a display cabinet) with the textile material. Heating elements should therefore be isolated from textiles.

Temperature and relative humidity

Do not expose textiles to high temperatures. Often the effects of heat damage are not immediately obvious but may be manifested by fibres becoming brittle or discoloured.

Relative humidity is a well understood agent of destruction. Fibres expand and contract in line with changes in relative humidity. Continual fluctuations of this type create stresses in fibres which eventually may lead to fragmentation of the textile.

Under low relative humidity conditions fibres shrink and textiles become desiccated and lose flexibility. They are then more susceptible to damage when handled. If on the other hand the textile is exposed to high relative humidity conditions the chemical stability of the textile will be threatened, the effects of light exposure enhanced and mould growth and insect attack encouraged.

Chemical degradation

As in the case of heat damage, many of the effects of chemical reactions occurring in textiles are not immediately obvious. They often only become evident when physical damage to the fabric has occurred. The effects of chemical degradation are irreversible.

Although cellulosic materials can tolerate a limited degree of alkalinity, they are sensitive to acidic and strongly alkaline conditions. Both acids and strong alkalis attack the molecular structures in the fibres, leading to a marked weakening of the textile, with the fibres becoming extremely friable.

Protein fibres, such as wool and silk, can tolerate exposure to weakly acidic conditions but are susceptible to attack by alkalis and strong acids. These latter substances attack the molecular structure, degrading the fibres and robbing them of tensile strength.

It is important to take these chemical reactions into account when designing treatments for textiles. For example, the type of cleaning processes applied to a fabric must be thought through carefully so that damage to the textile is avoided. For instance, do not use highly alkaline cleaning agents on cellulose-based textiles.

Pollution

Air pollutants such as sulfur dioxide, oxides of nitrogen and ozone all contribute to degradation of textile materials. These pollutants are more likely to cause problems in towns and industrial areas where emissions from car exhausts and factories are the greatest.

Dust

Dirt and dust inevitably end up embedded in textile fibres. Dust particles can cause physical damage through the abrasion of fibres, or promote degradation by acting as a nucleation centre for condensation, mould formation and accelerated chemical attack by adsorbed chemicals.

An indirect effect of dust and dirt is the impact of cleaning on textiles. All cleaning, no matter how carefully it is carried out, has the potential to weaken textile fabrics.

Insects

Insects cause damage in two main ways. Insect larvae destroy fibres by eating them and soiling and disfiguration occur when insect faeces accumulate on textile materials. The presence of moths flying about is really only indicative of a potential problem as it will be the larvae that emerge from the eggs laid by the moths that will cause problems for textile collections.

Textiles made from naturally occurring materials are most susceptible to insect attack whereas synthetic materials are rarely damaged.

Of the naturally occurring textile materials, protein-based textiles (wool, silk and fur) are most vulnerable to insect attack whereas cotton and other cellulosic materials are more prone to microbiological attack. However, under conditions that favour mildew growth, wool will be attacked. Similarly cotton and other cellulosic fibres are still at risk from attack by insects such as silverfish and termites.

Damage also may be caused to textiles by wood-boring insects which penetrate textiles in contact with their preferred food source.

Mould

The most damaging of the microorganisms are fungi that attack cellulosic materials. Under conditions of high relative humidity and low air circulation these fungal types are capable of rapidly breaking down cellulose and drastically weakening the fabric.

Staining of textiles is also caused by fungi. Many stains are very difficult, often impossible, to remove.

PREVENTIVE CONSERVATION

All textiles have a built-in tendency to decay. A prime objective of conservators is to minimise the impact of factors which contribute to degradation processes. A further aim of textile conservators is to preserve the integrity of an artefact so that it reflects not only its basic nature but also its history of usage. In realising this aim, it may be necessary to avoid treating certain artefacts. Such would be the case where treatment is likely to result in the loss of historical information.

There will be times when decisions must be made regarding the removal or retention of historically significant material, which will contribute to the degradation of the textile itself if retained. Each case must be judged on its merits.

As some historic textiles cannot be cleaned or softened, they will remain inflexible and therefore susceptible to fibre damage upon handling. Textile conservation is heavily based on non-interventionist techniques such as using correct methods to support and handle these materials and ensuring the best possible conditions exist in storage and display areas. In this way, degradative processes will be slowed and significant historical and technical information will be retained in textile artefacts.

Environment

The optimal temperature for a storage and display area is in the range 20-25°C with a relative humidity of 50-55 per cent. Relative humidity levels of 65% or greater increase the risk of mould infestation and encourage insect attack. On the other hand, relative humidity values of 45% or less, increase the risk of desiccation and subsequent embrittlement.

It is very important that conditions are kept as stable as possible. Placing artefacts in boxes, cupboards, drawers, showcases and even frames will help to stabilise the conditions by buffering the impact of external temperature and relative humidity changes.

Ensure light levels in storage areas allow examination of objects without any strain. Store textiles in the dark. Maintain light levels in display areas at 50 lux with a maximum UV content of 75 μwatts/lumen.

Storage and display

Guidelines which will enhance the longevity of textile collections include the following:

- inspect objects before adding them to any collection;
- store textiles under favourable environmental conditions;
- use archival quality materials, especially for those materials which come into contact with textiles;
- use appropriate storage and display techniques which buffer against environmental change and which minimise stresses within textiles;
- do not store textiles in plastics; and
- adopt practices which control dust levels and minimise problems with insect pests.

Before incorporating textiles into any storage or display area, thoroughly inspect them for signs of mould, insects or dust and treat accordingly. In this way, additional problems are not introduced into these areas.

Store and display textiles under controlled temperature, relative humidity, light and dust levels.

It is also important to have a shelving and storage system in which items are easily accessible, well labelled and easy to find. The use of a position identification system is recommended. Where possible, individually box items.

Materials used in storage and display systems should be of archival quality, particularly those materials in direct contact with textiles. Acid-free materials (pH 7) are recommended. Some acid-free materials are buffered with an alkaline buffering agent. While these materials are safe for use with plant-based textiles they should **not** be used with protein-based textiles such as wool and silk.

As plastics trap moisture, do not store textiles in these materials. Textile storage in plastic increases relative humidity and may contribute to either enhanced chemical or biological degradation.

Before being routinely discarded, previously-used textile storage media should be examined to determine whether they provide any useful additional information such as ownership, manufacture or other details of an object's history. The storage media then may be either discarded or stored separately.

Dust

The room chosen for storage or display should be one in which dust levels can be controlled. The area should be kept as dust-free as possible. The extent of cleaning needed depends on the influx of dust from external sources. If dust is allowed to accumulate the risk of insect infestation increases.

It is very important to have a program of maintenance in which all shelves, floors, vents and windowsills are cleaned. Carpets are not recommended for these areas as they attract dust and insects. Use a vacuum cleaner with very fine dust filtering capability for cleaning.

Insects

Insects found most commonly in collections (carpet beetles, moths and silverfish) are best controlled by thorough and regular cleaning.

Isolate and inspect new items for signs of infestation before bringing them into storage or display areas. This can be done by enclosing the item in a polyethylene bag and putting it aside for inspection two or three weeks later. Inspect the bag regularly during this period for signs of high humidity or condensation. If no evidence of insect activity is found, including larva, adult insects or frass, then place the item with other artefacts.

If pests are found, a textile conservator will be able to give advice on the safest way to exterminate the pest without damaging the artefact. Do not apply pesticides or other chemicals to textiles as these may be damaging.

Do **not** eat or drink in any areas where artefacts are housed as food fragments attract potential pests.

Mould

Damage caused by mould is largely irreparable. If mould is found on a textile, isolate it immediately, place it in conditions of lower relative humidity and seek the advice of a conservator. Mould can be controlled by ensuring that the relative humidity of storage and display areas is kept below 65%.

SYSTEMS FOR STORAGE AND DISPLAY

Flat storage

Store textiles flat where possible. This allows maximum relaxation for fibres while avoiding weight-bearing stresses.

Keep items as flat as possible with minimal folding. If folding is unavoidable, support folds with crumpled acid-free tissue. This will minimise damage along folds.

If possible, do not layer items. Textiles will develop creases and folds under their own weight, let alone under the weight of other textiles.

Large metal map cabinets can provide flat storage for textiles, with minimum folding. Large, low-profile, acid-free cardboard boxes are also excellent storage media for textiles. In addition to allowing for easy transportation, these boxes provide light and dust protection for textiles.

Roll storage

To save space, some strong flat textiles may be rolled onto acid-free cardboard tubes. Note the following points if considering rolled storage:

- rolled storage is generally not appropriate for painted textiles or for those that have been treated with adhesives;
- only use tubes with a minimum diameter of 150 mm;
- the tube should be at least 200 mm wider than the textile to be rolled;
- if no large tubes are available, the effective diameter of smaller tubes can be increased by wrapping bubble wrap around the outside;
- if there is no option but to use non acid-free tubes, isolate the textile from the tube with polyester or polyethylene sheeting and acid-free paper; and
- do **not** use PVC tubing for the long-term storage of textiles.

Roll a textile and prepare a roll for storage in such a way that minimal stresses are placed on the textile and it is protected against adverse environmental conditions. Steps include:

- place the textile face down and roll it along either the warp or the weft;
- while rolling, keep the textile firm, though not stretched, and interleaf it with acid-free tissue as it is being rolled;
- when rolling textiles that are either lined or have a second layer, take care to ensure that the inner layer does not become bunched or excessively creased;

- cover the roll with a prewashed cotton or white polyester fabric and tie it with cotton tape (but not too tightly);
- store rolled textiles by suspending them in a frame using a rod passed through the centre of the roll;
- do not allow rolled textiles to touch each other;
- cover the rack of rolled textiles with a prewashed fabric cover. Use a lightweight fabric with a tight weave, to give the textiles protection from light and dust; and
- identify each textile by tying labels onto each tube, making sure that the labels are all at the same end.

Hanging storage for costumes

Only costumes in excellent condition should be considered for hanging storage. Store weakened costumes or those that are heavily decorated, in boxes. Pad costumes with acid-free tissue to minimise folds and creasing (see Figure 5).

Figure 5: Padded costume in boxed storage

If costumes are to be hung, follow these general principles:

- pad and cover the hanger to fit the costume;
- spread the weight of the costume onto the hanger;
- use a protective cover over the costume; and
- store the costume in a tall cupboard that allows for full suspension without bunching.

The hanger must be smaller than the costume and padded, in the form of shoulders, to fit the costume. Polyester wadding (for example, dacron) may be used to firmly fill the shape. By padding the hanger, the weight of the costume is spread over a larger area, thereby reducing the load-bearing stress on the shoulders (see Figure 6). Cover the padded hanger with prewashed cotton fabric.

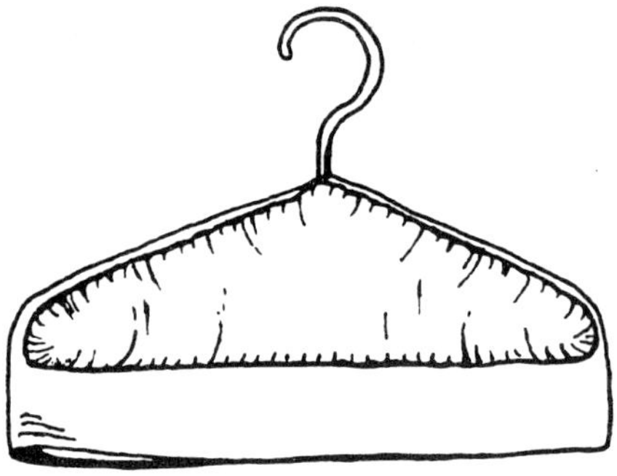

Figure 6: Fabric covered, padded hanger

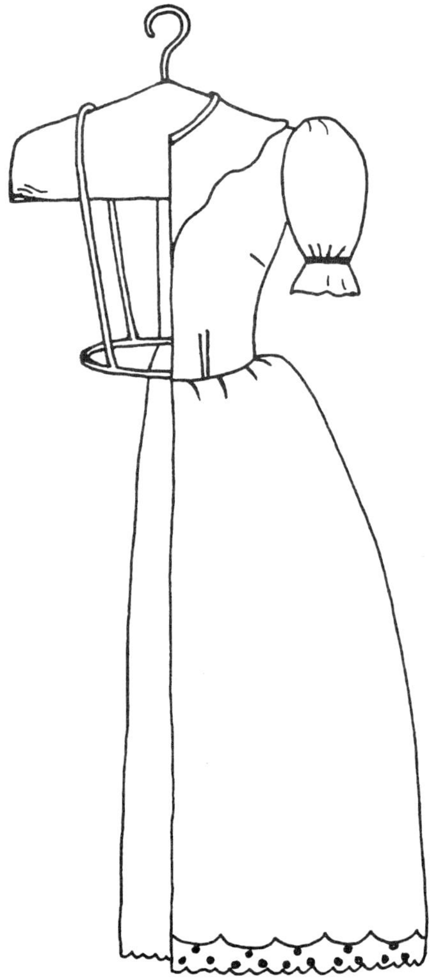

Figure 7: Hanging storage – padded hanger with cotton straps

If it is not adequately supported, the weight of the costume will cause damage in the long term. When hanging costumes it is important to spread the weight of the costume onto the hanger, but not to have the weight fully on the shoulders. For dresses, this can be achieved by sewing cotton tapes to the inside of the waist. Tie these tapes to the hanger to take the weight of the skirt off the bodice. Alternatively, and especially if the waist is weakened, a reinforcing cotton ‘hoop’ can be sewn to the inside of the waist. This is attached via cotton straps to the padded hanger. In addition to strengthening the waist this arrangement helps to ensure a more even weight distribution (see Figure 7).

Each costume should have its own removable and washable cover. Make covers from light, tightly woven fabrics such as white polyester lining. Avoid fabrics that have a tendency to cling or that have a strong friction hold (for example, cotton). Sew the cover so there is enough space inside for the costume to fit without restricting it. It must loosely cover the entire costume and have a closure at the bottom. Ensure the cover can be put on the costume from the side rather than over the top.

The cupboard in which costumes are hung must allow them to be fully suspended. As many dresses have trains it will be necessary to have very tall storage cupboards. The train should not be crumpled at the bottom of the cupboard. Do not overfill cupboards used for hanging otherwise stored costumes may become crushed.

Display

Textiles are most at risk while on display. Factors influencing the display of textiles include location, environmental conditions (relative humidity, temperature, light and dust), available space, public access and even the commercial and historic value of the materials themselves. Take all of these factors into account before deciding to display textile materials.

There are many ways to display textiles. Some examples of display techniques include:

- display on a flat surface;
- hanging;
- framing; and
- costume display on a mannequin.

Flat surface display

As long as the environmental conditions and the nature of the materials that contact the textile have been taken into account, **large flat textiles** may be displayed on any flat surface. It is important that any materials that come into direct contact with textiles are of archival quality. Display objects either completely flat, or slightly elevated for easier viewing.

Hanging

Physically strong textiles can be hung. Objects like tapestries, rugs and carpets can be suspended by stitching a Velcro strip to the top of the textile. The soft side of the Velcro is sewn to a strip of fabric, which is then sewn across the top of the textile to be displayed (see Figure 8).

Ensure the stitch tension is strong enough to support the weight of the textile evenly. If the tension is insufficient the textile will pull and bag, damaging its structure. If the tension is too great the textile will look 'quilted' and will be in danger of tearing.

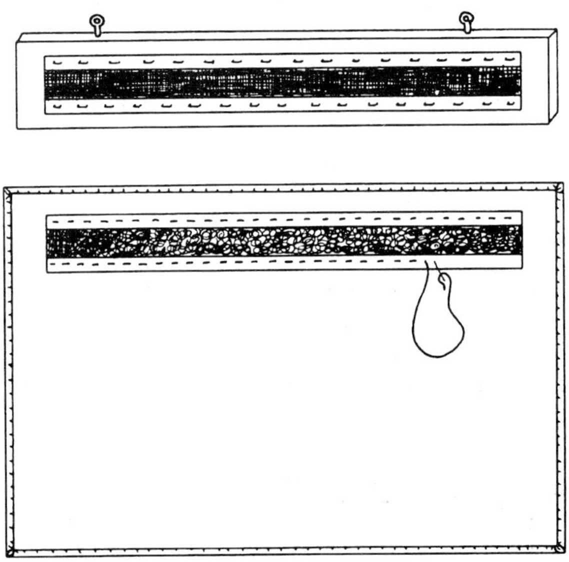

Figure 8: Hanging for strong, flat textiles

Attach the hoop side of the Velcro to a wooden batten, which has been sealed with a water-soluble polyurethane. Securely attach the wooden batten to the display wall.

Hang the textile by bringing the two Velcro sides together. To achieve the best result several pairs of hands will be needed. When removing the textile from display, do **not** pull on it; instead gently pry the Velcro strips apart. This will prevent damage to the textile.

Mounting and framing

Small flat textiles are less of a display problem. They easily fit into showcases or can be framed and placed on a wall. Lightweight textiles (such as samplers and lace fragments) which are in good condition, clean and chemically stable, are suitable for framing. Use archival materials for framing.

To frame a textile, first attach it to a mount, then frame it. Mounting involves covering a piece of board with cloth to which the textile can be attached.

Use a mount board of archival quality and a prewashed fabric of a neutral colour, preferably cotton or a polyester-cotton blend to cover it. If the fabric is dyed, assess its fastness (see Cleaning below). This is to reduce the risk of any colour transference from the backing to the textile. Remove all finishings from the backing fabric and preshrink it before use (see Figure 9).

To prepare a mount:

- cut a piece of good quality, acid-free 4-ply mount board, larger than the textile to be framed, with an edge around the textile of at least 30 mm;
- cut the backing fabric along the warp and the weft so that it is regular in shape and at least 50 mm larger than the board being covered;
- place this fabric face down on a clean work surface with the mount board then placed on the fabric;
- apply a small amount of adhesive (PVA is acceptable) to the back of the board with a small brush. Make sure that no adhesive gets on either the side or front of the board or fabric;
- fold the fabric over, onto the adhesive and press down;
- glue one side at a time. Glue the opposite side second so that the squareness of the fabric can be controlled;
- keep the corners of the fabric as square and flat as possible and leave the glue to dry completely; and
- cut any excess fabric from the back.

Attach the textile to the mount by stitching it to the mount board, as outlined below:

- place the textile roughly in the centre of the prepared mount board, allowing a slightly larger space at the bottom of the mount;
- using a fine needle, straight or curved, and colourfast thread, stitch the textile in place;
- use a running stitch, at least 10 mm from the edge, sewing through the textile and backing fabric only;
- cover at least three or four threads with the stitch at the front. It can be longer at the back where it is not seen; and
- if the textile is frayed or has weak use areas, use larger stitches to catch more of the textile and spread the weight, This will protect the textile from further fraying.

The mounted textile can then be framed, behind either glass or UV-absorbing perspex. To prevent moisture condensation, running of colours from the textile and mould formation, ensure there is no direct contact between the textile and the glass or perspex front. Leave an air space of at least 10 mm between the textile and the front of the frame.

Do not leave mounted textiles on permanent display as the effects of light exposure are both irreversible and cumulative.

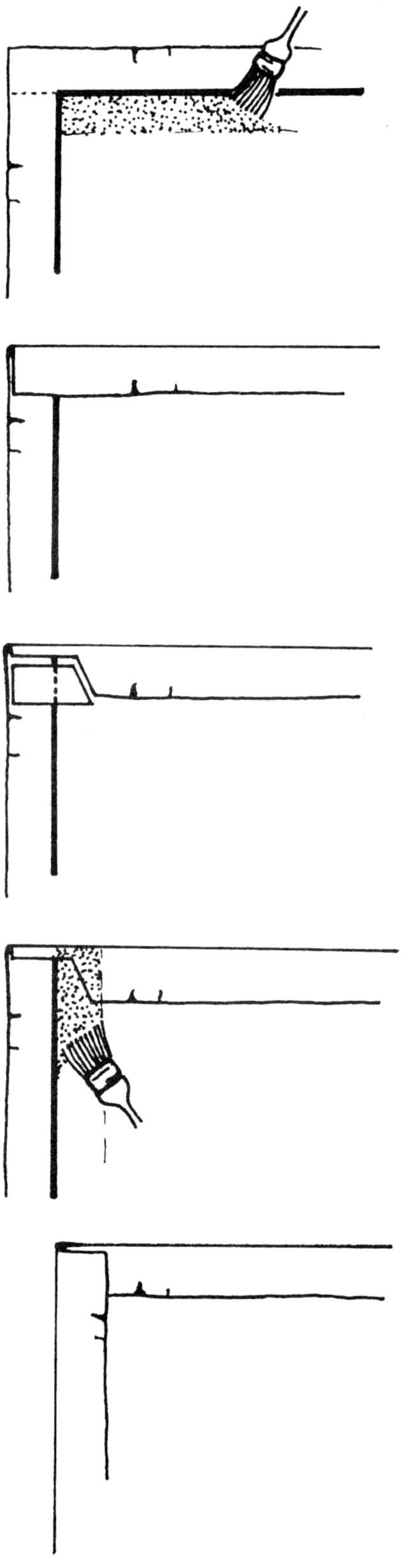

Figure 9: Steps for adhering backing fabric to mount board.

Sampler before treatment.
Damaged by insects, neglect and poor storage.

Sampler after treatment.
Supported on linen backing, framed.

Colours - Kings Park Memorial.
Mounted onto backing support.

3-D support - mannequin construction

When displaying textiles with a **three-dimensional shape**, questions of exposure and support must be addressed. Use support materials designed to suit the textile and ensure they are of the highest quality. An inadequate support will damage the textile. Support unavoidable folds with acid-free tissue. Be careful not to overstuff textiles as support is only needed to soften a fold. If a lot of tissue is placed in a costume it adds to the weight that the costume has to bear.

Never place a costume on a shop mannequin. Instead, manufacture a mannequin to fit the costume (see Figure 10). As people come in all shapes and sizes, so too do their costumes. Throughout the different periods there have been many varying shapes promoted by different styles of clothing. These styles and the development of particular corseting to accentuate shapes in costumes of certain eras must be taken into account when manufacturing mannequins.

The features, design and construction of a 'typical' costume mannequin are as below:

- the costume mannequin is a simple, single-legged stand with a body which slides on the central leg, allowing the height of the displayed costume to be adjusted;
- the body is made of a central frame to which a galvanised or painted wire net is attached;
- the basic body shape is a tube, smaller than the average person;
- polyester wadding is wrapped around the wire and areas where more shape is needed are built up to fit the costume;
- if the costume has a very small waist the wire net can be compressed;
- usually arms are not made for the mannequin. Instead a small amount of crumpled tissue may be placed inside the sleeves to give them shape;
- the mannequin is finished by covering it with a prewashed, neutral-coloured, cotton-knit fabric. This material allows finer adjustment to be made by further filling with polyester wadding; and
- stitching the mannequin in some areas will assist in developing the shape needed for each costume.

Mannequins can be reused for other costumes by refinishing and stuffing.

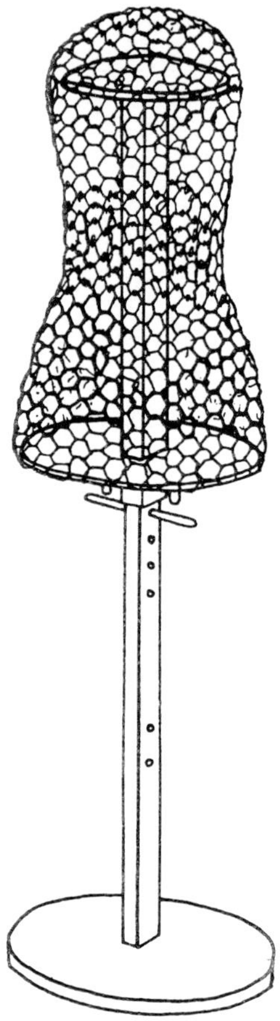

Figure 10: Costume mannequin before padding

TREATMENTS

Cleaning

Before cleaning a textile, establish whether it will benefit from cleaning and whether it is strong enough to withstand the treatment. Seek the advice of a conservator as cleaning, especially wet cleaning, may weaken textiles. Only an experienced conservator should attempt to clean painted textiles (such as flags and banners) and treated silks.

Remove loose dirt and dust from a textile before considering any other treatment. Use either a light-duty vacuum cleaner or a soft brush. Although the latter may be preferred in the case of small textiles or for localised treatments, brushing is generally inefficient, tending to relocate rather than remove dust.

Note that any other form of cleaning, such as chemical or aqueous cleaning, should be undertaken only by someone experienced in the cleaning of historic textiles.

Silk wedding dress attacked by rats.

Dress - before treatment.
Stained, torn, yellowed.

Dress - after treatment.
Washed and repaired.

Vacuum cleaning

As with all treatments, carry out vacuum cleaning only when necessary (for example, to prepare objects for storage, or after open display of textiles).

Very brittle or insect-damaged textiles are likely to be too fragile for this type of treatment. If weaker areas can be isolated and protected then the other parts of the textile may be vacuumed.

Vacuum cleaners used on textiles should be fitted with a mechanism that will allow the vacuum pressure to be adjusted. Either a variable speed motor or perforations in the hose system will allow the suction to be controlled. These controls should be at the user's hand so that adjustments can be made immediately the need arises. A low suction car vacuum cleaner is suitable.

When using a vacuum cleaner on textile material, consider the following points:

- fit the vacuum cleaner with a protective screen between the hose and the textile. A piece of muslin, nylon stocking or fine gauze, held in place by string or an elastic band are suitable for this purpose;
- hold the nozzle slightly above the surface of the textile while cleaning; and
- the fragility of the textile will determine the amount of suction that can be applied during cleaning.

As an alternative to placing a screen over the nozzle of the vacuum cleaner, place monofilament screening over the textile and move the vacuum cleaner over the screen. In this way, dust is drawn through the screen but neither the fabric nor its fibres are drawn into the vacuum cleaner. Bind the edges of the screen to prevent snagging with the textile.

Have very fragile textiles assessed by a conservator before attempting any cleaning.

Do **not** use beater-type vacuum cleaners and vacuum brush attachments on textiles.

Wet cleaning

Do **not** wash textiles as a matter of course nor as part of an annual maintenance or cleaning program. Avoid water cleaning textiles unless absolutely necessary for the survival of the textile in question.

Before wet cleaning historic textiles, consider these factors:

- possible loss of historic information;
- susceptibility to damage;
- colourfastness of dyes; and
- effects of washing on different fibre types, different weaves and on non-textile components.

Washing a textile in water can result in the loss of historic information or of the fabric itself. The look and feel of the textile may be altered permanently by this process.

Even the 'safest' of fabrics, the white cottons and linens, are susceptible to damage during washing. It is not always possible to ascertain areas of weakness in an old textile and the resultant fabric loss can be significant. For example, dark coloured stains of an unknown origin may fall out during washing leaving gaping holes in the textile. In addition certain finishing agents, incorporated in textiles to give them a particular look, may be washed out in water, irreversibly altering the appearance and characteristics of the textile.

Assessing coloured textiles is difficult as there are no foolproof tests to determine the colourfastness of the component colours. In the method described below, caution is advised as dyes may run unexpectedly, either in the wash or as the textile dries. If a soap is incorporated into the wash solution the resultant pH change may be enough for dyes that were previously set to become soluble and be lost.

Many textiles are made up of combinations of different fibre types, with cotton-silk and cotton-wool being common examples. Consider the 'wet properties' of different fibre types before washing and the reactions of individual fibre types to different pH conditions which result from using soap solutions.

Fabrics of the same fibre type but of different weave tension also are found in textile collections. Linings, for example, often have a coarser or a finer weave than the outer fabric. Washing in water may produce different shrinkage rates for the combinations, resulting in tensions in the textile between the differently woven fabrics. A further problem may arise if dust and dirt are trapped between the lining and the textile. Permanent staining of the outer textile has occurred when such a textile has been washed (Finch and Putnam 1985).

Also examine the different materials attached to textiles (buttons, beads, sequins, leather, piping) before washing as some of these may be affected adversely by water.

Bearing the above in mind, undertake washing if the textile is likely to deteriorate due to the presence of dirt or stains. Seek the advice of a conservator before washing, to ensure that this type of treatment will benefit the textile.

Regard washing as a one-off process which is followed up by correct storage or display to avoid the need for further washing in the future.

Pre-washing checks

Usually strong white textiles, such as linens and cottons, can be washed by the method described below. However, precautions must be taken before washing coloured fabrics. In particular, test each colour for **fastness** before any form of wet cleaning, as described below:

- dip one cotton bud for each colour into the soap solution to be used for cleaning;
- use buds that are only slightly damp;
- hold a cotton bud on each colour for a short time under light pressure; and
- use an unobtrusive part of the textile for this test.

Do not wash the textile if any colour transfers to the cotton bud. Consult a conservator.

Other checks are also necessary, as some attachments are not stable in water. Buttons and sequins made of gelatin and casein, for example, swell and disintegrate in water. Some fabrics, such as pressed velour, glazed chintz and crepes are not suited to water cleaning and treatments should be carried out only by a qualified conservator.

Surface clean the textiles, using a vacuum cleaner and screen, before wet cleaning.

Equipment for wet washing

To wash textiles, the following equipment is needed:

- a large flat tray;
- nylon curtain material, or similar, larger than the textile, to support the textile when lifting it;
- enough good quality water to cover the textile by about 20 mm;
- a pure soap; and
- clean, white towels to remove excess water from the textile.

The washing tray, such as a photographer's tray or bath, should be large enough to allow the textile to lay flat while immersed. Improvisation may be needed, especially if large textiles are to be washed.

Never lift unsupported wet textiles, as they are extremely fragile and the weight of the water could cause irreparable damage. Ensure that the support is lifted, **not** the textile. For larger textiles two or three people may be required to lift the support evenly and gently.

As an alternative to the use of a nylon curtain for support, a large textile such as a tablecloth can be rolled to reduce its size and facilitate handling. Rolling may also be used to allow a large textile to be washed in a container that is smaller than the textile itself. In such cases sections of the textile are washed progressively.

Although the use of distilled or deionised water is recommended for all stages of cleaning, softened tap water can be used for washing and for the first two rinses. However, distilled or deionised water must be used for the final wash. Borewater is not suitable and rainwater may contain impurities and particulate matter that could damage the fabric.

Commercial varieties of pure soaps are available. Use about five grams (about one level dessertspoon) of soap per litre of water. In most situations where washing is deemed essential, conservators use a non-ionic, pH-neutral soap solution. Before washing, establish which type of soap solution is best for the textile in question. Do **not** use commercial detergents because they contain harsh additives which are damaging to fragile textiles.

Washing, rinsing and drying techniques

Wash, rinse and dry textiles in a clean, dust-free room, according to the following procedures:

- dissolve the soap in a small quantity of water. Add this to the water in the tray and mix thoroughly;
- place the textile on its support and gently lower it into the solution, ensuring that the textile is wet evenly;
- gently press the textile all over with the palms of the hands or with the aid of a small sponge. This creates a mild suction which helps to remove dirt;
- **never** rub the textile or dip it in and out of the solution;
- if the textile is relatively strong, leave it to soak for five to ten minutes, then press again;
- note that colours can run with prolonged immersion, even after passing the colourfastness test; and
- after first wash has been completed for large rolled textiles, open it out, fold the washed end and repeat the process until the whole object is cleaned.

Rinsing is necessary to prevent dirt from resettling into the textile and to remove potentially damaging materials. To rinse the textile, follow these steps:

- using the support, or after rolling the textile, remove it from the wash solution and place it in clean water;
- repeat the pressing action with the palms of the hands;
- change the water again and repeat the process as often as required (usually two or three times) until

all traces of dirt and soap have been removed; and

- use distilled or deionised water for the last rinse.

Dry textiles as gently as possible. Never use sunlight or artificial heat. When drying textiles, observe the following guidelines:

- dry textiles right side up;
- using the support, remove the textile from the last rinse water and allow it to drain for a short time before placing it on clean, dry towels;
- cover the textile with more towels and gently press to absorb excess moisture. Gentle pressing should minimise any flattening of the weave;
- repeat the process with fresh dry towels;
- carefully remove the support and place the textile onto more dry towels and allow it to dry. Change the towels when necessary;
- spread large textiles, which have been rolled to facilitate lifting, as flat as possible for drying; and
- use a hairdryer on a cool and a low speed setting to accelerate the drying process. Avoid spot drying. While using a hairdryer, smooth folds or creases with the other hand. With three-dimensional items, such as dresses, separate layers of fabric and lift sleeves so that air can pass through.

Drying in this manner usually removes any need for ironing, which is a very harsh treatment that should only be carried out if absolutely necessary. If **ironing** is necessary, observe the following guidelines:

- iron the textile while it is still slightly damp (not wet);
- insert a cloth between the fabric and the iron;
- support the fabric fully, as while damp, it may not be able to support its own weight;
- set the iron at its coolest possible setting. **Never** use steam;
- **never** iron folds and creases into a textile as the fibres will eventually break along these lines; and
- pad sleeves and similar shapes with soft cotton to make ironing easier.

Do not starch textiles as it attracts insects and stiffens the fibres, which may lead to their eventual breakage.

Do not further treat stains that remain after washing. Do not try spot cleaning or bleaching as these usually weaken the textile.

SUMMARY

- Inspect textiles for mould or insect attack and treat before adding them to a collection.
- Identify the materials from which textiles are manufactured.
- Control temperature at 25°C or below and keep relative humidity in the 45-55% range.
- Keep light levels to 50 lux and 75 µW/lumen of UV.
- Wear cotton gloves when handling textiles.
- Where possible, store textiles flat, within boxes with acid-free tissue supporting any folds.
- Include sufficient padding to distribute the weight in hanging storage and use dust covers.
- Do not wash or starch as a routine procedure.
- Consult a qualified conservator before carrying out any treatments.

BIBLIOGRAPHY

Catling, C. and Grayson, J., 1982, *Identification of Vegetable Fibres*, Chapman and Hall, London and New York.

Finch, K. and Putnam, G., 1985, *The Care and Preservation of Textiles*, B.T. Batsford, London.

Landi, S., 1985, *The Textile Conservator's Manual*, Butterworths, London.

The Textile Institute, 1970, *Identification of Textile Materials*, 6th Ed., Manchester.

IVORY, BONE AND RELATED MATERIALS

INTRODUCTION

The use of bone and ivory dates back to prehistoric times. Early people, hunting animals for food and clothing, would use as much of the beast as possible. The teeth (ivory) and bones were used for arrowheads, handles and other implements. With time this usage extended to weaponry, musical instruments, religious pieces, personal artefacts, decorative items, artistic pieces and items for games.

When people speak of ivory, generally it is assumed the material is from the large incisor teeth or tusks of either the African or Indian elephant. The teeth of numerous other animals including the hippopotamus, sperm whale, narwhale, walrus, wart hog and wild boar also have been used for some of the purposes outlined above. Fossil ivories of the mastodon and the mammoth have been carved. An expert is able to distinguish these various ivory types by an examination which highlights differences in grain, colour, texture and hardness.

As the structure of bone is more open than that of ivory it is more easily stained and coloured. When worked and polished with oils and waxes bone can be difficult to differentiate from ivory.

Horn, baleen and tortoise shell are all skin-based materials that have been used for similar purposes to bone and ivory.

A vegetable-based substance, derived from the dried fluid of the seeds of the palm, *Phytelephas macrocarpa*, resembles ivory, stains easily and can be carved in the same way as authentic ivory.

In 1862 at the Great International Exhibitions in London, Alexander Parkes exhibited a material called 'Parkensine', a modified cellulose nitrate plastic. This material was substituted for ivory in billiard balls and laid the foundation for the plastics industry. Known as French ivory and, along with other materials such as mixtures of ivory and bone dust mixed with chalk, gelatin, gutta-percha and plaster of Paris, cellulose nitrate formed the basis of an extensive copy industry.

Today pigmented polyester resins are used to imitate these earlier works of art. Normally a silicone mould is made of the original and then pigmented resin is poured in. Once set, the surface can be treated with paint or dye to highlight any surface details. The opaque nature and uniform colour of these copies are usually sufficient to identify them.

Nature and composition

Bone-like materials (ivory, bone and antler) are made up of both organic and inorganic components. The major organic component is the fibrous protein collagen. This makes up about 35 per cent of these natural substances with the balance being inorganic calcium and magnesium phosphates and calcium carbonate.

On the other hand, skin derivatives such as horn, baleen and tortoise shell have the sulfur-containing protein keratin as the main constituent. These skin-based materials may be strengthened by the presence of inorganic salts.

Vegetable, or palm, ivory is composed of almost pure cellulose, the fundamental constituent of the cell walls of plants.

Synthetic ivory substitutes can be prepared from a variety of different materials (see above).

IDENTIFICATION

Although it is often difficult to differentiate between bone, ivory, horn and synthetic substitutes, an examination of the morphological, surface and structural features or of the chemical composition of a material usually allows a positive identification to be made.

A high quality hand lens and examination of photographs or photomicrographs which highlight structural features makes it easier to identify these materials (Penniman 1952).

Morphological features such as the shape and size of the materials in their unworked state, together with elements such as the marrow cavity in long bones and the pulp cavity in tusks may aid the identification process.

Ivory is basically another form of bone called dentine. Despite their different structures bone and ivory have similar chemical compositions. Thus, unless some material is available for destructive analysis, usually chemical tests cannot distinguish between bone and ivory.

Features which may identify elephant ivory include:

- the pattern of intersecting arcs, usually referred to as 'engine turning' or 'lines of Retzius', which are found on the cross-sectional (transverse) surface. It is more difficult to observe these lines on Indian elephant ivory;
- the presence of straight, continuous lines on the longitudinal surfaces;

- the presence of 'cloudy' areas, which are sometimes wavy, on longitudinal surfaces. These 'clouds' appear as areas which are whiter and more opaque than the material between them.

A further characteristic of all ivories is their fluorescence with a bluish light when irradiated with long wave UV light. Depending on the ivory type, this fluorescence varies from bluish-white to a deep violet blue (Penniman 1952). The difference in fluorescence from old ivories also may be useful in distinguishing old from new surfaces, as an aged patina fluoresces in mottled yellow tones while newer ivories and restorations usually appear deep blue-purple. Synthetic materials often exhibit a brilliant fluorescence, quite different from the natural substances.

Identifying features of bone include the following:

- generally lighter in weight than ivory;
- the presence of a porous cavity often visible on the back surface of an artefact;
- the presence of small pits that held the blood vessels and short longitudinal striations. These often appear as very small dots and darkened lines on the longitudinal surfaces, features which are enhanced by dirt which collects in them.

Microscopic examination, including the use of polarised light, or an examination of materials under UV light may allow materials such as horn, baleen, tortoise shell and vegetable ivory to be identified. Vegetable ivory is characterised by the presence of darker concentric lines on the transverse surface.

Vegetable ivory and man-made alternatives to the natural bone-like materials can be differentiated easily by spectroscopic or chemical methods. In particular, infra-red spectroscopy allows for rapid and usually unambiguous identification of polymeric substances (ivory copies). Analysis of this type must be carried out by an expert. Although this technique is destructive, only a small amount of material (less than one milligram) is required for testing.

A very simple, though destructive, method of determining whether a material is composed of a synthetic substance is the 'hot needle' test. Many of the polymeric materials used as substitutes for bone and ivory will melt when heated. A hot needle applied to an inconspicuous part of an object should give a quick, though not reliable estimate, of the composition of the object in question. Because of the destructive nature of this test, however, it is not recommended.

For a full description of the methods available to differentiate ivory, bone and related materials, refer to Penniman (1952), Thornton (1981) and Krzyszkowska (1990).

DETERIORATION

Bone and ivory have directional properties (are anisotropic) and are therefore susceptible to warping and cracking on exposure to moisture and heat. This is especially so for thin artefacts where even moisture from the hands may be damaging. Warping and cracking are essentially irreversible. Bone and ivory are also prone to chemical attack.

Deterioration processes which affect bone and ivory include:

- warping and cracking due to changes in relative humidity and temperature. Ivory is particularly sensitive to changes in relative humidity;
- chemical hydrolysis of the protein component of bone and ivory. This is enhanced by prolonged exposure to water;
- attack on the inorganic components of these materials by acids. Artefacts that were previously buried in an acidic soil will usually be degraded and fragile;
- attack on the organic components by alkaline reagents. A soft and crumbly matrix is the result of substantial collagen loss;
- bleaching by direct sunlight and UV light;
- damage by heat. When burnt these materials become grey or blue-black in colour;
- sulfur-containing compounds (for example, rubber and certain paints), which will turn ivory an unnatural yellow-orange colour if in contact with it; and
- staining due to contact with corroding metals such as copper and iron. The porous nature of these materials makes them susceptible to staining.

Ivory tends to develop an attractive yellow-brown patina as it ages. Do not attempt to remove this patina as it is part of its history, similar to the patina developed on a pewter tankard.

Horn, baleen and tortoise shell react in similar ways to those outlined above for bone and ivory. Avoid contact between thin films or delaminating surfaces of these materials and water as softening and deformation are likely to occur.

Cellulose nitrate, of which French ivory is composed, is an unstable chemical compound. As French ivory ages it develops a patina that is similar to that of ivory. Rather than being desirable however, the development of this

Tortoise-shell has been heated and shaped to fit these jewellery boxes. Objects loaned by Christina Sproule.

Closeup of box showing tortoise-shell overlaid onto bone.

Examples of scrimshaw on sperm whale teeth.

Elephant ivory showing intersecting arcs which help identify this material.

19th century ivory screen and stand showing cracking (Chinese).

A typical example of an ivory statue.

patina is an indication of the first stage of the potentially hazardous degradation of this material. As thin films of cellulose nitrate have been known to combust spontaneously, isolate artefacts showing signs of deterioration from other materials.

PREVENTIVE CONSERVATION

For conservation purposes ivory, bone, antler, horn, baleen and tortoise shell may be treated in the same manner, as they react in similar ways to given environments and treatments. For convenience, from this point all these materials will be referred to as 'ivory'.

Although ivory artefacts are reasonably durable, as is evident from the age and condition of many prehistoric materials, they can be damaged readily if improperly cleaned, handled, stored or exhibited.

Environment

Because of the sensitivity of these materials to changes in relative humidity, keep them within a temperature range of 19-25°C and relative humidity range of 45-55% (with no more than a 5% swing within a 24-hour period). It is desirable to maintain an environment with a steady relative humidity and temperature and, most importantly, prevent exposure to extreme conditions or rapid fluctuations.

If stored in the dark, ivory darkens in colour. On the other hand, these materials should never be placed in direct sunlight or bright artificial light as fading of colourings and dyes or an overall bleaching of the surface will occur.

If ivory is dyed, do not allow light levels to exceed 50 lux with the UV component restricted to 30 µwatts/lumen. For undyed material illumination levels should not exceed 200 lux with the UV component restricted to 75 µwatts/lumen.

Handling

To prevent staining of the surface, wear cotton gloves when handling ivory materials.

As ivory materials are affected by moisture, avoid dramatic changes in relative humidity. Usually, materials from tropical regions will have a higher moisture content than similar materials from drier areas. For this reason slow acclimatisation to a new environment is necessary in order to reduce the possibility of cracking or splitting (see the chapter, Preventive Conservation).

When packing ivory for transportation ensure there is an adequate buffer against both physical damage and changes in temperature and relative humidity. Wrap artefacts in acid-free tissue, place in a sealed polyethylene bag, wrap with bubble wrap and then pack in an insulated box. The aim is to control the temperature and therefore the relative humidity within the sealed bag.

Storage and display

If on display, place ivory within a display case or cabinet as these provide protection from dust and dirt and also buffer changes in temperature and relative humidity. Due to the emission of acidic vapours from some timbers, metal cabinets are preferred to wooden ones.

Store ivory under low light and low UV levels (see Environment above). As light bleaches the surface of ivory and constant darkness causes it to darken, considerable variation in colour may occur unless objects are moved in relation to the predominant light source. The effect of different exposures to light is usually evident in the differing colours produced on the front and back, or upper and lower, surfaces of objects.

Ensure lighting has no effect on the internal temperature, and hence the relative humidity, of the display case (see the chapter, Preventive Conservation).

Additional storage and display considerations include the following:

- inert materials, such as spun polyethylene or polypropylene, can be used to line storage shelves to provide cushioning;
- due to the discolouration induced by the sulfur in rubber, pads or adhesives made from this material should not be used near ivories;
- avoid contact with iron, copper alloys and coloured materials as staining may result; and
- horn is the material most likely to suffer from insect attack and should be inspected at regular intervals.

TREATMENTS

Very fragile ivory artefacts should only be treated by conservators. Artefacts in reasonably good condition may be cleaned of surface dirt and grime if proper precautions are observed. Refer stains caused by contact with corroded metals or coloured materials to a conservator for treatment.

Before cleaning or any other treatment, examine the object carefully to identify the nature of the material, to determine the strength of the object and to note whether it has been patinated or decorated. If the material is fragile it may need to be supported on a padded block which can be moved without direct handling of the object itself.

Examination

Guidelines for examination include:

- using a binocular microscope if possible. This will help estimate the depth and extent of cracks and the amount of deterioration;
- using microtests to determine the material of any decoration and how it is applied, as well as to determine its condition and ability to undergo any proposed treatment;
- noting and recording the presence of cracks (extent and depth), accretions, stains, old repairs, and new or recent damage; and
- observing objects under a long wave UV light. This is usually helpful in locating old repairs and some accretions.

Cleaning

Objects in good physical condition may need only dusting with a soft brush.

If brushing is not sufficient to remove the dirt and grime then wet cleaning may be attempted. Great care is needed if wet cleaning techniques are used. Water is potentially very damaging to these materials and non-polar organic solvents, such as toluene, have been shown to affect the organic components of ivory (Matienzo and Snow 1986). Ivory, for instance, has been damaged by even the application of damp swabs. Consultation with a conservator is recommended.

Follow the guidelines below if wet cleaning is necessary:

- **never** immerse an ivory object in water and do **not** apply water to cracked or porous surfaces;
- roll a cotton bud, moistened with solvent (see below), over the surface to remove dirt. Clean only a small area at a time;
- immediately dry the surface with another cotton bud or soft tissue;
- if necessary, remove residual soap with a cotton bud moistened in distilled water. Dry the surface immediately; and
- test any solvents on an inconspicuous part of any painted or decorated surface before any cleaning is attempted.

Solvents which have been used to clean ivory include:

- water;
- water and alcohol or methylated spirits (50:50);
- water containing a non-ionic detergent (see the chapter, Ceramics);
- white spirit;
- white spirit containing a soluble detergent (such as Vulpex B-30); and
- leather cleaner (see the chapter, Leather).

Leather cleaner has been found to be very effective. This cleaner has appeal as it has a low water content and its combination of a non-polar solvent and non-ionic detergent, allows a range of surface contaminants to be removed.

Care must be taken when cleaning ivory materials which have been deliberately painted as these attempts at cleaning may damage the original work. Even more care is needed when dealing with thin films of ivory as these are particularly susceptible to water damage.

Repair and consolidation

Only carry out repairs and consolidation after consultation with a conservator.

Objects that are broken or cracked can be repaired using pigmented resins.

Do not use epoxy-based resins as they yellow with age and may also cross-link over time. This latter property makes future removal and retreatment difficult. A further disadvantage of epoxy-based adhesives is that the adhesive is stronger than bone and ivory. Should further breakage occur it is best that the repair fail rather than cause a new break adjacent to the previous join.

If the ivory is flaky, powdery or delaminating, it may require consolidation using a resin and solvent combination such as Paraloid B-72 in acetone. For better penetration, work of this type should be carried out by immersion in a vacuum chamber.

Colloidal dispersions such as Primal WS 12, WS 24 and WS 50 also can be used. These have better ageing properties than emulsions and due to their smaller particle size and viscosity, are better able to penetrate.

SUMMARY

- Ivory is extremely sensitive to changes in relative humidity and temperature. Maintain relative humidity at 45-55% with no more than a 5% swing within a 24-hour period.
- Never immerse ivory in water or wet the surface.
- Always wear cotton gloves when handling ivory.
- Keep light levels **low** and **even**. Recommended levels are below 200 lux and 75 μW/lumen of UV.

- Acclimatise ivory from tropical regions slowly to minimise cracking and warping.
- Display ivory objects in a case to help buffer against rapid changes in relative humidity or store wrapped in acid-free tissue in an acid-free box.
- Obtain advice from a conservator before attempting cleaning or other treatments.

BIBLIOGRAPHY

Krzyszkowska, O., 1990, *Ivory and Related Materials: An Illustrated Guide*, Bulletin Supplement 59, Institute of Classical Studies, London.

Matienzo, L.J. and Snow, C.E., 1986, The chemical effects of hydrochloric acid and organic solvents on the surface of ivory, *Studies in Conservation*, vol. 31, pp. 133-139.

Penniman, T.K., 1952, *Pictures of Ivory and Other Animal Teeth, Bone and Antler*, Occasional Paper on Technology, 5, Pitt Rivers Museum, University of Oxford.

Thornton, J., 1981, The structure of ivory and ivory substitutes, in *Preprints, 9th Annual Meeting of the American Institute for Conservation of Historic and Artistic Works, May 27-31, 1981*, American Institute for Conservation of Historic and Artistic Works, Washington D.C., pp. 173-181.

WOOD

INTRODUCTION

Wood is a widely used and well known material. Although its general properties are familiar to most people, there is an underlying complexity to wood that is not widely appreciated. It is a natural substance made up of countless individual cells. These cells and their contents are composed primarily of:

- water;
- polysaccharides (hemicelluloses and cellulose);
- polyphenolics (lignin); and
- extractives. These materials, which are usually present in small quantities, may affect the colour and odour of the wood.

Examination of the cross-sectional surface of a tree trunk reveals three distinct zones: the bark, the light-coloured outer region (the sapwood) and the dark-coloured inner region (the heartwood). It is the heartwood that is used in furniture, building, sculpture and the variety of other common uses to which wood is put.

The tangential and radial directions may also be identified on the cross-sectional surface (see Figure 11). Wood properties vary in these and the longitudinal direction. For instance, when wood dries its shrinkage is greatest in the tangential (5-10 per cent) and least in the longitudinal (less than 0.1%) directions.

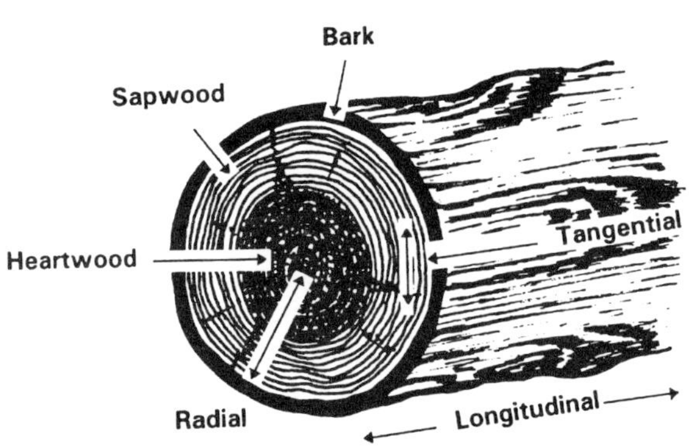

Figure 11: Wood – tree trunk – cross-section

From the time a tree is felled it begins to lose moisture, first at the surface and eventually from deeper within the wood. The rate at which green timber dries depends on environmental conditions and the type of wood. It is a challenge to timber specialists to dry wood without warping, cracking and splitting.

Seasoned wood continues to interact with its surroundings, absorbing or releasing water in response to changes in the relative humidity of its environment.

Wood samples are usually grouped into hardwood or softwood classifications. These classifications are not related to the hardness or the softness of the materials, being based primarily on the presence of pores (hardwoods) or their absence (softwoods). Balsa, for example, despite its inherent softness, is a hardwood.

There are also fundamental differences in the usual physical characteristics of the trees from which these timber types are derived. These are listed below:

Hardwood	Softwood
broad leaves	needles
deciduous or evergreen	evergreen
flowers or seeds	cones or seeds
complex cellular structure	less complex

DETERIORATION

Damage to wood and wood products may be caused by:

- poor handling or exposure to changing relative humidity (physical degradation);
- heat (thermal degradation);
- light and UV radiation in particular (photochemical degradation);
- biological agents such as fungi, bacteria or insects (biological degradation); and
- acidic or alkaline chemicals (chemical degradation).

Poor handling, exposure to fluctuating relative humidities and insects usually cause physical damage to wood whereas heat, light, fungi, bacteria and corrosive chemicals cause chemical changes to the wood substance. These latter changes can lead to the complete destruction of the wood.

Physical degradation

Wood may be physically damaged by either poor handling or as a result of stresses induced by changing moisture gradients. Its relative softness means that it is easily damaged by contact with harder and sharper objects.

Note that historic furniture which forms part of a collection should not be treated as furniture. For example, do not sit on the chairs in such a collection.

Excessively hot and dry conditions cause wood to shrink and crack. Conversely, cold and damp conditions cause wood to swell and warp. Substantial damage may be caused by large, rapid fluctuations in relative humidity. This is particularly so if wooden parts are closely joined and if their respective grains run contrary to one another. The restriction of free movement often leads to warping and cracking.

The rate of change of relative humidity and the way in which the wood has been sawn (along or across the grain, radially) determine whether bowed, cupped, twisted, cracked or split wood will result from exposure to inappropriate or changing relative humidity conditions.

The expansion and contraction of wood may damage either the wood itself or materials attached to it. Paint layers, for example, will tend to craze and flake if the underlying wood is subjected to alternating periods of expansion and contraction.

Physical damage may occur if no precautions are taken when wooden objects are transported from one climatic region to another. For example, wooden sculptures obtained from tropical regions which are transported to drier regions commonly develop serious cracks as moisture is lost from the wood. Similar damage may occur if items composed of wood or other organic substances are exposed to hot sunlight during the day and cold, moist conditions at night.

Thermal degradation

The most severe form of thermal degradation is obviously the complete destruction of wood by burning. The individual components of wood (hemicellulose, cellulose and lignin) also are affected by heat before the state of combustion is reached.

Heat weakens the bonds between fibres, leading to increased brittleness and fragility. For example, the embrittlement of newspapers with age can be attributed largely to thermal degradation of hemicelluloses present in the groundwood pulps.

The extent of degradation is determined by the type of wood concerned, the temperature and the duration of exposure. As chemical breakdown usually occurs more rapidly in an aqueous environment, the presence of moisture increases the effects of thermal degradation.

Physical damage will occur if a wooden object is placed close to a heat source. The resultant loss of moisture often results in shrinking and cracking of the wood. Thermal degradation is considered to be the most serious threat to wood kept indoors.

Photochemical degradation

Chemical, mechanical and light energy factors combine to contribute to the deterioration of wood that is exposed outdoors (**weathering**). The general appearance and surface finishes of historic structures often are affected in this way.

When wood is kept reasonably dry and exposed to sunlight or UV radiation, the surface tends to turn brown. A grey finish is observed when the effects of light and moisture are combined. The reactions are believed to be chiefly due to changes in the lignin caused by UV radiation. Usually colour changes are restricted to the surface of the wood.

In addition to the problems associated with photodegradation of wood itself, excessive light exposure will cause bleaching of certain dyes or pigments and fading or discolouration of surface finishes.

Biological degradation

Given the right conditions, a variety of different organisms will attack wood. These include:

- bacteria;
- fungi (such as the brown, white and soft rots); and
- insects (such as termites, furniture beetles and powder post beetles).

The type and quantity of extractives present in the heartwood are important in determining the biological resistance of wood.

The sapwood of most species and the heartwood of many others are prone to attack by a number of different wood-rotting and wood-staining fungi. **Wood-staining fungi** (mould) flourish in damp, dirty and unventilated conditions. Although moulds merely stain the surface of wooden items, **wood-rotting fungi**, such as dry rot, severely damage structural timbers. Wood-rotting fungi require moisture, some air, moderate temperatures and the absence of toxic influences to develop.

Termites (white ants), black ants and other insects are also responsible for serious damage to wooden materials. The most commonly occurring wood-boring insects found in museums are the furniture beetle and to a lesser extent, the powder-post beetle.

The **furniture beetle** usually attacks softwoods such as pine and fir and is commonly found in damp floorboards. It also will attack mature hardwood such as oak and walnut and is responsible for considerable damage to old furniture.

The **powder-post beetle** only attacks hardwoods and occurs most frequently in damp timber or in structural timbers of recent buildings.

Chemical degradation

Wood is generally resistant to a large number of chemicals, but it is still vulnerable to chemical attack, particularly under conditions of high acidity (pH less than 2) or high alkalinity (pH greater than 11). Under these conditions the long chains of the cellulose and the shorter chains of the hemicellulose molecules are broken, producing a softer, more friable object.

Chemical degradation is enhanced by high temperatures and the presence of iron salts, sulfur dioxide and oxidising agents, such as chlorine and nitric acid.

PREVENTIVE CONSERVATION

In order to ensure wooden objects are well cared for, take the following factors into account:

- light, temperature and relative humidity;
- handling techniques;
- modes of storage, display and support; and
- protection from insects, fungi and dirt.

Environment

To maintain wooden objects in the best condition, the following environmental conditions are recommended:

- relative humidity in the range 45-65%;
- temperature range of 18-25°C; and
- light levels of up to 200 lux for undyed or uncoated wood with levels of 50 lux for other objects. Exposure to UV light should be less than 75 μwatts/lumen.

Never place wooden objects in direct contact with outside walls or in areas in which large variations in temperature and relative humidity are expected. Avoid placing wooden objects near fireplaces, heaters, airconditioning vents and doorways. Maintaining relative humidity below 65% should ensure that fungal attack does not occur.

Where both metal and wooden components exist in an object, a compromise may be needed. In these cases, it is preferable to bias conditions in favour of wood as this material is more sensitive to changes in environmental moisture levels.

Never expose furniture and other wooden artefacts to direct sunlight. In addition to causing photochemical damage to the wood itself, veneers and glues are likely to be affected, often resulting in lifting, shrinkage, warping and cracking.

Handling

Common sense is the best guide when moving or handling any object. Follow the guidelines below:

- seek help when moving large pieces of furniture;
- grip objects only in areas that can support their full weight;
- remove any detachable pieces before movement;
- lift furniture clear of the floor when moving it. Otherwise the side thrust on feet or legs can place undue pressure on joints; and
- to reduce the risk of dropping wooden objects, do not use gloves.

Storage and display

To store, display and support wooden objects safely, follow these guidelines:

- use stable, inert materials for the construction and support of artefacts (see the chapter, Preventive Conservation);
- the mode of storage is largely determined by the size of the objects themselves - drawers, shelves, cupboards or even the floor itself may be appropriate;
- if drawers are used for storage, enamelled metal drawers are preferred. Wooden drawers may also be used but avoid chipboard and other composition boards;
- store flat objects on level surfaces while specially constructed supports or padding may be needed for objects with irregular surfaces;
- padding, such as polyethylene or polypropylene foam, may be used but only if the object's stability is not compromised;
- large flat-bottomed objects may be stored on the floor but should be raised on padded blocks to allow for air circulation;
- use dust covers for shelving and keep furniture clean and dust-free;
- maintain a stable, clean environment;
- do not store or consume food and drink near wooden artefacts; and
- inspect objects regularly, looking for signs of insect attack such as flight holes or frass that may have fallen from such holes. Regular inspection

Homemade gramophone.
Manufactured from a variety of Western Australian timbers.
Main: after conservation.
Inset: before treatment.

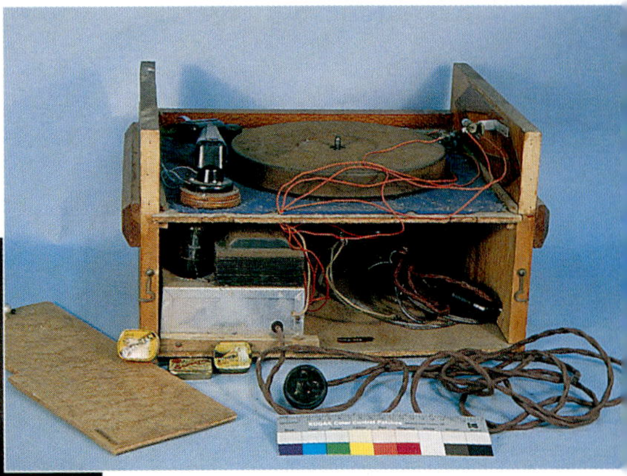

Below: Ivory inlaid chest (Japanese).
Rapid or large changes in relative humidity can cause the inlay to separate.

Child's merry-go-round.
Manufactured from painted wooden clothes pegs.

is even more critical for objects which cannot be stored under cover.

Large wooden objects kept outdoors should be placed on a concrete pad, under cover, to protect them from weathering elements and to prevent easy access by black and white ants. Additional protection from weathering can be attained by maintaining painted or varnished surfaces. Dust these objects regularly.

Use stands to raise wheeled objects from the ground. This takes the weight of the vehicle from the wheels and reduces access by ants.

If transporting wooden objects between regions of differing relative humidity, take precautions to allow the object to acclimatise to its new environment. Packing and equilibration regimes are described earlier (see the chapter, Preventive Conservation).

TREATMENTS

Before treating a wooden object, examine it carefully, noting significant features which may affect the type of treatment chosen. Factors such as the type of original surface, the presence of maker's marks, evidence of usage and previous repairs or alterations need to be considered when deciding on a treatment strategy.

Cleaning

As wooden objects and certain surface finishes are particularly sensitive to moisture, dry cleaning methods are recommended. The abrasive nature of dust must also be considered when contemplating cleaning, especially with objects that have highly polished surfaces.

For all wooden surfaces, but especially unsealed and polished surfaces (including French polished), the best approach is to use a soft brush and vacuum cleaner to remove dust and loose dirt.

Objects that have a surface that is not permeable to water (for example, waxed, polyurethane finish) may be cleaned using the approach described above or by using a sponge that has been slightly moistened in water. Do not allow water to lie on the surface of the wood.

Do not use wet cleaning techniques on polished wooden surfaces.

Consolidation or repair

Wooden objects requiring conservation or restoration can range from large structures and vehicles to extremely fine, delicate carved objects.

Understanding an object's past and possible future roles may affect the type of treatment undertaken. For instance, repairs to a horse-drawn vehicle that is to be used will differ from those for a similar object to be placed on static display.

There is a variety of techniques and consolidants that may be used to 'repair' damaged or friable wood. These repairs include consolidating friable components, filling gaps and gluing dislodged pieces.

Materials used to repair wooden objects include a variety of resins, waxes and adhesives. Some of these, not all of which are recommended for use, are listed below:

- resin and wax;
- polyester resins (for example, Paraloid B72);
- polyvinyl butyral;
- polyvinyl acetate;
- epoxy resins (for example, Araldite);
- cellulose nitrate; and
- silicone rubbers;

Unfortunately, inappropriate materials are often used to replace missing wood or as fillers for gaps and cracks. Some of these include newspaper, plaster, concrete, bitumen and motor car body filler.

The type of adhesive and the filler type will be determined by the proposed use of the object. If the object is to perform a structural role then the combination of materials will be different from those that would be used for non-structural fills. For structural fills where movement of the wood is likely to be slight, an epoxy resin and microballoon fill has been recommended (Grattan and Barclay 1988). The use of a fill of epoxy resin and sawdust is described elsewhere (see the chapter, Case Studies). A summary of traditional fillers is provided in Appendix 5.

As the techniques and chemicals used in consolidation are specialised, seek the advice of a conservator.

Furniture

Usually older style furniture is constructed and held together by dowels or pegs and animal-based glue. Although these glues are quite strong, they deteriorate with age, become very brittle and are easily broken, especially if excessive stress is placed upon the joints. Wooden screws, brackets and hold down clamps (table tops) were used in later furniture.

If restoring period or historic furniture, take care to use correct restorative methods. Incorrect procedures can undermine both the value and the historical importance of the furniture. If animal glues and dowelling were used originally, use the same materials in any restoration work.

Note, despite the recommendation above, there is some support for using modern materials so repairs and restoration work can be distinguished from the untreated components.

If a new piece has to be constructed and fitted to an old object, use original methods. Retain any remaining damaged, original pieces for future repairs.

As with all restoration procedures, research into the methods of construction of furniture is very important, often yielding valuable information which can guide any restoration process.

Staining and marking of furniture

Staining or marking is virtually inevitable on furniture that has been used throughout its life. These stains and marks often enhance the character and patina of the piece. Some attempts to eradicate staining and marks have damaged some fine pieces of furniture.

As the removal of stains and marks may involve the loss of both wood and patina, consider the available options before bringing the sander and sandpaper into action. Seek advice from a conservator. Drastic treatment may result in the loss of value of the piece, especially if problems are encountered with reproducing the surface finish and colour (often difficult tasks).

Inlays

A variety of materials, including brass, ivory and different woods, is used for inlays. Their differing compositions and reactivities to changing environmental conditions complicate repairs. Extremes of temperature and humidity will affect each of the materials differently.

The treatment of inlays is highly specialised. Do not attempt treatment before seeking professional advice.

Surface finishes

Surface finishes applied to wooden objects include:

- waxes;
- shellac (French polish);
- polyurethanes;
- oils; and
- veneers.

Exercise care when selecting a surface coating to apply to wooden objects. The purpose of the coating may be to either protect a friable surface or to confer a pleasant sheen to a surface that has become dull. In the past it was customary to apply drying oils, such as linseed oil, or waxes such as beeswax. The former suffer from the disadvantage that they yellow with age, a tendency that is accentuated under tropical conditions, and the latter often leave the surface of the wood slightly sticky. Sticky areas attract dust, particularly in the crevices in the wood. This creates favourable conditions for the laying of eggs by woodboring insects.

Depending on the nature of the object, **waxes** may be suitable as protective surface coatings as long as care is taken to choose a suitable wax mixture which leaves a relatively hard, non-sticky surface finish. Such a wax mixture may be prepared using some commercially available synthetic waxes. A useful formulation and method of preparation is given below:

microcrystalline wax	100 g
polyethylene wax	25 g
white spirit	230 g

- melt the waxes together and stir well to ensure that they are thoroughly mixed; and
- pour the molten mixture quickly into the white spirit and stir constantly while cooling so a smooth paste is obtained.

Several varieties of these waxes are available and the sheen of the resultant wax film can be varied by altering the grades or the proportions of the waxes used.

The high dispersive power of the microcrystalline wax helps to remove ingrained dirt from the wood as well as providing a protective coating of pleasant appearance.

Formulations made from beeswax and carnauba, mixed with turpentine, have been found to work well.

Several suitable commercial wood waxes are available and these give satisfactory results. Avoid waxes containing silicones (stated on the container) as they are very difficult to remove. This may cause problems if subsequent treatments are necessary.

Only use coloured waxes after careful thought, as these can alter the appearance of the wood. Clear finish waxes are preferred.

French polished furniture has a beautiful and lustrous finish but it can be damaged easily. As French polish is shellac dissolved in methylated spirit, any wet object or alcohol will either mark or dissolve the surface. Restoring damaged surfaces usually will require the services of a professional restorer.

Polyurethane finishes are clear, hard and resistant to wear but are virtually impossible to remove without damage to underlying wood. Their use on period or antique furniture is not recommended.

Oil-based finishes also give a lustrous shine but unless wiped down carefully can leave a 'tacky' finish which will attract dust. Oils which may be used on furniture include poppy seed, walnut and Danish oils.

Veneer is a thin layer, normally of some exotic timber, laid and glued over a frame of a different type of wood. If animal glue has been used and is deteriorating, lifting of the veneer may occur. If regluing is attempted, all traces of the old glue must be removed to ensure a flat finish is obtained. Refer large areas of lifting veneer to experts.

Upholstery

Upholstery is a general term which includes carpets, bed hangings, curtains, chairs, sofas and the components of seat furniture. Information concerning the deterioration, care and conservation of these objects may be obtained by reading the appropriate chapters that deal with the particular material types associated with these objects.

Discussion in this section concentrates on the wooden frame, rather than with the webbing, springs, stuffing, lining, cover and other non-wood upholstery components. Despite this focus, these latter components are important (Burgin 1990, Twichel 1990, Perkins 1990). Some general aspects related to their care and conservation are listed below:

- if extremely disintegrated material is replaced, clean and store it;
- use materials such as plywood and perspex to support deteriorated webbing;
- soft brushes and low suction vacuum cleaning can be used to clean stuffing;
- place and mould stuffing to its original shape during replacement;
- stabilise acidic hessian by using water poultices; and
- use ethafoam if reconstruction of the underupholstery is necessary for display purposes and the original materials are unable to be used.

As long as the original fabric has been retained, the colours, patterns and types of textiles used on **covers** often provide evidence of the style of a period. The conservation of covers is somewhat contentious, especially the issue of removal of the cover for treatment. Replacement is often difficult and cannot always be accomplished.

Apart from cleaning robust covers with soft brushes and low suction vacuum cleaners their conservation is best left in the hands of conservators.

The **frame** can provide useful information about the history of an object. Breaks in the joints or members and nailing patterns, for instance, may give an insight into past wear, abuse and repairs.

Repairing a frame raises many ethical questions regarding the use of adhesives, the replacement of parts and the general extent of intervention (James 1990, Podmaniczky 1990, Graves 1990). The following principles are useful guides when considering conservation of a frame:

- if part of the frame has to be replaced, document this and retain the removed section;
- minimise intervention so that as much of the original object is retained as possible;
- if an adhesive is required for a mechanical joint, use a reversible adhesive, such as PVA;
- analyse and document any original adhesive;
- strengthen weak components by using metal plates to bridge joints or low molecular weight consolidants; and
- when re-upholstering, minimise damage to the frame by using the original holes or by nailing into plugs of white pine which have been used to fill holes.

Heavy vehicles or machinery

Although every artefact must be assessed individually, repairs to heavy wooden equipment and horse-drawn vehicles normally require strong consolidating agents. As maximum strength is required, animal glue is not recommended (see the chapter, Case Studies).

The application of oils to the wood is not advised as dust quickly adheres to it. This in turn attracts moisture and subsequent mould development. Preventive measures, such as those outlined earlier in this chapter (see Preventive Conservation) are recommended.

SUMMARY

- Carefully check wooden objects for insect infestation or mould before adding them to a collection.
- Keep temperature and relative humidity within the ranges 18-25°C and 45-65% respectively. Hot, dry conditions will cause wood to shrink and crack while excessively moist conditions will cause it to swell and warp.
- Never expose wooden objects to direct sunlight. In addition to causing photochemical damage, veneers and glues may be affected, resulting in lifting, warping or cracking.
- Do not put objects on top of polished surfaces as they could scratch the polish.
- When storing large objects, place bubble wrap over them and dust covers on top.

BIBLIOGRAPHY

Burgin, A., 1990, Eighteenth- and nineteenth-century chair and sofa treatments, in *Upholstery Conservation*, Preprints of a Symposium held at Colonial Williamsburg, East Kinston, N.H., American Conservation Consortium Ltd, pp. 323-337.

Grattan, D.W. and Barclay, R.L., 1988, A study of gap-fillers for wooden objects, *Studies in Conservation*, vol. 33, pp. 71-86.

Graves, L., 1990, Conservation of an 1811 sofa with nearly intact original upholstery, in *Upholstery Conservation*, Preprints of a Symposium held at Colonial Williamsburg, East Kinston, N.H., American Conservation Consortium Ltd, pp. 356-376.

James, D., 1990, *Upholstery - A Complete Course*, Guild of Master Craftsman Publications, East Sussex.

Perkins, Z.A., 1990, Conservation of a Leon Marcotte side chair, in *Upholstery Conservation*, Preprints of a Symposium held at Colonial Williamsburg, East Kinston, N.H., American Conservation Consortium Ltd, pp. 409-421.

Podmaniczky, M.S., 1990, Wooden frame conservation techniques, *ibid*, pp. 29-41.

Twichel, J., 1990, Experiments with 'tackless' upholstery: Successes (and trials) at SPNEA, *ibid*, pp. 232-245.

PAPER AND BOOKS

INTRODUCTION

Paper is one of the most commonly used materials, far outstripping textiles and plastics. Almost the complete history of mankind is recorded on paper.

Paper-making

The word paper is derived from papyrus, a long-stemmed plant *Cyperus papyrus*. The method which used this plant as a writing support was developed by the Egyptians about 4000 years ago.

Although paper, as it is known today, was developed by the Chinese in about AD 100, it was not introduced to Europe until the 12th century. The Chinese used the mortar and pestle method of papermaking, where cloth or bark was rinsed with water and then reduced to a pulp through the action of the mortar and pestle. In Europe, hammers driven by water power were used to produce pulp from cotton or linen and water by beating these materials in stone or metal-lined wooden troughs.

Beating is a very important part of the papermaking process as it increases the area for interfibre bonding and the overall strength and flexibility of the paper. Paper made without mechanical treatment is usually weak. Occasionally straw from wheat and rice plants was added to cotton and linen. The end result, however, is a weaker paper. Very high quality paper is produced from cotton or linen. Due to a shortage of the raw materials this type of paper was highly valued.

It was not until the 1850s that paper was produced from groundwood pulp. This paper, which usually consisted of 80 per cent groundwood and 20% cellulose, was both cheap and of low quality. Wood pulp consists of both fibrous and non-fibrous components.

The low quality and low durability of wood pulp paper are due to the rapid breakdown of the non-fibrous components when exposed to air and light. Newspaper, for example, which is made from low grade wood pulp, yellows very rapidly when exposed to light. Prolonged exposure leads to increased yellowing and brittleness.

Techniques developed in the early 20th century to separate the fibrous and the non-fibrous components of wood pulp led to the production of higher quality paper.

PAPER CHEMISTRY

Usually paper is made up of the following combination of materials:

- raw plant matter;
- sizing agents;
- fillers; and
- brighteners and colouring agents.

The **basic raw materials** of paper are fibres derived from wood and other plants. Good quality paper contains a high proportion of cellulose molecules with a correspondingly low lignin content.

Cellulose is a polymeric substance made up of linked glucose units. The arrangement of these units and of the resultant polymeric chains determine the overall quality and mechanical properties of a paper sheet. In good quality rag paper about 1000 glucose units are linked.

High cellulose, low lignin papers usually are prepared from cotton rag or linters, whereas paper with a higher lignin content is derived mostly from wood pulp. Depending on the use of the paper, wood pulp may be chemically treated to produce papers of varying qualities.

Paper is **sized** so that it repel liquids such as inks, making it suitable for writing and printing. A high degree of size is used for the purpose of writing, to prevent ink from feathering, and a lesser degree is used for printing so that ink can be absorbed as quickly as possible.

Traditionally sizing was carried out as a separate step. By the second half of the 19th century, however, it became possible to add the sizing agents directly to the pulp (internal sizing). Combinations of alum and rosin were used in this process. Unfortunately these sizing agents elevated acid levels in the paper, which meant the paper deteriorated more quickly. Now synthetic cellulose components are used as sizing agents to overcome the problem of acidity, allowing papers with neutral or alkaline pHs to be produced.

Clay, titanium oxide and calcium carbonate are among the most commonly used **fillers**. These materials, added during stock preparation, serve to produce different finishes, for example, calendered paper.

Originally indigo was used as a **colouring agent**. This substance has been replaced by synthetic fluorescent dyes and optical brighteners.

Map - Shark Bay.
Laminated in self-adhesive contact. This shows staining, mould, as well as folds and creases.

Maps.
Showing damage from adhesive tape and acidic backings.

A.

B.

C.

Ink drawing.

A: Example of tightly rolled paper after being stored inside a tube.
B: Unrolled after humidification and during dry-cleaning.
C: After treatment and mounted for storage or display.

Some examples of storage boxes for paper material.

Types of paper

Paper types are many and varied. Paper quality depends on the raw materials and chemicals used in processing and the actual production practices used. Archival quality papers, made from rag material and which use an alkaline processing system, last longer than those made from the type of wood pulp used for newspapers. As described previously the latter discolour and distort rapidly.

A list of paper and board types, which describes their components and chemical characteristics, is supplied in Appendix 6.

DETERIORATION

Paper is prone to attack and subsequent degradation by chemical, biological and environmental agents. Deterioration may be caused by:

- the presence of potentially damaging chemicals within the paper;
- exposure to external pollutants;
- environmental factors such as light and relative humidity;
- biological attack by moulds, insects and rodents; and
- inappropriate intervention or lack of care by those responsible for collections.

High levels of **acidity in paper** may be brought about by the presence of material introduced both during and after processing. These materials include alum or rosin sizing agents, high lignin pulp material, coatings and certain inks, such as iron gall ink.

Acidic substances attack the long cellulose chains, causing them to break into smaller units. A more brittle paper, or one containing holes, may result.

Absorption and chemical reaction with oxides of nitrogen and sulfur from the air, combined with the natural ageing of paper components, also may contribute to increased acidity levels in paper.

Chemical processes can affect the appearance as well as the mechanical structure of paper. Oxidation of cellulose, catalysed by iron or copper impurities or by the presence of atmospheric ozone produced as a by-product of the photocopying process, may lead to the development of foxing stains similar to those produced by moulds. High relative humidity enhances this type of degradation.

Light-induced photochemical degradation, initiated by exposure to both white and UV light may either yellow or bleach paper. Heating of paper, caused by overexposure to light, accelerates deterioration processes.

Dust and dirt may lead to a combination of chemical, biological and mechanical damage. The abrasive nature of dirt particles may cause physical damage to fibres. Dirt particles also act as nucleation centres, encouraging condensation, chemical attack and mould development.

Mould formation is enhanced by high **relative humidity**. Moulds which develop on paper cause stains known as foxing. These stains are usually brown in colour and are especially disfiguring to works of art on paper.

Fluctuating relative humidity levels can cause physical damage to paper. Under conditions of high relative humidity swelling of paper may lead to cockling, while low relative humidity can result in paper becoming brittle.

Insects such as silverfish, cockroaches, flies and book lice, and rodents such as rats and mice cause physical damage by feeding on paper. Additional damage is caused by their excreta.

Do not underestimate the influence of careless handling or treatment on the deterioration processes that affect paper. Some examples of this type of damage include:

- the application of adhesive tapes to paper;
- the use of metal paper clips;
- the inappropriate use of backing and other materials;
- poor quality framing or mounting; and
- rough and inappropriate handling.

Do not use **adhesive tape** as a means of repair. Inevitably the adhesive tape fails, leaving behind a yellow stain that is very difficult, if not impossible, to remove.

Do not use pressure-sensitive or gummed tapes, sold as archival repair tapes, without first consulting a conservator.

Metal paper clips are prone to rusting, cause indentations in the paper and have sharp ends which may tear paper.

Acidic mount boards and **inappropriate backing** (such as plywood, card, straw boards) can destroy or discolour the paper objects they were meant to support. They also can cause matburn, the brown line that imprints itself into the artwork along the window mount.

Poor **framing**, in which there is direct contact between the work of art and the glass or perspex, may lead to the transfer of part of the image to the glass or perspex. An obvious loss of part of the original image is the result.

PREVENTIVE CONSERVATION

Preventing damage to artefacts must always be the highest priority. Any treatment involves intervention, which may alter the originality of an artefact or contribute to changes within its constituents.

Preventive action does not have to be complex. Simple measures and precautions go a long way toward protecting paper objects. Some of these measures include:

- hygiene and regular, careful cleaning of storage and display areas;
- storage and display under appropriate environmental conditions;
- regular monitoring of objects;
- careful handling;
- use of archival quality materials for storage and display; and
- use of appropriate storage and display techniques.

Environment

Maintaining appropriate environmental conditions within storage and display areas will enhance the longevity of paper-based materials.

Light levels of about 50 lux, with a UV content of 75 µwatts/lumen, are recommended if photochemical degradation is to be minimised. Do not expose paper objects to direct sunlight nor place light sources close to these items. Monitor light levels carefully. To minimise deterioration of paper artefacts limit their exposure to light.

As light levels associated with photocopying are very high, indiscriminate photocopying will damage paper objects. If copying is necessary, as in the case of materials needed for study or viewing (for example, newspapers, certificates), only copy the documents once. Observe copyright restrictions and use archival quality paper for copies. Some papers may yellow, even after only one exposure.

Maintaining relative humidity levels within the range 45-60% and temperatures of 18-22°C are recommended. Information on temperature and relative humidity control has been provided earlier (see the chapter, Preventive Conservation). Buildings have zones that tend toward dampness and zones in which conditions fluctuate more often. Doorways, chimneys, areas near heating and airconditioning vents and outside walls are examples of such zones. These should be avoided.

Should it be difficult to establish the above environmental conditions, strive to maintain conditions that are relatively steady. Slow changes during seasonal variations should allow most objects to adjust accordingly and will minimise damage. Rapid and frequent fluctuations in relative humidity levels, in which paper objects swell and contract repeatedly, will increase the rate of deterioration. While buffering of seasonal changes in environmental conditions is recommended, prolonged elevated relative humidity levels will increase the risk of mould development.

Handling

Paper is particularly susceptible to physical damage. Careful handling and a commonsense approach is necessary to minimise damage to paper and paper products. To prevent the transfer of oils, fats and acids from the skin, wear disposable latex (rubber) or cotton gloves when handling books, documents and paper artefacts. Pick up paper objects with both hands, not by one corner.

Keep fragile papers secured and on a suitable support until treatment begins.

Use pencils for documentation purposes since accidental marking with inks, biros, felt pens or similar may prove indelible.

Storage and display

Hygiene and regular, careful cleaning are important to maintain paper artefacts' condition. Guidelines for storage and display of paper artefacts include:

- keep storage areas clean, dry, well ventilated and free from insect and rodent infestation;
- regularly inspect stored material; and
- do not store items in cellars and attics as they are likely to be overlooked.

Depending on the type of paper object the following storage and display techniques and media may be appropriate:

- archival quality boxes or folders;
- cardboard boxes lined with acid-free tissue or barrier paper;
- flat storage in metal drawers;
- rolled storage on the outside of large diameter, acid-free cylinders;
- mounting;
- framing; and
- encapsulation.

Archival quality boxes or folders provide protection for paper artefacts. In addition to providing support, protection from dust and the danger of being squashed, boxes act as buffers to environmental fluctuations.

Do not use alkaline-buffered boards and paper for the protection of paper materials that also have leather, parchment, photographic, woollen or silk components. Use neutral, acid-free materials instead.

Although archival storage boxes, made from either acid-free paper board, polyethylene or polypropylene, are commercially available, they tend to be expensive and may not be of the desired size. A do-it-yourself box is a perfectly acceptable alternative. Acid-free boards such as foamcore, archival mount and corrugated boards are all suitable and pre-gummed acid-free paper or linen tapes can be used for their manufacture. Storage folders can be manufactured from a variety of suitable buffered and unbuffered acid-free card (see Figure 12).

Should the above not be applicable, or if suitable materials are not available, store artefacts in ordinary **cardboard boxes**, provided these are lined with acid-free tissue or special barrier paper. This paper must be changed at regular intervals (every 12 months). Items in boxes are not immune from danger and should be checked regularly for insect infestation and for any changes in condition.

Flat storage, preferably in metal drawers, is recommended for items such as documents, maps, newspapers and certificates. They should be stored flat, unfolded and interleafed with acid-free tissue paper, which is slightly larger than the items themselves. Do not fold aged paper as in time the creases become tears.

Take special precautions with documents that contain attachments like seals and ribbons. Ensure these are not crushed or allowed to imprint themselves onto other documents. Place these items on top of a stack to avoid damage.

To reduce pressure on items on the bottom of a box or drawer, do not try to cram in too many items. Arrange items according to size so large ones are beneath smaller ones. Store objects of a similar nature, size and condition together.

If an item such as a map is too large to store flat, roll it onto either a large **acid-free cylinder** or a large cylinder covered with mylar (polyester) and then with acid-free tissue (minimum diameter of 150 mm). Cover the entire object with acid-free tissue paper before rolling to prevent individual layers from pressing or rubbing against each other. Protect the outer surface of the item with a further layer of acid-free paper. Do not roll painted or fragile objects, or those that are thick and inflexible.

Framing is a useful method of storage and display as it protects paper from outside influences such as dirt and handling. To reduce the amount of damaging UV light reaching the item, use UV-absorbing perspex in preference to glass. Unfortunately, framing is often expensive or impractical, especially for large items like maps.

Mounting (matting) provides safe support for flat paper objects such as watercolours, engravings, drawings and documents (see Figure 13). When

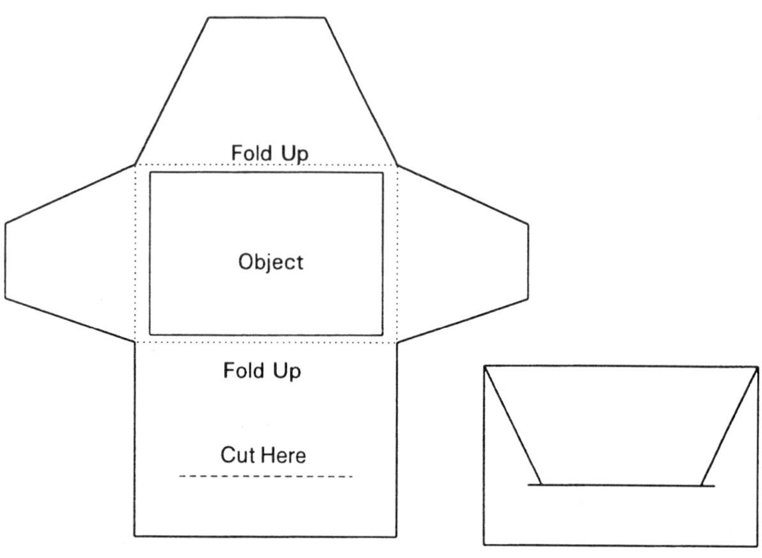

Figure 12: Storage folder

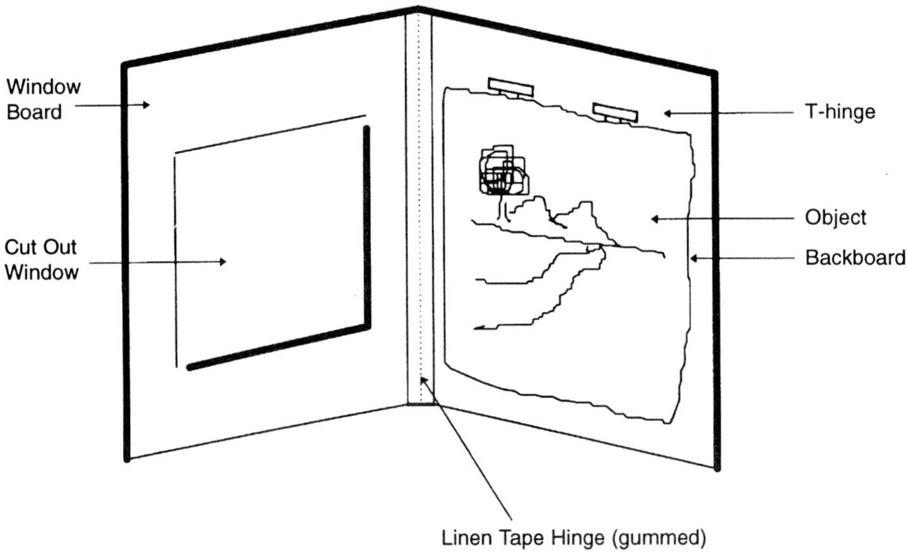

Figure 13: Standard window mat support

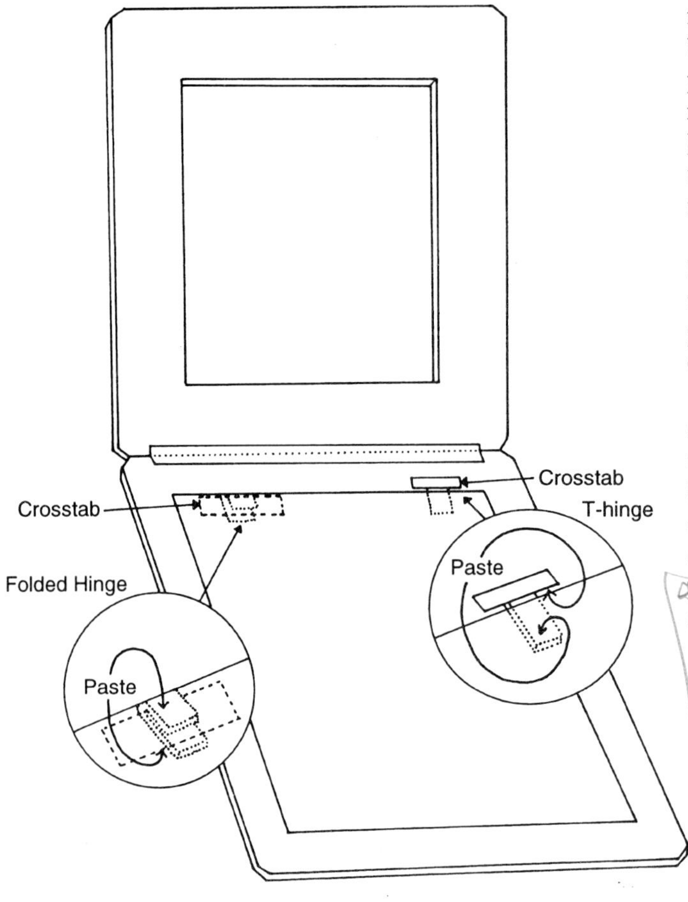

Figure 14: T–hinge and folded hinge

mounted, they can be handled and viewed without being touched. Use acid-free mount board, preferably 100% rag mount or alkaline-buffered rag mount board for this purpose. The latter will be able to counteract acidity (present or latent) in the paper item. When choosing coloured board make sure that it is 100% acid-free.

Use acid-free hinges or make them using book-binders' pre-gummed (not self-adhesive) paper tape or Japanese tissue paper and starch paste, depending on the weight and condition of the paper. Consult a conservator before attempting this.

Examples of two different types of hinging are shown below (see Figure 14). The T-hinge can be used when the edges of the object are to be covered by a window mount. Since they are covered by the object itself, folded hinges allow the edges of the object to be exposed.

Never glue paper objects to their backings. Many adhesives change their composition, turn yellow and may become insoluble as they age. Gluing also restricts the natural movement of paper. Hinging allows objects to move freely while they are held securely in place.

For storage and protection, cover artefacts with acid-free tissue paper. Alternatively, insert a sheet of mylar the size of the mount between the window mount and the artefact. Do not use mylar in the case of flaking paints, chalk, powdery pastels or charcoals as its electrostatic nature may dislodge pigments from the paper support. It also may burnish some surfaces. In these cases, use acid-free glassine paper instead.

A cheaper alternative to framing or mounting is **encapsulation**. In this technique, the paper artefact is sandwiched between two pieces of mylar or polypropylene film. Cut these pieces about 15-20 mm larger than the paper on all sides. Use clear, double-sided tape to join the two pieces of film on all sides, leaving a small uncovered length, about 20-25 mm (minimum), along one corner for air circulation and exchange (see Figure 15). For increased air circulation, leave one entire side unadhered.

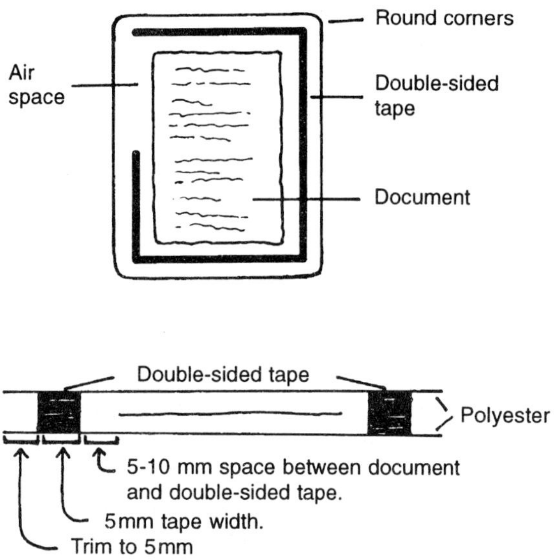

Figure 15: Encapsulation

Do not encapsulate highly acidic material as the restricted air movement will accelerate deterioration. In some cases an alkaline buffered sheet can be inserted behind a document that is being encapsulated. Although this will assist in countering acidity, it has the obvious disadvantage of obscuring one side of the document.

Because of mylar's electrostatic nature, encapsulation is not appropriate for chalk drawings, pastels and watercolours. Materials which have attachments such as seals and ribbons also are not suitable for this method of storage. Disadvantages of encapsulation include the glossiness of mylar and its lack of UV protection.

Photographs may be encapsulated in mylar or polypropylene film. Store them upright in a folder or file so that there is no weight pressing the encapsulating film against the photographic emulsion.

Tracing paper

Tracing papers are usually translucent and have a smooth and hard surface, making them very receptive to aqueous inks. Of the variety of available tracing papers the most commonly used ones are:

- prepared tracing paper;
- parchment paper; and
- natural tracing paper.

Prepared tracing paper is manufactured from cotton pulp. The transparency of this paper is due to its impregnation with assorted gums, oils and resins.

Parchment papers (also known as pergamyn and papyrine) are produced by a process in which unsized sheets are immersed briefly in sulfuric acid and then neutralised with ammonia. This treatment alters the cellulose structure. Sometimes glycerine or glucose are then used to coat the paper. Parchment papers are greaseproof.

Natural tracing papers are produced by physically modifying the cellulose fibres. This treatment increases the surface area of the fibres without shortening them. Heat and compression treatment produce a very dense paper free of internal gaps. The surface is usually sized to make it more receptive to inks (Dobrusskin 1991).

Due to their high densities, tracing papers are very susceptible to damage caused by either exposure to high relative humidity conditions (greater than 60%) or by contact with water. These factors cause expansion, deterioration and permanent damage.

Tracing papers are among the most difficult to treat since all repairs will be obvious, due to the transparency of the paper. Any treatments must be carried out by a conservator.

Because of the difficulty of treatment, preventing damage assumes even greater importance. Keep tracing papers flat and fully supported in an environment in which relative humidity and temperature fluctuations are minimal.

Books

Handling

Do not remove books from shelving by pulling the headcap or spine. Rather, ease them out by carefully grasping them around the centre of the spine. Wear gloves when handling books.

Minimise photocopying pages of books, as the process places the spine of the book under stress. In

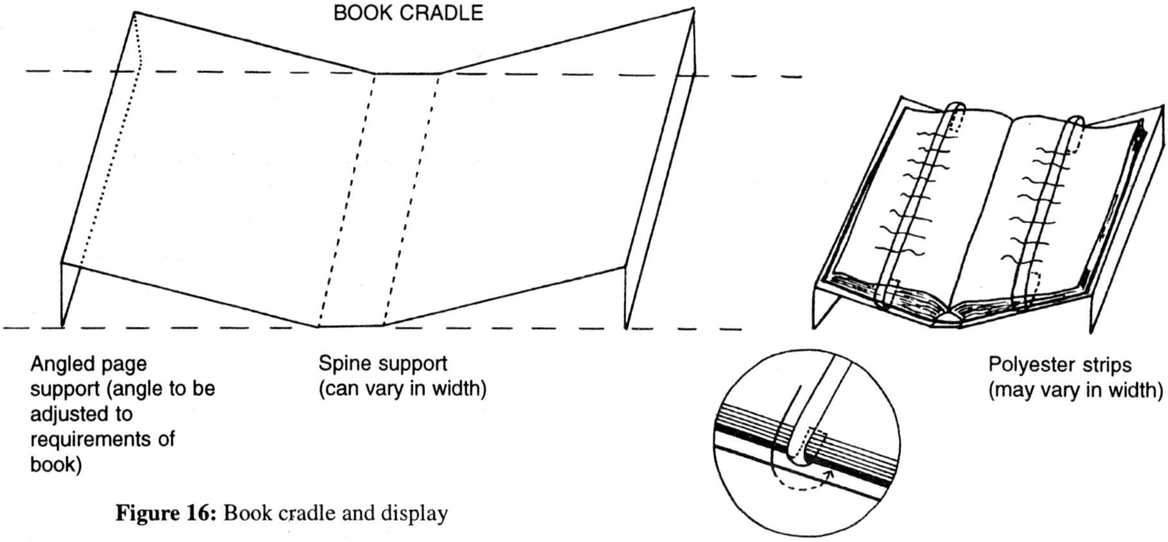

Figure 16: Book cradle and display

addition, the very high light levels associated with photocopying increase photochemical degradation of the paper.

Storage and display

Should it be desirable or necessary to display certain pages of a book, then use book cradles or blocks. These support both parts of the book, preferably on a slight angle, to avoid stress on any part of the book or spine. Keep the spine itself flat. These cradles or blocks can be bought or made using acrylic (perspex) or acid-free card (see Figure 16).

To hold pages flat while on display, use mylar strips, made into hoops, to 'strap' particular pages, including the cover. Form the loop by applying a small piece of double-sided, acid-free tape to one end of the mylar strip. This join can be hidden underneath the book. A thin, flexible version of mylar (0.002-0.003 mm) is suitable for this purpose; thicker versions may cut the paper. Polyester or polypropylene films are also suitable. Turn pages regularly to avoid overexposure of any particular page.

Enclosed steel shelving is ideal for book storage. Use a curtain made from washed calico or similar material if enclosed shelves are not available. Store books vertically and according to their size unless they are large volumes or softcovers; store the latter flat, with minimal stacking.

Do not pack vertically stored books too tightly, otherwise they will not be able to be removed easily by grasping around the centre of the spine. Bookends offer good support, preventing books from falling over or sagging.

To prevent the migration of acids from timber shelves, cover them with acid-free card (for example, mount board), Cell-Air or similar, cut to the width of the shelf. Treat new timber shelving with a water-based polyurethane to seal the surface. The card, or similar, can be replaced when dirty, worn or damaged.

Do not put shelving against outer walls as these areas are prone to dampness and temperature and relative humidity fluctuations.

Store pamphlets, magazines, brochures and journals in special archival folders or boxes. These are commercially available or may be tailor-made.

Avoid the use of dressings on leather-bound books as their presence often complicates future conservation treatments.

Stamps

History

The first adhesive postage stamp, the famous Penny Black, was produced in the United Kingdom in 1840. This stamp carried the head of Queen Victoria of England as its central design. The image was hand engraved, while the background was produced by a mechanical engraving process. To achieve the high detail in the printing a very smooth, good quality paper was needed. The individual corner letters in this very early example served as a precaution against forgery. Stamps were usually coated with a starch adhesive after printing. They were not perforated.

Use of the cancellation mark, to prevent the re-use of stamps, was soon introduced. Initially these marks were produced using red, water-soluble dyes (the

Maltese Cross hand stamp). To minimise the opportunities for the removal of the cancellation mark and re-use of the stamps, these early dyes were replaced with carbon black printers' ink.

Modern stamps are printed by offset lithography or photogravure techniques. Sometimes oxide pigments are added to create a holograph-like effect. The tiny pigment particles act like prisms and produce different patterns when the angle of light is changed.

Environment

Control of relative humidity and light conditions is critical to prevent damage to stamps.

As some cancellation marks are water soluble and many of the adhesives (usually starch or gum arabic) used on stamps are hygroscopic (attract or absorb moisture), control of relative humidity is important. Damage to the adhesive usually devalues the stamp. If relative humidity is not controlled, the stamp may become distorted.

Storing stamps in albums ensures that they are not exposed to the fading influences of strong lights. If stamps are put on display, exert strict control over the level and duration of light exposure. A maximum intensity of 50 lux is recommended.

Storage

Although traditional stamp albums are both widely available and used, they are often not of archival quality. Plastics used to cover stamps can have serious effects. Plasticisers have the potential to act as solvents for stamp printing and writing inks.

Philatelic pages and folders manufactured to archival specifications are now commercially available. These materials provide full protection and support to the stamps without affecting the original adhesive.

Treatments

Stamp conservation treatments are extremely specialised and require the attention of a conservator.

TREATMENTS

Using quality materials and adopting practices which minimise damage to paper-based materials are preferable to applying remedial treatments to these objects. The susceptibility of paper to deterioration, however, means that a discussion of some of the available treatments is necessary.

As with all conservation treatments, a thorough assessment of an artefact's condition is essential before any treatment is applied. It is also important to test any potential treatment on an inconspicuous part of the object to minimise further damage or loss.

Familiarise yourself with the particular technique to be used by applying it to an expendable piece. Where there is any doubt about the condition or the treatment of an object, consult a conservator.

Invasive techniques such as washing, deacidification, bleaching and use of solvents should be left in the hands of a conservator. Approach the numerous published recipes with care, particularly as treatment procedures are modified continuously.

There is no such thing as a routine or standard treatment. Each object deserves special attention that takes into account condition, age, constituents, manufacture, origin, colour or discolouration and so on.

Carry out pretreatment tests carefully to ensure the object can withstand the treatment. Test each colour individually. Some colours may be stable at low relative humidity levels but bleed when exposed to conditions of prolonged higher relative humidity.

Deacidification can cause certain papers to darken and bleaching may fade colours or delaminate certain paper types. Do not use ordinary household bleaches under any circumstances.

Cleaning

Paper

The first step in most cleaning treatments is to remove dust and dirt. If paper is dirty but has no other signs of deterioration, such as flaking or brittleness, it may be surface cleaned.

Surface cleaning may be achieved by using:

- a soft brush;
- a soft, high quality eraser;
- grated eraser; and
- proprietary document cleaners.

A **soft brush**, such as a squirrel or cosmetic brush, can remove dust, bearing in mind that dust particles can be quite sharp or may smear.

If brushing is not effective, try a soft, high quality **eraser**, but only after the type of media has been established. For instance, charcoal or pencil drawings and pastels cannot be cleaned in this way and care must be taken to avoid smudging inks and scuffing paper.

When erasing, use even strokes, going in one direction or rotating movements, covering only small areas at a time. This will minimise the risk of slipping or crushing. Use a thin, flexible slice of eraser to reduce pressure on the document. Wear a disposable latex (rubber) glove on the hand holding the document to avoid the transfer of grease and perspiration. Alternatively, wash hands before treatment to ensure they are grease-free.

Grated eraser also may be used to remove dirt. Grate an art eraser or cleaner (for example, Artgum, Faber Castell) finely using a plastic kitchen grater. Plastic is preferred as the metal variety may rust or shed small metal particles, which could damage the paper. The resultant grains are spread over the paper and lightly rotated with the palm of the hand or the flat of the fingers until the entire area has been covered. The residue is then brushed off.

An alternative is to use a commercially available, non-abrasive **document cleaner**. *Draft Clean Powder* is similar to the grated eraser discussed above and is used in the same way, but the granules are of different size and texture. Fine powder is mixed with coarser and firmer particles but with some extra care it can be used safely.

Document Cleaning Pads use the same ingredients as the Draft Clean Powder but are ground more finely. The powder is held in a cloth pouch and with manipulation is released onto the document. With circular motions of the pouch, dirt and dust are absorbed. Dirt is not transferred to the object even though the cloth becomes dirty during the cleaning process.

As the object is obscured by the pad during cleaning test this method before using it. A potential disadvantage of this technique is that residues of the fine powder may remain in the paper grain after cleaning.

Books

Clean books by using a dry lint-free cloth, a soft brush or even a low suction vacuum cleaner such as a car cleaner.

Brushing is preferred, with the use of a vacuum cleaner being limited to those objects in very good condition. Brush dust away from the spine.

If using a vacuum cleaner, cover the nozzle with a piece of loose weave cloth (for example, cheesecloth, gauze) and hold it a few millimetres above the paper surface. This prevents scratching and will stop any pieces from being sucked into the vacuum cleaner accidentally.

Due to the complex composition of paper-based materials such as books, maps and stamps, apart from removing surface dust, only attempt treatment after consultation with a conservator. The mix of leather, paper, fabric, adhesive, dyes, inks and pigments found in these objects means that any treatment must be considered very carefully.

Removing residual Sellotape glue

Where the plastic carrier of Sellotape is stuck to the paper, a conservator is needed to remove it safely. This carrier, however, often becomes detached with age, leaving behind the sticky adhesive. This is undesirable as it is unsightly, attracts dirt and pages could stick together.

To remove the sticky residue rub a piece of crepe rubber (available from art and craft stores) in light circular motions over the particular area. This will gather the adhesive in a small ball, which can then be carefully lifted with tweezers.

This method can only be used on strong, sturdy papers as brittle and fragile papers are likely to be damaged during this process. The stain left by the adhesive, however, will remain. Usually, removing this stain will require a qualified conservator to apply a solvent treatment, a very slow and time-consuming process.

Interleafing

Interleafing with acid-free or buffered tissue paper is a protective measure that will counteract acidity to a certain extent, especially if the documents are then stored in boxes or folders manufactured from archival materials. Interleafing also minimises abrasion between documents.

High acidity levels may be countered to some extent by placing affected papers in an alkaline or neutral environment such as that afforded by boxes or folders.

Cut buffered or unbuffered acid-free tissue paper used for interleafing to a size slightly larger than the document in question. If the documents are of varying sizes, cut the tissue to the dimensions of the largest document. This will prevent slipping and ensure there is complete coverage of the documents. The resulting documents can be stored in a folder or box that has been made to size. Do not cram too many items into one box or folder.

Certain pages of books can be interleafed with unbuffered acid-free paper, especially where transfer of images, inks or smudging may be a danger. Take care to limit interleafing to a few pages as too much added bulk will put pressure on the spine.

Damp or waterlogged paper

If an object is damp or wet, dry it out as quickly as possible using fans or hairdryers on a cool setting. Keep papers flat and held in place as any movement could cause further damage. Hold books upright with the pages opened as evenly as possible.

An even more critical situation involves complete waterlogging, which may follow flooding of a storage area. For books, insert sheets of blotting paper, slightly larger than the book pages, every fourth or fifth page so that excess water is absorbed.

If large numbers of paper objects are involved, freeze items that cannot be treated immediately. This will minimise further damage through prolonged wetness and possible mould attack. Treat frozen objects individually at a later date.

Mould

If mould is present on paper, quick action is necessary to prevent damage. To avoid the spread of fungal spores, isolate the object immediately in a plastic bag.

As slightly damp conditions are usually needed for mould to develop, allow the object to dry partially before further treatment is attempted. This will make it easier to remove the mould. Dry the mould-affected object in a well-ventilated area, such as a fume cupboard, or outside.

After partial drying, remove visible mould with a soft brush using gentle strokes away from the person to avoid inhalation of fungal matter. Treat each page of an affected book. If the paper is fragile or flaking, or fumigation is required, consult a conservator.

Mould is difficult to treat. Freezing techniques are suitable for most paper-based objects. Do not use thymol as it can damage and discolour paper. It is important to seek professional help.

After treating the object and cleaning the previously occupied storage space, ensure there is no recurrence of the conditions that allowed the mould to develop in the first place. Regular, careful cleaning and preventive conservation are the best solutions.

SUMMARY

- Maintain high cleaning and hygiene standards.
- Store and display paper in appropriate environmental conditions. Relative humidity and temperature ranges of 45-60% and 18-22°C respectively are recommended.
- Keep light levels to 50 lux and 75 μW/lumen of UV.
- Do not use adhesive tape or metal paper clips.
- Use only archival quality materials for storage and display.
- Handle objects carefully using cotton or rubber gloves. Never hold by corners as mounts may be brittle.
- Always use a reputable conservation framer for mounting artworks on paper.

BIBLIOGRAPHY

Bass, S., Paper conservation, Information Sheet, Museums Association of Australia, WA Branch.

Canadian Conservation Institute, 1986, Storing works on paper, *CCI Notes, 11/2*, Ottawa, Canada.

Clapp, A.F., 1987, *Curatorial Care of Works of Art on Paper: Basic Procedures for Paper Preservation*, Lyons and Burford, New York.

Dobrusskin, S and Banik, G., 1991, Flattening of tracing papers and selected case studies, Course Notes, ICCROM Paper Conservation Course, Austria.

Hamburg, D.A., 1992, Library and archival collections, in *Caring for Your Collections*, The National Committee to Save America's Cultural Collections, Arthur W. Schultz (Chairman), Harry N. Abrams Inc., New York, pp. 52-63.

Holben Ellis, M., 1992, Works of art on paper, *ibid*, pp.40-51.

Institute of Paper Conservation, *The Paper Conservator* and *Paper Conservation News*, Secretary, Institute of Paper Conservation, PO Box 17, London, WC 1N 2PE, England.

Johnson, A.W., 1988, *The Practical Guide to Book Repair and Conservation*, Thames and Hudson Ltd, London.

Rickman, C., 1992, Conservation of philatelic materials, in *Conference Papers Manchester 1992*, Institute of Paper Conservation, G.W. Belton, Lincolnshire

Smith, M.A. and Brown, M.R., 1990, *Matting and Hinging of Works of Art on Paper*, 2nd Revised Edition, Consultant Press, New York.

S & M Supply Company, 1992, *Glossary, Useful Hints*, PO Box 4296, Kingston, ACT, 2609.

Wächter, O., 1982, *Restaurierung und Erhaltung von Büchern, Archivalien und Graphiken*, Herman Böhlaus Nachf. Q.M.B.H., Graz, Austria.

Zetta Florence Pty Ltd, 1995-96, *It's Our Heritage*, Zetta Florence Catalogue, PO Box 109, Fitzroy, Victoria, 3064.

PHOTOGRAPHS

INTRODUCTION

The camera obscura, described by Leonardo da Vinci in his notebooks had been used by artists for centuries as an aid to sketching landscapes. The effects of light on silver salts also had been known for some time. In the 1820s Frenchman Joseph Niépce produced images, which he called heliographs, using bitumen on a pewter plate. The first photograph was taken in 1826 and needed an eight-hour exposure. It was not until the 1830s, however, that the French scenic painter, Louis Daguerre, discovered a practical method of producing a photograph.

In the early 1830s Thomas Wedgewood experimented with making images using silver salts on paper, but it was not until 1835 that Daguerre achieved a major breakthrough. By accident (a broken thermometer) he discovered that mercury fumes were able to develop a latent image on an exposed silver plate that had been sensitised with iodine. By 1837 he had developed a working process and in 1839 he formally announced his discovery. The images produced by this process became known as **daguerreotypes**.

Daguerre's work prompted Fox Talbot, an English gentleman scientist, to present papers on his own discoveries. In 1835, at the same time as Daguerre, he had produced negative images, on silver sensitised paper, which he called **calotypes**. On hearing of Daguerre's discovery he sought to improve on his imperfect images. Eventually, in 1840, he was able to produce a paper negative from which a positive paper print could be made. These he called photogenic drawings.

Also at this time another Frenchman, Hippolyte Bayard, was experimenting with sensitised paper prints, exhibiting them on June 24, 1839, before either Daguerre's or Talbot's methods were announced.

The French Government offered Daguerre a lifetime pension if he would reveal the details of his discovery. This he did in August 1839. The process was offered free of charge throughout the world, except in England, where patents were enforced.

The daguerreotype was far superior to the calotype in detail and far more popular. The advantage of the calotype, which allowed a number of copies to be made from one negative, was outweighed by the fact that it could not match the quality of the daguerreotype.

The major drawbacks of Daguerre's method were the cost and its inability to produce multiple copies. The product was a direct positive, being exposed in the camera and then developed to produce a one-off positive image. If a second copy was required then a second sitting had to be arranged and the same price paid.

In 1851 the English sculptor and photographer Frederick Scott Archer started using collodion, a mixture of a cellulose nitrate compound with alcohol and ether, on glass photographic plates. A negative image could be produced if a glass plate, coated with collodion and sensitised with silver nitrate and potassium iodide, was exposed and then developed while still wet or tacky. This image was of greater sensitivity than either the daguerreotype or the calotype. It was noticed that when this image was backed with a black card a positive image was produced. This new photographic method was called the **ambrotype** and it rapidly superseded the daguerreotype and the calotype.

A cheaper offshoot of the collodion process was the **tintype** or **ferrotype**. Despite its name it was iron and not tin which was used in this process. A sheet of iron was coated with tacky collodion and exposed in the camera while still wet. It was then developed, fixed, dried and varnished. Popular from the late 1850s, it was used by travelling photographers until the 1940s.

It was the wet plate negative, however, that dominated photography till the 1880s. When contact printed onto albumen paper and toned the result was a lovely warm, purple-brown image.

The development of the gelatin dry plate in 1880 and its use on paper signalled the end for the wet plate and albumen process. The gelatin negative and positive system is the basis of modern photography.

Photographic applications have become as diverse as its practitioners. There are photo-ceramics, photo-jewellery, cloth prints, prints on glass, leather, metal and ivory. There are photo-mechanical processes, pigment prints and numerous colour processes. The main photographic types normally found in collections are outlined below.

PHOTOGRAPHIC PROCESSES

Daguerreotype (1839-1860s)

Direct positive

The process of producing a daguerrotype, involved the following:

- a thin silver sheet was sweated onto a copper plate and then highly polished;
- after sensitising with iodine vapour the plate was exposed in the camera; and
- the latent image was then developed using mercury fumes.

Because the image was easily damaged, daguerreotypes were housed behind glass with attractive brass mounts and leather-covered cases. Plastic cases, known as union cases, were introduced in 1854. These cases were made by heating and pressing into moulds a mixture of gum shellac and sawdust (or other fibrous material), making this the first commercial example of a thermosetting plastic.

Daguerreotypes are recognised by their silver surface, sometimes being called the 'mirror with a memory'.

Calotype (1840-1860s)

In its strictest sense the term calotype refers to the negative produced when a silver-sensitised sheet of paper is exposed in a camera.

The positive prints produced from this negative, often called calotype prints or salted prints, lacked detail due to the paper fibres which produced a fuzzy appearance.

Salted prints (1840-1860s)

Salted prints have the following features:

- good quality paper was coated with light-sensitive silver salts and printed out in sunlight to produce the image; and
- prints from glass negatives gave a sharper image than those from a paper negative.

Initially the image was fixed using a strong salt solution. After 1841, however, sodium thiosulfate (hypo) was used. The hypo dissolved out unexposed silver chloride, producing a brighter image.

Ambrotype (1851-1870s)

Direct positive

An offshoot of the wet collodion process, the ambrotype is an underexposed negative with a black backing. This backing gives it a positive appearance.

Ambrotypes were packaged the same way as daguerreotypes, behind glass within a gilded, leather embossed case.

Tintype (1852-1940s)

Direct positive

Similar to the ambrotype, the tintype is in fact a sheet of japanned iron, coated with a sensitised collodion emulsion. Exposed in the camera, then immediately developed, the tintype exhibits a dull positive image with creamy highlights.

Sometimes mounted in the same manner as ambrotypes and daguerreotypes, they were more commonly mounted in cards or albums. They are found in a range of sizes right down to buttonhole size. Abraham Lincoln's presidential election campaign used his image on a tintype badge.

Wet plate process (1851-1880s)

Collodion negative

Features of the wet plate process include the following:

- a glass sheet, coated with collodion and sensitised with potassium iodide and silver nitrate, was exposed in the camera while still wet;
- developed immediately after exposure, the resulting negative produced fine detail;
- if allowed to dry before exposure a lot of sensitivity was lost; and
- the wet plate is identifiable by its creamy-grey appearance.

Most commonly used in conjunction with albumen paper to produce prints, it was very popular until the introduction of the gelatin dry plate in 1880.

Albumen print (1850-1920s)

The albumen print:

- is coated with light sensitive silver salts and egg white solution;
- was normally produced by contact printing in daylight from a wet plate negative; and
- the image has yellow highlights with reddish-brown density areas.

The albumen print is the photograph most often found before the turn of the century. Most visiting cards are albumen prints. Although it was still manufactured in the 1920s, the albumen process went into a decline after 1880.

Gelatin dry plate negative (1880-present)

The fumes from preparing and exposing the wet plate affected photographers' health.

In the 1870s Dr Leach Maddox developed the gelatin emulsion, which is the basis of modern photography. The gelatin plate needed no sensitising by the user and it came packaged, ready to be exposed. This ease of use meant it quickly supplanted the wet plate method and glass plates. It was in common usage until recent times.

Gelatin paper prints (1880-present)

The advances made during the 1870s with gelatin emulsion resulted in the preparation of a gelatin bromide developing out paper (DOP). DOP uses a chemical solution to produce a black and white image which is developed using artificial light in a darkroom.

It was not popular with photographers, who were geared to printing out paper (POP) and the warm tones they produced. POP are contact printed using daylight. The particle size of the silver in these images is very small. This tends to scatter the light that hits them, giving the image its characteristic warm tone. Once the image density was satisfactory it was then fixed.

The silver in DOP is larger than in POP, producing images which exhibit a neutral hue.

The introduction of a baryta layer (barium sulfate mixed with gelatin) below the gelatin layer added brilliance to the print. Gelatin POP rapidly replaced both albumen and collodion POP as the preferred print material.

Improved sensitivity and speed in papers in the early 1900s increased demand for developing out papers and by 1920 POP was rarely used.

Platinum prints (1880-1920s)

Platinum prints:

- were admired for their tonal range and soft image;
- did not fade; and
- although normally steel grey in colour, sometimes were produced with a brown tone.

As platinum became increasingly expensive in the early 1900s, imitations using silver-gelatin, and also collodion, were manufactured. As the paper fibres of the platinum print are discernible under low magnification microscopic examination, it is easy to differentiate the original from the copy.

Collodion prints (1880-1920)

Collodion prints exhibited the following characteristics:

- the same high gloss and reddish-brown tones as gelatin POP;
- could be manufactured with a matt finish to imitate platinum prints. With gold and then platinum toning the image is very stable and this, coupled with its resistance to moisture, means that these prints have resisted fading extremely well; and
- are easily distinguished from platinum prints as they have a baryta layer below the emulsion. The paper fibres are not visible under microscopic examination.

Cyanotypes (1880-1920)

Originally developed in the 1840s this process was soon forgotten, only to reappear some 40 years later. Its bright blue appearance meant it never really gained widespread popularity and its main claim to fame was its use in the reproduction of engineers' drawings. From this came the term 'blueprint'.

Celluloid (cellulose nitrate) (1889-1950)

A refinement of Alexander Parkes' 1861 invention, cellulose nitrate film was coated with a silver gelatin emulsion. Available in both sheet and roll format, eventually it was to dominate as the preferred negative material.

Using roll film in a suitably controlled camera, it was possible to expose a number of negatives rapidly. The smaller size of these negatives necessitated the use of developing out print material, signalling the end of the glass plate and printing out paper method of photography.

Cellulose acetate (1930-1960s)

The inherent instability and flammability of cellulose nitrate resulted in the production of 'safety film' (cellulose acetate). This was in turn superseded by cellulose triacetate film (1950) which was in turn overtaken by polyester (1965).

Photomechanical processes

Photomechanical prints include:

- collotype (1870 on);
- photogravure (1880 on); and
- letterpress halftone (1885 on).

They are not true photographs as they have no emulsion and are printed by machine. Low magnification shows up the printed pattern.

Cyanotype c1890.
Inset: closeup of surface showing image within the paper fibres.

Opaltype.
Hand-tinted image on opal glass c1890.

Postcard – Letterpress half-tone.
Inset: detail of child's face showing dot pattern.

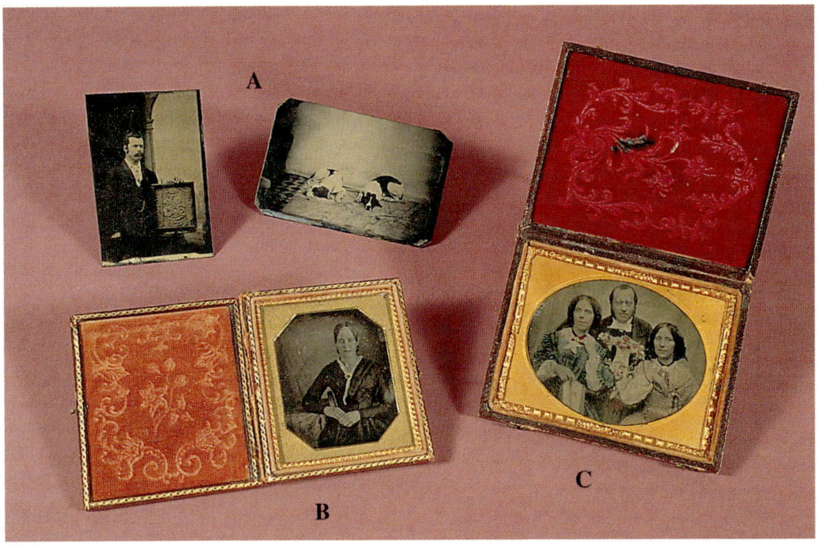

A) Tintype
B) Daguerreotype
C) Ambrotype

Examples of enclosures for photographic images.

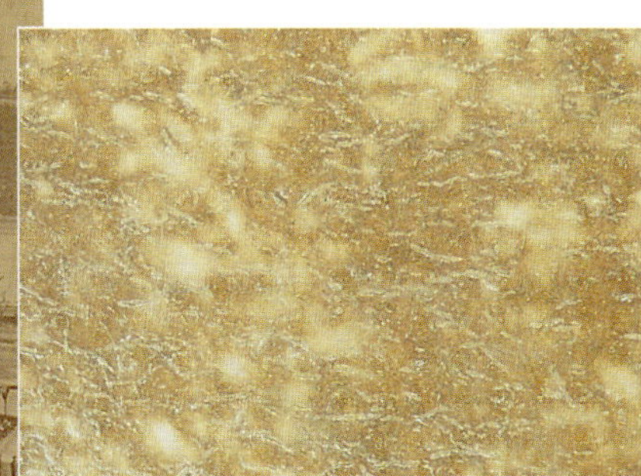

Albumen print of Swan River, Perth, Western Australia c1897.
Inset: closeup of surface showing paper fibres below emulsion.

Pigment prints

Using inorganic pigments and the reaction of bichromates to render gelatin or gum arabic insoluble, these prints do not fade. Although a large range of pigments could be used, the colours chosen were normally warm chocolate browns.

Examples of pigment prints include:

- carbon print (1860-1900s);
- gum bichromate (1890-1930s); and
- woodburytype (1865-1890s).

The woodburytype was an early photomechanical process that used pigmented gelatin to produce the image.

Opaltypes (1880-1920)

Opaltypes are characterised by:

- a positive image on milky white glass;
- many are hand tinted or retouched; and
- the image layer can be either carbon, silver-gelatin or platinum.

Lantern slides (1851-1900)

Lantern slides can be identified by the following:

- the emulsion layer can be either collodion albumen, carbon pigment or silver-gelatin;
- these were often tinted or hand painted; and
- the slide was usually formed by sandwiching two sheets of glass together to protect the image.

Stereograph (1851-1920)

Although there are examples of stereoscopic daguerreotypes and calotypes, the vast majority of these images are in the form of albumen prints. Silver-gelatin and collodion prints also were produced in stereographic pairs.

Photo-ceramic (photo enamel) (1950s-present)

The photo-ceramic process involves:

- using pigments in a variety of ways to produce an image on metal or porcelain;
- the image is sealed by glazing; and
- the images do not fade.

Colour (1860s-present)

Hand-colouring of images began at the inception of photography. There are many fine examples of early hand-tinted daguerreotypes, ambrotypes, prints and emulsions of all sorts. Before 1900 all colour photography involved either hand-tinting, pigment prints or photomechanical processes. In 1904 the Lumière brothers invented the autochrome process, an additive process, but it was not until 1935 that the modern era of colour photography started with the introduction of Kodachrome films.

A few of the major developments of colour processes are listed below.

- carbon print (1860s-1930s);
- gum bichromate (1890s-1930s);
- collotype-photomechanical (1868-present);
- autochrome-additive process (1904-1940s); and
- modern colour photography (1935-present).

A tabular summary and guide to the identification of the various photographic processes is provided in Appendix 7.

DETERIORATION/CONSERVATION

General considerations

In addition to suffering the same problems as other paper-based materials, photographic images have other in-built problems. Some of these problems include:

- the emulsion layer is particularly attractive to insects as a food source;
- gelatin emulsions are very susceptible to mould attack caused by high humidity;
- continual changes in relative humidity may cause silver mirroring;
- images on glass are easily scratched; and
- tinted emulsions may fade due to prolonged exposure to light.

As restoring damaged images is expensive, it is essential that they are accurately identified and correctly stored or displayed to minimise deterioration.

The conservation treatment of photographic images is a highly specialised subject and is fraught with potential difficulties for the amateur. Consultation with a conservator is recommended for almost all problems.

Daguerreotypes

Deterioration

The kind of deterioration likely to affect daguerreotypes includes:

- tarnishing of the silver image;
- damage of the fragile image by handling when out of its frame;
- mechanical damage from the brass mount or broken glass; and
- high humidity causing corrosion.

Conservation

Exercise great care when handling these images. Treatment should be attempted by a qualified conservator only. Note the following points:

- the silver-mercury amalgam image is formed on the surface of the plate and can be wiped off if carelessly handled;
- wear gloves and handle the plate by the edges only;
- physical damage, such as scratching, is irreparable. Damaged images should have photographically restored prints made;
- store daguerreotypes in a low relative humidity environment (45-50 per cent relative humidity is acceptable); and
- if condensation is present on the inside of the glass cover, disassemble the mount and clean the glass with alcohol. Hold the daguerreotype plate by the edges when reassembling. If inexperienced, only carry out this process in consultation with a conservator.

Although thiourea silver dips have been used to remove tarnish from daguerreotypes, this treatment is **not** recommended. It is extremely hazardous as surface coatings may have been applied or the image may have been hand tinted.

Unless the tarnish is so bad as to almost obscure the image, it is not worth attempting to remove it. Consultation with a conservator is essential.

Ambrotypes

Deterioration

Deterioration of ambrotypes involves:

- mechanical damage to the emulsion layer by scratching; and
- breakage of glass.

Conservation

Methods of conserving ambrotypes include:

- minimising mechanical damage to the emulsion by placing a black acid-free card behind the image; and
- if the image bearing glass is broken, do not attempt to glue it. Instead copy it and sandwich it between two sheets of modern glass.

Remove dirt by using a soft brush or a moistened cotton bud. Do not use organic solvents as they may dissolve the emulsion.

Tintype

Deterioration

Factors most likely to cause deterioration of tintype plates include:

- not housing them in a case or mount so they become bent, causing the collodion emulsion layer to crack;
- high humidity, which causes the iron plate to rust, resulting in further blistering of the emulsion; and
- scratching, tarnishing and dirt also damage unmounted tintypes.

Conservation

The simplest way to conserve Tintypes is to mount them. A mount, comprising unbuffered acid-free backing board, spacer, window mount and glass or perspex cover, will protect the image.

Prints

Deterioration

All prints will suffer damage if:

- handled carelessly;
- exposed to inappropriate storage or display conditions, such as high light, temperature and relative humidity levels; and
- exposed to insect attack.

Staining and foxing of prints disfigures them. Lignin in paper causes it to discolour and become brittle, while metallic impurities and localised mould growth can result in foxing. Light and high humidity will accelerate these forms of deterioration.

Silver prints are susceptible to damage from:

- sulfide formation;
- oxidation and reduction; and
- deterioration or staining from poor quality mount boards.

Sulfiding of the silver may result from impurities in the mounting material or the presence of residual processing chemicals such as the fixer (sodium thiosulfate). The result is a general fading and yellowing of the print or image.

Oxidation of silver is caused by the reaction of oxidant gases with particles of silver, converting them to highly mobile silver ions. These silver ions can migrate through the emulsion layer and, if reduced back to metallic silver, be redeposited in a new area. This results in fading of the image and colour changes. Sources of oxidant gases include industrial pollutants and poor quality mount boards.

The extremely small particles of silver in POP are more susceptible to oxidative damage than the coarser particles present in DOP. In POP the image tends to become more yellow and red whereas DOP tends to exhibit a bluish-silver mirroring effect.

Platinum prints and **pigment prints** usually do not fade. The main damage to these images is usually caused by the support material becoming stained or brittle.

For platinum prints high temperature and relative humidity or pollution can cause image transfer with close contact mounts or covers.

Conservation

Conservation of photographic print images is enhanced by:

- careful control of temperature, relative humidity, light and pollutant levels;
- the use of unbuffered, acid-free storage containers; and
- the use of archival quality, acid-free mounting materials.

Specialist conservators and some professional photographic organisations carry out photographic restoration work. Some problems that can be tackled include:

- the removal of mounts and remounting. Many photographic prints are brittle or may suffer if exposed to aqueous treatments. Removal of mounts is extremely difficult in these cases;
- the repair of physical damage such as that caused by insect attack or tearing. Repairs can be made using infill paper fibres, retouching and then coating, with gelatin or methyl cellulose as the binder; and
- restoration of silver mirroring. Silver mirroring can be tackled by applying a gelatin layer over the top of the mirrored emulsion. This masks the effect and makes for easier copying.

Specialists are required for these tasks, particularly in the case of important, original photographic works.

Make copies before beginning **any** restoration work. Make retouched copies for display if the originals are badly deteriorated.

Because of the catalytic effect of the platinum in platinum prints, store these print types in polyester or polypropylene sleeves, to separate them from direct contact with other photographic materials.

Some of the chemical treatments used to restore images include:

- intensification;
- bleaching;
- redevelopment; and
- reduction.

These chemical treatments are **not** recommended.

Glass plate negatives

Deterioration

The most common problems encountered include:

- scratching of the emulsion;
- breakage; and
- silver-gelatin may exhibit silver mirroring or the effects of inadequate processing.

Conservation

Store plates on edge in an enamelled metal box. Other materials that can be used for boxes are unbuffered acid-free board, heavy duty polyethylene and foamcore.

Fit polyethylene channel of the same width as the glass, along two adjacent sides of the plate, to allow them to stand separately. This allows an airflow between the plates and prevents them sticking together.

Cellulose nitrate

Do not store cellulose nitrate near any other material as it is inherently unstable. In addition to giving off noxious gases as it deteriorates, cellulose nitrate has been known to ignite spontaneously. Seek specialist advice if you have a substantial collection of cellulose nitrate materials.

Modern negatives

Modern negatives, if stored in the correct environment, should last for hundreds of years. Careless handling is the most common cause of damage.

Colour material

Although colour photography has been around since just after the turn of the century, the initial additive process was cumbersome and did not gain widespread popularity.

With the introduction in the 1930s of the chromogenic system, a subtractive process, colour photography gained popularity. In the 1960s the more stable silver dye bleach was reported but was not used for negative print material.

It is important to differentiate between true colour photographs and hand-tinted black and white images or pigment prints.

Deterioration

Colour photographs are inherently unstable. This is because the image is formed using organic dyes rather than metallic silver. Organic dyes fade in response to light, temperature, relative humidity and pollutants.

The most popular types of photographs, such as the colour negative and print system favoured by the majority of the public, is the least stable. This system, the chromogenic process, uses colour couplers during processing to produce the dyes. As well as fading at uneven rates this process can exhibit yellow staining even when stored in the dark.

A more stable system is the silver-dye-bleach system in which dyes are incorporated in the emulsion during manufacture and selectively removed during processing. This process is often used for making prints from colour slides.

While modern colour material has improved stability, images from the 1940s and 50s are often found in a severely faded or stained state.

Photos from the 1960s and 70s may also show severe deterioration, depending on their method of manufacture and storage and display conditions.

Conservation

Descriptions of the full range of colour material, from the 1940s to the present, is too extensive for inclusion here. Obtain advice from photographic conservators and by consulting appropriate specialist publications.

Some basic guidelines do apply:

- restrict light levels to no more than 50 lux for displayed items;
- exclude sources of UV light, in particular daylight to maintain levels less than 75 μwatts/lumen;
- maintain relative humidity in the range of 35-45%;
- as long as relative humidity is controlled, store colour materials in a cool place. The lower the temperature, the longer colour material will last. Storage temperatures in the range 18-22°C are recommended;
- mount prints with unbuffered acid-free board behind perspex or glass. Glass is cheaper but perspex does not break as easily. Never use chipboard, hardboard, plywood and particle board to mount prints; and
- avoid direct contact with glass or perspex to prevent any transfer of the image.

Correctly storing photographic prints, negatives and slides will increase their durability. Ideally each photograph should have its own enclosure to protect it against rapid changes in relative humidity, dust, insect attack, pollutants and excessive handling. Archival products are available from conservation supply companies and high quality photographic albums can be obtained from most photographic stores.

The following storage guidelines will increase the life of colour prints:

- **never** use self-adhesive or magnetic albums for storing prints as they are harmful to the image;
- slides are best stored in their boxes or in uncoated polypropylene or polyester sleeves;
- store negatives in uncoated polypropylene or polyester sleeves. Glassine or paper envelopes are not recommended;
- only use acid-free boxes, or those manufactured from polyethylene, polypropylene or polyester, and enamelled metal cupboards for storage;
- wrap large prints with unbuffered acid-free tissue and store them in an acid-free cardboard box, which should then be stored on a shelf or in a metal cabinet;
- if using paper envelopes to store prints, ensure they are unbuffered acid- and lignin-free
- never use PVC plastics, rubber bands, paper clips and poor quality adhesives;
- do not store glass plates and cellulose nitrate material in plastic enclosures;
- regularly inspect and clean storage areas to ensure there is no insect attack. Change tissue regularly as it will become contaminated with impurities from original mount boards; and
- as long as relative humidity can be controlled, store colour material at lower temperatures (a range of 18-22°C is acceptable).

SUMMARY

- Treat and store most photographic collections in the manner as described for paper objects.
- Control temperature and relative humidity to 18-22°C and 35-45% respectively.
- Avoid direct sunlight and control light levels to 50 lux and less than 75 μW/lumen.
- Do not use self-adhesive albums under any circumstances.
- Do not touch emulsion with bare hands.
- Support prints evenly. Do not lift by a single corner.
- Inspect regularly to avoid insect attack.

BIBLIOGRAPHY

Booth, L. and Weinstein, R., 1977, *Collection, Use and Care of Historical Photographs*, American Association for State and Local History, Nashville.

Davies, A. and Stanbury, P., 1985, *The Mechanical Eye in Australia*, Oxford University Press, Melbourne.

Martin, E., 1988, *Collecting & Preserving Old Photographs*, Collins, London.

Reilly, J., 1988, *Care and Identification of 19th Century Photographic Prints*, Kodak Publication No. G-25, USA.

Rempel, S., 1987, *The Care of Photographs*, Nick Lyons Books, USA.

Wilhelm, H., 1993, *The Permanence and Care of Colour Photographs*, Preservation Publishing, Grinnell, Iowa.

PAINTINGS

INTRODUCTION

Ancient cave and rock paintings provide evidence of the lifestyles and relationships between prehistoric people and their environments. These earliest of works, as with modern paintings, vary greatly in their subject matter, style, techniques and use of materials.

The term paintings most often evokes thoughts of a framed image in oils or watercolour on canvas or board. There are, of course, a great many types of supports as well as finishes and materials. If we consider some of these materials it is obvious that the traditional term needs to be viewed in a broader context. Inks, chalks, acrylics, pastels, charcoal and other materials, either alone or in combination, together with a variety of grounds or varnishes may all be applied to a variety of supports. The addition of other materials, as in collage or ethnographic material, may blur the boundary between painting and object.

Structure

Paintings, and oil paintings in particular, usually comprise the following elements:

- a support, which may be made from many materials (for example, canvas, cloth, wood, metal, ivory, leather);
- a ground, such as gesso or pigments mixed with oil, usually to produce a white background;
- pigments such as natural ochres or minerals; and
- binders, which include oils or egg yolks or whites, glue or varnishes (may include dammar, gum arabic, acrylics).

Added to the above could be other material such as feathers, sand and wood, all of which react differently to the agents of decay.

DETERIORATION

Factors likely to contribute to the deterioration of paintings include:

- overexposure to light which will cause fading, especially of watercolours;
- exposure to elevated temperatures which will accelerate chemical deterioration;
- changes in relative humidity conditions which can cause separation of layers, sagging or stretching of the support and even mould growth. Prolonged exposure to low relative humidity levels can cause desiccation and splitting;
- dust which will attract moisture and insects;
- airborne pollutants which may cause discolouration;
- inferior materials in restoration work which may lead to changes in colour; and
- poor handling or storage which may lead to tears in paintings or chipping, abrasion, loosening or even breakage of frames.

In addition to the environmental and other factors described above, paintings may suffer because of the inherent instability of the materials from which they are made. This is particularly so for paintings produced in the 20th century due to the immense range of synthetic materials that have become available. Examples of these additional problems include:

- flaking of ochres as the support material for a bark painting attempts to return to its original shape;
- breakdown and yellowing of varnish layers;
- embrittlement, foxing, or matburn on works of art on paper due to the use of poor quality mounting materials; and
- changes in colour and material failures as a result of using less stable, non-traditional materials.

PREVENTIVE CONSERVATION

Environment

Maintaining a stable environment and controlling lighting will slow the ageing processes that contribute to deterioration of paintings. A stable environment is also important to minimise the damage to aged and less flexible canvas and to prevent distortion of wooden backing panels.

Ideally the storage and display environment for paintings should have a relative humidity in the range 45-65 per cent with a temperature range of 15-25°C.

Most of the common backing materials, such as paper (stretched or unstretched), cloth, wood, parchment, vellum or even bone and ivory will respond to changes in relative humidity. Take care not to encourage embrittlement and desiccation or too much flexibility or even mould growth. Methods for controlling relative humidity fluctuations are described earlier (see the chapter, Preventive Conservation).

As watercolours are most sensitive to damage by exposure to light, restrict light levels to 50 lux with a maximum UV level of 75 μwatts/lumen. Oil and tempura paintings may be displayed under conditions of up to 200 lux and 75 μW/lumen.

Never expose paintings to direct daylight or hang them in areas prone to large variations in temperature and relative humidity. Hanging a painting above a fireplace, for example, is not recommended due to the increased temperatures of the brickwork and the possibility of smoke damage. Other inappropriate areas are described elsewhere (see the chapter, Preventive Conservation).

Although glazing is usually only necessary for particularly valuable or fragile paintings, **framing** does assist in preventing the ingress of dust and buffering against changes in ambient conditions. A backboard, for example, minimises relative humidity changes for the painting support and may help to prevent flaking of the paint surface.

Commonly used glazing materials include glass and acrylic materials such as perspex. Although chemically safe, glass can shatter and damage a framed object whereas acrylics are shatter-resistant. A further advantage of acrylic glazing is the opportunity to use acrylics that filter UV light. Do not allow direct contact between the painted surface and the glazing as this will increase the risk of mould growth and pigment damage.

Seek advice from conservation framing specialists as there are many factors to consider in framing a painting. These are additional to the aesthetics of the frame itself. Some of these factors include:

- depth of the frame;
- method by which the painting is fixed within the frame;
- types of packing materials; and
- types of backing boards and glazing materials.

To provide additional protection for particularly valuable paintings, incorporate conditioned silica gel into the frame. Do not attempt this type of treatment without professional advice as there are risks if correct procedures and conditioning are not carried out.

Handling

Avoid contact with the painted surface when handling paintings. This will reduce the chance of leaving fingerprints on varnishes or of dislodging fragile surfaces. Although wearing white cotton gloves is generally recommended when handling paintings, take care with impestos and similar artworks, as there is the possibility of the gloves catching on the protruding paint.

As some of the older, ornate frames may have sections that are loose, inspect paintings and frames before moving them. As long as the frame is in good condition, carry the framed painting with one hand underneath the bottom of the frame and the other on the side. If the frame is in poor condition, place it on a support and carry the support.

Storage and display

Before hanging a painting for display, check the frame and wires to ensure they are in good order, are sufficient for the weight of the painting and are arranged so the weight is evenly distributed. If there are no wires in place, take the painting to a framer for advice on the most appropriate hanging method. Do not hammer in nails or use string or cord to hang paintings.

If framed images are not hung, store them according to the following guidelines:

- stand upright;
- place sheets of acid-free board or foamcore between each frame;
- place padding, such as foamcore, underneath the stack to protect the edges of the frames; and
- raise this stack slightly from the floor and place a wedge against the outermost frame to prevent slipping.

Protect unframed paintings by storing them in custom-made boxes. Construct these boxes from archival materials and store them in enamelled metal cupboards or on enamelled shelves.

Inspect paintings, particularly if in storage, on a regular basis.

Do not use inks or sticky labels on the backs of paintings as they may bleed through to the front. Catastrophic damage can be caused by spilling inks or other liquids.

Do not use aerosols near exposed paintings, as they have the potential to cause softening and damage to paint surfaces.

TREATMENTS

Documentation

Carefully document both the history and condition of artwork as soon as it enters any collection. Provide details concerning the painting and the frame, and include:

- notes about the artist, the date of the painting and the title of the work;
- colour and black-and-white photographs, taken from various angles to highlight special features such as labels or damage; and

Acrylic painting showing damage from careless handling of ink.

Oil painting damaged by poor storage.

Water-colour painting showing fading due to light exposure.

- a condition report recording the dimensions, materials used in the painting, details of any previous restorations or irregularities, descriptions of the type and condition of all materials present (even if unsure of their nature), labels or writing on the edges or back.

There may be evidence of an underlying work which may require special examination using infra-red, UV or X-ray photography.

Cleaning

Conservation treatment of paintings is a specialised area of work, requiring high levels of skill and training. As inappropriate treatments have the potential to damage and compromise the integrity and value of a painting, any decision to treat a painting must be made only after consulting conservation and curatorial professionals.

Each painting is unique and no general guidelines can be set as to the extent of treatment required. Bearing the above cautionary notes in mind very brief details are given below of the type of work that would require the services of a conservator. These include:

- removal of yellowed varnish to reveal the true colours of a painting. Solvents are often used to do this;
- remounting or cleaning of water colours or works of art on paper (some details are given in the chapter, Paper and Books);
- repair of tears or holes in canvas or paper;
- reattachment of loose or flaking paint;
- flattening of dents or bumps (cockling) of paper by using a combination of heat and relative humidity;
- restretching of canvas. Great care is needed to prevent splitting as aged canvas loses its flexibility; and
- removal of dirt and stains.

It is important that all conservation work is reversible. Thus, when a recently applied varnish eventually yellows, it will be able to be removed. Similarly, materials used in retouching may age at a different rate to the original and may have to be removed at some time in the future.

An example of a painting that required treatment is described below. This painting, a modern, acrylic, Aboriginal bark painting was in the process of being given a collection number when ink was accidentally splashed onto it. The proposed treatment of this work of art was as follows:

- photograph the painting, including close-ups of damaged areas;
- sketch stained areas to highlight those areas which may not show up sufficiently in a photograph;
- determine the chemical nature of the ink;
- search the literature for all known solvents or reagents which will dissolve the ink;
- spot test to determine if the chosen reagent will remove the ink without damaging the underlying image;
- remove the ink area by area; and
- if the reagents affect the paint layers then it may be best to overpaint the ink. This treatment must be fully documented and reversible.

SUMMARY

- Document all aspects of a painting, including details of the artist, title of the work, photographs, sketches and condition report.
- Use correct attachments for hanging paintings and obtain professional framing advice for large and heavy works.
- Control temperature and relative humidity to 15-25°C and 45-65% respectively.
- Restrict light levels to 50 lux and less than 75 μW/lumen of UV.
- Do not touch front or back surfaces with bare hands.

BIBLIOGRAPHY

Simpson, M.T. and Huntley, M., (Eds), 1992, *Caring for Antiques*, Conran Octopus, London.

Leisher, W.R., 1992, Paintings, in *Caring for Your Collections*, National Committee to Save America's Cultural Collections, Arthur W. Schultz (Chairman), Harry N. Abrams Inc., New York, pp.30-39.

CERAMICS

INTRODUCTION

Pottery and pottery fragments are extremely durable, having survived from ancient times until the present. This durability has resulted in these materials forming an important part of the archaeological record.

The term ceramic is used to describe a variety of fired clay objects which include porcelain, stoneware, earthenware and terracotta. The basic criteria for categorising ceramics are the type of clay or body and the nature of the firing process.

Porcelain and *glaze* are closely related to glass in nature. Porcelain has a high-fired, vitrified white clay body and glaze is the vitrified or glassy coating found on ceramics. White clay, or kaolin, the raw material for porcelain is a hydrated aluminium silicate.

Stoneware is also high-fired and vitrified, but is made from secondary clay; that is, clay which contains material other than the basic aluminium silicate. It is generally opaque, with a range of colours which includes white, grey, black and buff. Stoneware usually has a fine-grained body with a porosity of less than 3 per cent.

Earthenware has a low-fired porous body made from secondary clay. Its strength is much less than that of stoneware or porcelain and its porosity is more than 15%. Both earthenware and stoneware must be glazed if they are to retain water.

Terracotta is low fired and unglazed.

Many further distinctions may be made within these groups according to the type of body, decoration, style or function of the object. It is important to assess ceramic objects before treatment, as the type of ceramic will influence the choice of treatment.

DETERIORATION

The most common ceramic conservation problems include:

- breakage;
- deterioration of previous repairs;
- flaking painted decoration or glaze;
- soiling or staining;
- loss and cracking; and
- damage from salt efflorescence.

Damage from salt contamination may occur in unwashed objects recovered from buried or underwater sites. As the object dries, chloride and sulfate salts form crystals which expand and break up the ceramic. Signs of salt damage are white crystals on the surface, shallow pits on the ceramic body or missing spots of glaze.

PREVENTIVE CONSERVATION

Environment

Store or display ceramic objects in a stable environment, with temperatures in the range 15-20°C and within a relative humidity range of 40-55%.

Extremes, or sudden changes in temperature and relative humidity may cause ceramics and glazes to crack. Adhesives used for repairs may also be adversely affected. If an object has been contaminated by soluble salts, fluctuations in relative humidity may cause disruption to the clay fabric and glaze as the salts crystallise or redissolve.

Avoid heat build-up from lighting sources. For display, place lighting outside showcases and if possible direct onto ceramic objects by reflection.

Handling

Take care when handling ceramic materials as they are often fragile and easily broken. Observe the following guidelines when handling ceramics:

- use clean, bare hands or disposable rubber gloves;
- check for any breakages, cracks or old repairs;
- remove any loose parts such as lids before moving;
- do not pick up objects by handles or protruding parts;
- carry only one object at a time. Place one hand underneath the base and use the other hand to support the side of the object; and
- if a quantity of objects need to be moved, use a tray lined with bubble wrap, a thick, clean towel, cottonwool or crumpled tissue paper and pad between each object.

Storage and display

Protect ceramic objects against dust, harmful vapours and physical damage in storage. Achieve these aims by:

- storing ceramic objects in boxes or closed cupboards;
- using metal cabinets in preference to unsealed wooden cupboards or display cases. These latter

units may emit organic acid vapours which are harmful to low-fired, unglazed ceramic objects;
- padding objects in boxes with bubble wrap or acid-free tissue paper;
- lining shelves with inert polyethylene foam sheet or acid-free paper and leaving enough space around each object for easy access; and
- not stacking objects. If stacking is unavoidable, as in the case of plates, separate objects with acid-free paper that has been cut to size.

If using wooden or wood-based composites for storage and display, seal them properly (see the chapter, Preventive Conservation).

TREATMENTS

Examination

Before beginning any treatment, thoroughly examine the ceramic, noting:

- the condition of the ceramic body;
- the extent of previous repairs;
- any unfired decoration or blistering, weak and flaking glaze; and
- the presence of stains and residues.

Pay particular attention to any unfired decoration or weak and flaking glaze, because if these are undetected they could be damaged during treatment.

Note the presence of any stains and residues as these indicate the history and use of an object and it may be appropriate to retain them.

Use notes, drawings and photographs to document the condition of the ceramic before it is treated. Record all observations and pertinent investigations.

Cleaning

As cleaning removes dirt which could otherwise be embedded further during subsequent treatment stages, it is often the first stage of a conservation treatment. Cleaning techniques which may be applied to ceramics include:

- brushing;
- vacuuming;
- wiping with damp swabs; and
- wet chemical cleaning.

Start the cleaning process by using the most gentle and least toxic materials. Always attempt dry cleaning before wet or chemical cleaning. Remove loose dirt using a brush and gentle vacuum suction. Wooden sticks will remove accretions. Do not use metal probes as they are likely to cause damage.

Do not wash objects with flaking glaze or soluble painted decoration and if extremely fragile do not brush them. Clean robust sections of vitrified glaze on such objects using damp swabs. Never immerse ceramics in water, as cracks in the glaze could retain water, leading to further damage.

Test any solvents to be used on an inconspicuous area and on decoration or gilding before application.

Some dirt can be removed using cotton swabs moistened in distilled or deionised water. Roll the swabs over the surface, do not scrub them back and forth. To remove grime, use a solution containing a few drops of a concentrated, non-ionic detergent (such as Lissapol) in water (100 ml).

Alternatively, add pure soap solution to water as outlined below:

- dissolve one gram (about one teaspoon) of pure soap flakes in a little hot water;
- add enough cold water to make a total of one litre of solution;
- add 100 ml of soap solution to 100 ml of water; and
- apply with a cotton swab by rolling over the surface.

Remove detergent or soap residues using cotton swabs moistened with distilled water.

This method particularly suits small intricate objects and porous, unglazed ceramics.

Poulticing

Poulticing is also suitable for cleaning porous, unglazed ceramics. The steps in preparing and applying a poultice are detailed below:

- tear acid-free blotting paper into small pieces;
- wet the paper with distilled water;
- mash the blend to make a pulp. A heavy-duty domestic blender is a very effective 'masher'. Note that a large amount of water needs to be added to the paper for correct functioning of the blender (about 300 ml of wet paper to 1500 ml of water);
- drain excess water from the poultice, using either a strainer or hands, before application;
- cover the ceramic surface with an acid-free tissue to avoid the paper pulp becoming trapped in the ceramic pores;
- apply the poultice. As it dries, it absorbs dirt from the pores of the ceramic;

A.

B.

C.

Repair of ceramic dish.

A. Materials used.

B. Application of Paraloid B-72 adhesive.

C. Adhesive tape holding parts together until adhesive sets.

- cover the poultice with a polyethylene sheet if the environment is dry. A poultice which dries too quickly may not be effective;
- leave the poultice to dry completely and fall away; and
- several applications may be required to clean the ceramic surface satisfactorily.

Wash ceramics which are sound, glazed or less porous using a more conventional method, as outlined below:

- use a large plastic container or line a sink with towels and wash only one object at a time;
- use cold or warm water (1 L) which contains either a concentrated, non-ionic detergent (1 ml or 0.25 teaspoon) or 100 ml of soap solution (see above for preparation);
- use small brushes to remove stubborn dirt;
- rinse the ceramic thoroughly with distilled water; and
- drain the ceramic on cloth or paper towelling and dry it with a soft cloth.

Stain removal

Try solvents such as methylated spirits, alcohol and acetone on stubborn stains. Apply these with cotton swabs.

On porous, unglazed ceramic surfaces, use a paper poultice prepared with tissue paper and the chosen solvent. To slow the evaporation of the solvent, cover the poultice layer with polyethylene film.

Take care if using acetone. Avoid contact with skin, wear eye protection and do not inhale vapours.

Remove stains found in the bottom of old tea cups and in cracks by using oxygen-releasing detergent powders. These powders, which are often marked 'Contains Oxygen Bleach', contain sodium perborate, which is converted to hydrogen peroxide in water. To remove these stains:

- prepare a 2% solution by dissolving 20 g of powder (about one tablespoon) in 1 L of water;
- leave the porcelain or other glazed ceramic in the solution for about two hours;
- check the object periodically, brushing the stained area gently at these times;
- begin the treatment in the morning and continue until the stain is removed;
- if necessary, store the ceramic in clean water overnight and place it in fresh bleaching solution the following day;
- when the stain has been removed, rinse the object thoroughly by soaking it in distilled water for two hours; and
- drain and dry the ceramic.

Although it is more expensive than the oxygen-releasing detergent powders and has a limited shelf life, hydrogen peroxide is effective in removing stubborn stains from porcelain. **Always test decorative elements first to make sure they will not be affected**. If there are no adverse effects then apply hydrogen peroxide as described below:

- pre-soak the porcelain in distilled water before applying the hydrogen peroxide;
- lightly roll some cotton wool and soak it in 3% v/v hydrogen peroxide. Up to 30% hydrogen peroxide solution may be used;
- place the swab directly over the stain, leaving it in place for two or three hours;
- check periodically, repeating the process until the stain is removed;
- if the treatment needs to continue the following day, place the porcelain in water overnight and then continue the application of hydrogen peroxide until the stain is removed;
- rinse the porcelain thoroughly by leaving it to soak for two hours in distilled water; and
- allow the porcelain to drain and dry.

As hydrogen peroxide is a very powerful oxidising agent, wear rubber gloves and eye protection when using it.

Copper and iron stains may result from clamps or dowels used in old repairs or from contamination on burial sites. Removing these stains is difficult and requires the use of stronger chemicals. Consult a conservator before attempting treatment of these types of stains.

Desalination

If a ceramic shows signs of salt damage (see Deterioration) it must be desalinated.

For ceramics with a friable surface, poulticing is recommended, rather than washing. Apply a fine tissue that will not 'catch' on the ceramic surface before the paper pulp (see Poulticing above). In the case of very friable ceramics seek advice from a conservator.

Porous ceramics whose surface is not friable should be wet gradually to avoid further damage. This may be achieved by:

- placing the object in a large plastic container,

adding enough tap water to cover the base of the ceramic and covering with a tight-fitting lid;
- check the ceramic periodically;
- water will be drawn up into the ceramic by capillary action, allowing air to escape;
- add more water, up to the 'wet mark' on the ceramic; and
- continue this process until the object is submerged. Desalination then proceeds.

Keep objects recovered from damp burial (terrestrial) or underwater sites wet until desalination can begin. Transport them in individual, sealed polyethylene bags, with some wet sand or water to cushion them. Place the bags in rigid containers, then transfer the objects to plastic containers, buckets or tubs for treatment. Keep containers covered to avoid evaporation of the wash solution.

Desalinate ceramics recovered from marine sites by following the regime below:
- place the ceramic in a 50:50 seawater/tap water solution for two weeks;
- transfer to pure tap water and leave for four weeks;
- transfer to distilled or deionised water and wash until no more chloride salts are released. This will involve periodic changes of solution after several months in each bath; and
- if slime forms on the ceramic, indicating that bacteria are active, add a biocide to the wash solution. Consult a conservator if bacterial contamination is suspected.

The time required to complete desalination varies greatly from object to object. Ideally the chloride content of the solutions should be monitored and the solutions changed when the chloride levels in solution have stabilised. This process requires access to sophisticated equipment. A simpler approach is described below.

As a general guide, test wash solutions monthly for chloride salts and change the solutions if salts are present in the wash solution. To test for chloride salts, use the following procedure:
- place 2 ml of wash solution in a test tube;
- add two drops of 10% v/v nitric acid to the wash solution;
- add two drops of silver nitrate solution to the nitric acid/wash solution. The silver nitrate solution is prepared by dissolving about 15 g of silver nitrate in 100 ml of distilled water;
- if a white precipitate forms, then chloride salts are present. Change the wash solution and continue desalination for a further month; and
- continue washing until tests show that no chlorides are present (four to five months in most cases).

Previous restorations

Previous restoration attempts may be indicated by the presence of large metal staples, dowels, glues, resins and fills.

Staples and dowels are usually left in place as removing them can cause damage. If, however, they are corroding and damaging the ceramic, treat them for corrosion or remove them. See a conservator for advice on the most appropriate procedure.

Adhesive repairs and residues are usually apparent as they often become yellow and unsightly over the years. Some common adhesives used to repair ceramics include starch paste, animal glues, shellac, cellulose nitrate, soluble nylon, epoxies and emulsions such as PVA. Depending on the type used, old adhesives can often be redissolved. Unfortunately the solubilities of many adhesives change as they age. Soluble nylon, for instance, is probably better referred to as insoluble nylon! Comprehensive information regarding the preparation and properties of consolidants, adhesives and coatings is provided elsewhere (Horie 1987).

A conservator can provide advice regarding adhesive type and solubility. If solvents are used to soften or dissolve adhesives, always test painted surfaces to make sure they will not be affected.

To test the solubility of an old adhesive, follow these steps:
- carefully cut a small chip of adhesive with a sharp scalpel;
- place it in a covered glass container;
- soak it in water initially;
- if the adhesive does not dissolve in cold water then try warm water, alcohol (ethanol) or methylated spirits (95% ethanol and 5% methanol) and acetone (in that order);
- stronger solvents are needed to dissolve adhesives like epoxy resins. Consult a conservator before attempting to remove these adhesive types; and
- if a chip of adhesive cannot be removed then apply the solvent to an exposed spot of adhesive and note its effect.

Take the usual precautions (rubber gloves, eye protection and non-inhalation of vapours) when using organic solvents such as acetone and alcohols.

To dismantle an old repair, try the following techniques:
- work on a padded surface, or line the container so that pieces that fall apart will not be damaged;

- keep an accurate record of each fragment's position in the ceramic so that reconstruction will be easier;
- paint the solvent repeatedly over the joins while very gently manipulating the fragments to test for any movement;
- when using alcohol, methylated spirits or acetone, cover the joins with cotton wool wicks soaked in solvent. Place the object in a plastic container with a tight fitting lid;
- clean excess adhesive from the edges of separated fragments while the adhesive is still soft (use a stiff brush dipped in solvent or a sharpened stick). Take care not to remove any of the clay fabric; and
- leave fragments to dry.

If it is necessary to immerse the join fully in solvent, wet the porous ceramic gradually. Avoid full immersion in acetone or alcohol if possible, due to the cost and exposure to the solvents themselves. Consult a conservator if this step is deemed necessary.

Joining

Adhesives selected for joining ceramics should be reversible and have good ageing properties. They should be able to be redissolved if necessary, should not yellow, become brittle or lose adhesion with age.

Certain acrylic and polyvinyl acetate adhesives meet the above criteria and are suitable for ceramic repairs. Paraloid B-72, an ethyl methacrylate and methyl acrylate copolymer, has been used widely (Koob 1986) and UHU All Purpose Adhesive, a polyvinyl ester, has shown good results. Both adhesives can be removed or diluted with acetone. Paraloid B-72 is available from conservation materials suppliers and UHU is available from art materials or stationery suppliers.

Joining fragments requires both skill and patience, as illustrated in the following procedure:

- have a practice run of the joining sequence, holding the fragments together with tape (no adhesive);
- degrease all broken edges before joining. Apply methylated spirits (or alcohol) with a small cotton swab. Take care to remove any cotton fibres that may cling to the broken edges;
- prime porous ceramic fragments with a dilute adhesive solution before joining together. Dilute the adhesive with an appropriate solvent by mixing one part adhesive to four parts solvent. Brush the dilute solution over all broken edges and allow to dry;
- to repair a broken ceramic vessel commence by joining the base fragments and proceed upwards
- small fragments can often be joined together first to make a few large fragments which can ultimately be fitted together;
- use a sand tray to support ceramic fragments while the adhesive dries. Use only clean white sand and place a piece of soft tissue under the ceramic;
- stand the larger of the two fragments being joined in the sand - the weight of the other fragment (if correctly balanced) will tighten the join;
- select two fragments to be joined and apply adhesive along the centre of one edge;
- push the fragments together and pull apart slightly to check for an even distribution of adhesive;
- press the fragments together and manipulate to get the correct position. Running a fingernail across the join can help to check for a good fit;
- should the join need realigning, apply solvent with a brush to soften the adhesive and allow time for adjustments;
- remove excess adhesive while still wet, or semi-dry, with an appropriate solvent or if necessary with a sharp scalpel when dry. Apply a minimum amount of solvent to prevent weakening of the join; and
- apply a suitable tape across the join, on both sides of the ceramic and leave the fragments supported in a sand tray until the adhesive sets.

Work methodically so that fragments are not locked out at the end of reconstruction. A practice run of the joining sequence should ensure this. Use a tape which will not bond too strongly to the ceramic for the test run. By doing this no adhesive residue will be left behind nor will the ceramic surface be damaged when the tape is removed.

Some of the self-adhesive (pressure-sensitive) tapes available from stationery or art suppliers are suitable. Archival quality paper tapes, which are self adhesive and pressure sensitive, are preferable but these are only available from conservation materials' suppliers. They range from strong, thick paper tapes, such as Filmoplast P90 and Tyvek Tape, to finer tissue paper tapes, such as Document Repair Tape and Filmoplast P.

Do not apply tape to fragile glazes, painted decoration or friable, unglazed ceramics.

Dowelling is not generally recommended as it involves removing part of the object by drilling holes. If an object is too heavy to be joined with an adhesive, display it on a support which holds fragments as if they are joined.

Gap filling is not always necessary, as there is some tolerance for loss in artefacts. If ceramic loss is visually disturbing or provides structural problems, filling may be carried out. Note that the aim should not be to make the object look new. Restrict filling and inpainting to areas of loss and do not cover original parts of the object. Filling and inpainting require considerable practice and a conservator's assistance should be sought.

SUMMARY

- Maintain ceramics in a stable environment with temperature and relative humidity ranges of 15-20°C and 40-55% respectively.
- Avoid extremes or sudden changes in temperature and relative humidity to minimise damage to glaze, ceramic or adhesives.
- Store in a dust-free environment. Avoid stacking.
- Handle carefully, with disposable rubber gloves or clean, bare hands.
- Carry objects one at a time, with support provided at the base and side. Use a padded tray to carry a group of objects.
- Examine and document objects thoroughly before beginning any cleaning or other treatment.
- Use dry cleaning methods before wet or chemical treatments. Test water, solvents and any other chemicals which come into contact with ceramic materials, on an inconspicuous part of the object.
- Desalinate objects recovered from burial or marine sites. Do not allow objects to dry before desalination is complete.
- For repairs, choose adhesives that are reversible and have good ageing properties. Plan and execute the joining of broken ceramic methodically.

BIBLIOGRAPHY

Craft, M., 1992, Decorative arts, in *Caring for Your Collections*, National Committee to Save America's Cultural Collections, Arthur W. Schultz (Chairman), Harry N Abrams Inc., New York, pp. 96-107.

Horie, C. V., 1987, *Materials for Conservation*, Butterworths, London.

Koob, S., 1986, The use of Paraloid B-72 as an adhesive: its application for archaeological ceramics and other materials, *Studies in Conservation*, vol. 31, pp. 7-14.

Williams, N., 1983, *Porcelain Repair and Restoration*, British Museum Publications, London.

GLASS

INTRODUCTION

Glass manufacture is believed to have originated in Mesopotamia or Egypt, some time before 3000 BC. The glass beads, figurines and vessels produced were similar in appearance to ceramic objects. They were made using the techniques of core forming, mosaic, fusion, mould casting and cold cutting. Glass blowing was developed in the 1st century AD, probably in Syria. The techniques for handworking glass have continued, essentially unchanged, for 2000 years.

Ancient glass was formed from a mixture of silica (sand, crushed quartz or flint), alkali (soda or potash from plant ash) and lime (probably included as an impurity in the sand). Glass was coloured by the addition of oxides of metals such as copper, iron, cobalt and manganese.

Some glasses which were not purposely coloured had yellow or green tinges. This was due to iron oxide impurities in the sand. A colourless glass was achieved by adding manganese dioxide. This process of decolourisation dates from the 1st century AD.

Until the 10th century soda from the ashes of marine plants was used universally to modify the silica network. After this time the glass makers of Northern Europe replaced soda with potash, obtained from beechwood ash. The resultant glass was known as 'forest glass' and was mainly green or brown in colour.

By the 15th century Venice was established as the most prominent glass manufacturing centre in Europe. 'Cristallo', a fine clear glass was developed by adding lime to the soda-silica mixture.

In Bohemia in the early 16th century, a clear, solid crystal glass was produced when lime was added to the potash-silica mixture. This glass was ideal for cutting and engraving.

Lead glass, also known as 'glass of flint', was developed in Britain in the 17th century. This glass, with a 30 per cent lead oxide content, is characterised by its clarity and brightness.

Mould casting was revived in North America in the early 19th century. The use of press moulding allowed intricate patterns to be produced cheaply and quickly. Early pressed glass objects were made predominantly from colourless lead glass.

In 1864 a 'lime' glass was developed which was most suitable for pressing. It resembled lead glass but cost less. This was important as production of glass containers became mechanised in the late 19th century. Hand blown bottles were still produced as late as the 1930s but only for certain types such as pharmaceutical bottles and cosmetic ware.

Most of the glassware used during the 18th and 19th centuries in Australia and other parts of the then British Empire was imported from Britain. In comparison with the common 'black' glass bottles, there is a scarcity of the colourless and pale green, flint glass objects on early Australian sites. This is due to manufacturing limitations and differences in excise duty that existed between flint glass and black glass in Britain from 1746 to 1845 (Boow 1991). Older, cheaper methods of manufacture, such as those using wooden moulds and push-ups, were continued for black glass bottles until about 1870.

DETERIORATION

Apart from the obvious fragility of glass and its tendency to crack and break, there are other forms of deterioration which occur when glass is in contact with moisture and aqueous solutions.

Surface weathering produces effects which vary greatly, from a loss of transparency to the formation of iridescent layers, crizzling and scaly encrustations.

The reaction of glass with water can be described as "an inward diffusion of water molecules, which then react with non-bridging oxygen atoms to produce hydroxyl ions that migrate out with the alkali cations" (Newton 1989). The surface layer of the glass becomes alkali depleted and protons (H^+) replace the alkali ions in the glass network. As protons are smaller, this results in shrinkage of the leached surface layer of glass. When the glass dries various forms of deterioration may be observed. The surface may become opaque or iridescent and fine lamellae or thick flakes may fall away.

When flat sheets of glass are stored 'face to face' in a humid environment, the trapped moisture will quickly form a leaching solution and attack the glass.

Crizzling, the formation of very fine surface cracking, occurs in glass with a disproportionate composition (excess alkali and insufficient lime). This type of composition is often found in glass of the 16th to the 18th centuries. Crizzled glass objects 'weep' when placed in a humid environment, with the droplets of moisture on the surface continuously leaching the excess alkali.

Other environmental influences which adversely affect glass include:

- carbon dioxide and sulfur dioxide which combine with moisture in the air to produce weathering crusts of calcite ($CaCO_3$) and gypsum ($CaSO_4$), for example, on old window glass;
- slightly acidic or alkaline soils;
- soluble salts which are inevitably present in glass recovered from a marine environment. If the glass is allowed to dry before being thoroughly washed, crystallising salts will cause surface exfoliation; and
- exposure to sunlight. Decolourised glass, which contains manganese salts, develops a purple hue after prolonged exposure. This effect has even been found in shards recovered from shallow water.

PREVENTIVE CONSERVATION

Environment

Optimum conditions for storage and display of stable glass objects are 40-55% relative humidity and a temperature range of 15-20°C.

Relative humidity control is important as a moist environment will affect any glass surface adversely and a desiccating environment will cause further damage to weathered glass. In addition, adhesives used for repairs may 'cold flow' if exposed to high relative humidity or high temperatures.

High temperatures may damage painted, crizzled or weathered glass. After appropriate treatment, keep chemically unstable, crizzled and weeping glass at 42% relative humidity. This strict condition is necessary as higher relative humidity levels will dissolve salts and lead to their migration while lower relative humidity levels increase the risk of cracking. Use a sealed container and conditioned silica gel or an appropriate saturated salt solution and seek advice from a conservator.

Light levels are not critical for most glass as fading is not often a problem. Sunlight and other UV sources will affect decolourised glass, giving it a purple hue. Light levels of up to 300 lux, with a UV content of 75 μwatts/lumen are acceptable for stable glass objects.

It is important to avoid heat build-up from lighting. Place display lighting outside showcases and if possible direct light onto glass objects by reflection.

Handling

Glass is a fragile material which is easily broken if not handled carefully. Take the following guidelines into account when handling glass objects:

- check for breakages or failing adhesive;
- remove any loose parts, such as lids or stoppers, before carrying;
- only carry one object at a time with the weight supported uniformly and one hand under the base;
- do not wear cotton gloves as glass surfaces are smooth and slippery. Instead handle objects with bare, clean hands or disposable rubber gloves;
- line trays used to carry objects with bubblewrap or cottonwool covered in tissue paper. Insert bubblewrap or crumpled tissue paper padding between objects; and
- keep handling of iridescent or weathered glass to a minimum.

Storage and display

Do not store flat glass 'face to face' as trapped moisture will damage the glass surface. Use perforated acid-free board to separate the glass sheets and allow air exchange.

Store glass vessels in rigid cardboard boxes padded with inert polyethylene foam, bubblewrap or crumpled acid-free tissue paper. Special cradles can be built from foamcore and ethafoam for top heavy or damaged objects.

Unless the surfaces are properly sealed (see the chapter, Preventive Conservation), do not use wooden cupboards or showcases for storing or displaying glass objects. Acid vapours given off by hardwoods such as oak and birch and by composite boards, are damaging to glass that has a high soda content. Enamelled metal cabinets or shelving are recommended. Line shelves with a non-slip material such as closed cell polyethylene foam. Attach this foam firmly to the shelving.

TREATMENTS

Examination

Thoroughly examine glass objects before storing, displaying or treating them in any way. Photographs, as well as notes and drawings, are useful for documenting the condition of objects before and after treatment.

Identify and clearly describe signs of deterioration. These include the presence of:

- cracks;
- old repairs;

Examples of glass deterioration in bottle collection.

A.

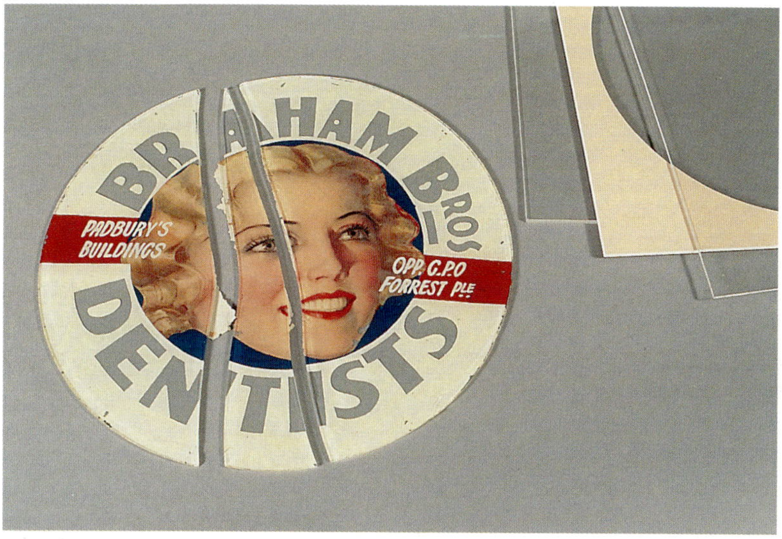

B.

Broken glass - advertising sign.

A. Before restoration.

B. Mounted behind perspex.

- missing parts; and
- surface deterioration such as opacity, iridescence (or opalescence), crizzling, pitting, delamination and encrustations.

Also note any marks that indicate the place, date or method of manufacture and original contents of bottles and jars.

Record the presence of any content residues. Ensure these residues are maintained during any subsequent treatment.

Keep accurate records of any treatments carried out and any changes that occur to the object while it is in storage or on display.

Cleaning

Only clean glass if it is in sound condition. Do not brush, or allow to become wet, glass that has poorly adhering paint or surface weathering. Do not clean or chemically treat degraded glass (for example, exfoliated, crizzled, weeping, encrusted) or painted glass without consulting a conservator.

Guidelines for cleaning **sound glassware** are described below:

- use dry methods of cleaning first;
- remove surface dirt with a soft, clean cloth or a brush and gentle vacuum suction;
- if wet cleaning is necessary, then examine the object for any previous restoration, as some adhesives may be affected by water;
- clean the surface of repaired objects by applying distilled water with cotton swabs;
- to wash sound glassware, use cold or warm water (one litre) and add either a few drops of a concentrated, non-ionic detergent (such as Lissapol) or about 100 ml of pure soap solution. (The soap solution is prepared by dissolving one gram or about one teaspoon of pure soap flakes in a little hot water and adding enough cold water to make one litre.);
- use a large plastic container or a sink lined with towels;
- do not leave glass to soak in the water ;
- only wash one object at a time;
- use soft brushes, cotton swabs or pliable sticks to remove stubborn dirt from wet glass;
- thoroughly rinse the glass with distilled or deionised water (in a large container) and drain on cloth or paper towelling;
- dry glass immediately with a soft cloth or by immersing it in a bath of methylated spirits; and
- use methylated spirits to remove stubborn dirt. Apply with a cotton swab, after testing any painted areas.

Rinse **'weeping' glass** gently in deionised or distilled water. Do not leave it to soak; dry it quickly and thoroughly by passing through two baths of methylated spirit. The ideal storage conditions for this type of glass is in an environment maintained at a relative humidity of 42%. This will avoid repetition of the 'weeping'.

Desalination

Place glass recovered from waterlogged land sites or marine environments **immediately** into sealed polythene bags to prevent dehydration. For glass recovered from the sea, partially fill the bags with seawater.

Washing is necessary to remove soluble salts, especially chloride salts, which will otherwise damage the glass when it is dried. Guidelines for desalination are described earlier (see the chapter, Ceramics).

Removing encrustations

During desalination, calcium encrustations can be removed mechanically from sound glass using pliable wooden spatulas and brushes. Calcium encrustations harden if allowed to dry and then are more difficult to remove. Remove surface encrustations with great care as some forms of surface degradation, such as iridescence and exfoliation, are not apparent when the glass is wet.

Using polyphosphate water softeners, such as 'Calgon', to remove calcium encrustations is **not** recommended for any weathered glass. These have been shown to cause damage (Horie 1989).

Use water softeners with caution for the treatment of **strong, unweathered glass**. A 2% solution of Calgon in cold or warm water, sufficient to cover the object, may be used for this purpose. Initially the glass may be soaked for a few hours, periodically brushing away the calcium encrustations as they soften.

Repair

Joining broken glass is made difficult by the transparency of the material, its smoothness and the lack of 'tooth' or 'key' on broken edges.

Although epoxy resins have been used in the repair of glass, their general use is not recommended. They tend to yellow badly as they age and are difficult to remove.

A few epoxy resins have been developed specifically for conservation use and these have good ageing properties. They are available from conservation materials suppliers but appear to have a limited shelf life and are very expensive.

Some acrylic and polyvinyl acetate adhesives used for ceramic repair, Paraloid B-72 and UHU All Purpose Adhesive respectively, are also suitable for glass repair (see the chapter, Ceramics).

The principles, guidelines and techniques for repair and reconstruction previously outlined for ceramics apply equally for glass fragments (see the chapter, Ceramics). Points specific to glass are described below:

- before joining, degrease the edges of glass fragments with a cotton swab soaked with either methylated spirits or acetone;
- do not place tape, used to hold fragments together, on fragile surfaces;
- if the artefact is flat, lay fragments together on a flat surface and hold with tape;
- place a release material, such as wax paper or silicone release paper, under the glass fragments to prevent excess adhesive adhering to the support;
- paint the adhesive lightly over the joins. The adhesive will be drawn into the joins by capillary action; and
- remove excess adhesive later, using a sharp scalpel.

Often synthetic casting resins are used for filling losses in glass. **Gap filling** causes some stress to the glass and the resins have a tendency to yellow. Only carry out filling if it is structurally or aesthetically necessary. It is a complicated procedure and consultation with a conservator is essential.

To strengthen a **crack** in glass to avoid further damage, dilute adhesive with an appropriate solvent and paint along the crack. Even a well repaired join in clear glass usually remains visible. This occurs because the refractive indices of the glass and that of the adhesive are usually different.

A **broken glass stem** may require dowelling as well as adhesive for a successful repair. The difficulty of drilling precise holes into the broken glass stem can be overcome by using a metal collar and a glass drill bit (Jackson 1982). The dowelling technique is complex and it is best to seek advice from a conservator.

Consolidation of glass is not generally recommended. If it is considered necessary, consult a conservator. Exfoliating, iridescent glass will lose its 'rainbow' colouring if a consolidant is applied.

BOTTLES

Bottles and jars form the basis of many collections. As most bottles are made from glass the aspects of deterioration, care and conservation outlined earlier in this chapter apply to these objects.

It is most important to be aware of the history of collected bottles, as the burial environment from which they were recovered will influence deterioration processes.

Deterioration

In addition to the usual factors which affect the deterioration of glass, internal stresses will be present in hand- or machine-blown glassware. This is due to differences in cooling and shrinkage rates between the thin and thick sections of the molten glass vessel. Exposing bottles to sudden changes in temperature may upset the balance of these internal stresses, resulting in the glass fracturing. For this reason always allow glass to adjust gradually to new environmental conditions. Such allowances should be made following excavation, washing and movement from one climatic region to another.

Weathered glass attains a variety of colours and textures depending on the environmental conditions to which it has been exposed. Bottles that have been in a moist environment will become iridescent or silvery and the surface may exfoliate. Glass buried in an alkaline environment, guano sites for example, is characterised by pitted, opaque surfaces.

Clear glass exposed to sunlight for a long time will become purple, indicating that manganese was used in its manufacture. Some clear glass will become amber, an indication that selenium rather than manganese was used as a decolourising agent. As selenium was used between 1915 to 1930 and manganese was used predominantly between 1880 to 1915, these forms of deterioration are important for dating.

As long as it is placed in a suitable environment, most weathered glass will not deteriorate further after soluble salts have been removed from them.

Preventive conservation

During and after excavation, do not allow wet bottles to dry. Keep plastic containers with tight-fitting lids, polyethylene bags and bubblewrap on hand to store the glass as it is recovered.

Store and display glass bottles under the conditions previously recommended for glass objects. In view of the internal stresses present in bottles, control temperature and relative humidity conditions carefully.

Treatments

Cleaning

Before washing, allow bottles excavated from wet sites to stand for 24 hours in a partially closed bucket with 10 millimetres of water covering the base. This will allow the bottle to adjust to the ambient conditions.

Gradually humidify dried bottles that require washing in a similar fashion.

Remove softened accretions with a nylon brush, such as a toothbrush. Loosen any sand packed inside bottles with a pointed, wooden tool and then gently shake it out. Avoid using metal probes as these may scratch and mark the glass. Water also will help loosen and remove packed material from inside bottles.

Soften stubborn accretions and remove soluble salts by immersing the bottles in tap water. Soaking for a few days may be necessary. Do not use warm or hot water as the temperature change may crack the bottles.

Chemicals are generally not recommended for cleaning glass bottles. Although a quick result may be achieved with the use of acids, soda or household bleach, these chemicals will attack weathered glass or leave harmful residues.

An alternative cleaning technique involves the use of an ultrasonic bath. A high frequency sound produces shock waves, which loosen dirt from the glass object. Use this technique cautiously, as friable glass may disintegrate in the process.

Corks, caps and labels

Some bottles may retain the original contents, cork, lead cap or paper label. In order to keep as much information about the bottle as possible, conserve these objects intact.

Paper labels are very fragile and may be obscured by dirt and mould. Remove dirt from the glass and paper by gentle, dry brushing. Take precautions so that dust which contains mould spores is not inhaled. A cotton bud moistened with water and wooden points can be used to clean the glass. Do not wet the paper during the cleaning process.

Lead caps on bottles are usually corroded and require chemical treatment to stabilise them. Although details of lead treatment are given in the chapter on Metals, consult a conservator before embarking on any treatment of lead caps.

Following all treatments, microcrystalline wax paste can be applied to the lead and any exposed cork to seal the bottle and contents. A suitable wax paste and its method of application are described below.

microcrystalline wax	5 g
white spirit	10 ml

- apply the paste with a small, stiff brush and allow it to dry; and
- repeat the process until a layer approximately 2 mm thick coats the lead and exposed cork.

If no lead cap is present but the cork is sound and the contents have been retained, the bottle may be cleaned and washed as described in the section above for empty glass bottles.

After cleaning, seal the bottle to ensure the cork remains moist and swollen and that the contents do not evaporate. Apply microcrystalline wax paste to the cork and lip of the bottle (as described above).

Consult a conservator if more information on sealing bottles is needed.

Polishing glass

Do not use abrasive powders or chemicals to polish glass. In these processes a layer of the original object is destroyed, breakage may result from heat build-up and chemical residues may be deposited which may cause further damage.

SUMMARY

- Store glass in a stable environment with temperature and relative humidity ranges of 15-20°C and 40-55% respectively.
- Handle glass objects with disposable rubber gloves or clean, bare hands.
- Carry objects one at a time, with support at the base and side. Alternatively use a padded tray to move a group of objects.
- Never store flat glass face-to-face. Separate the sheets to allow for air exchange.
- Examine objects thoroughly and record their condition, old repairs, makers' marks or content residues before undertaking any cleaning or other treatment.
- Consult a conservator before treating degraded or painted glass.
- Desalinate glass recovered from burial or marine sites. Keep the glass wet following excavation and during desalination.

BIBLIOGRAPHY

Boow, J., 1991, *Early Australian Commercial Glass: Manufacturing Processes*, Ed. J. Byrnes, Heritage Council of NSW, Sydney.

Craft, M., 1992, Decorative arts, in *Caring for Your Collections*, National Committee to Save America's Cultural Collections,

Arthur W. Schultz (Chairman), Harry N Abrams Inc, New York, pp. 96-107.

Horie, V., 1989, Materials used for glass conservation, in *Conservation of Glass*, Eds R. Newton and S. Davison, Butterworths, London, pp. 165-185.

Jackson, P.R., 1982, A dowelling technique for glass restoration, *The Conservator*, vol. 6, pp. 35-36.

Newton, R., 1989, Deterioration of glass, in *Conservation of Glass*, Eds R. Newton and S. Davison, Butterworths, London, pp. 135-164.

STONE

INTRODUCTION

Rocks are essentially aggregates of different minerals. Some rocks, such as limestone and quartzite, are composed of only one mineral, calcite and quartz respectively. Once cut and dressed, a rock is then referred to as a stone.

Rocks are classified into three major groups:

- igneous;
- sedimentary; and
- metamorphic.

The distribution of rocks in the first 16 kilometres of the earth's crust is about 95 per cent igneous, 4% clay rocks, 0.75% sandstone and 0.25% limestone. Of the rocks outcropping on the earth's surface (including the underwater surface) 5% are igneous rocks, 4% are metamorphic and 75% are sedimentary, the rest being covered by ice.

Igneous rocks are formed as magma cools. They are either glassy, such as obsidian and pumice (frothy glass), or crystalline, such as granite, porphyry and dolerite. Igneous rocks are primarily silica (35-80%) with smaller amounts of alumina (up to 25%), potash, soda, lime, magnesia and iron oxides also present.

Sedimentary rocks are formed following cycles of weathering, sedimentation and lithification. Transportation of the sediments is followed by settling and then lithification (transformation into rock). All rock types (igneous, sedimentary and metamorphic) are subject to weathering.

Sedimentary rocks are generally stratified, fine grained and heterogenous. They may contain pebbles, sand, clay, shells, mineral grains and fragments of older rocks.

Sandstone is formed from sand particles cemented by secondary silica or calcite. *Shale* is formed from clay minerals plus mica and quartz. *Limestones*, which represent 25-35% of all sedimentary rocks, are formed from either the precipitation of fine calcite ($CaCO_3$) or from the build-up of fossilised shells. *Soapstone* is formed by the weathering products of talc (steatite). *Alabaster* is an aggregate of gypsum formed by chemical sedimentation.

Metamorphic rocks are formed when existing rocks are transformed by intense pressure, stress or heat. Their mineral components are recrystallised in the solid state, without melting or solution. All rock types, igneous, sedimentary and metamorphic, may undergo metamorphosis. For example, as a result of metamorphic processes, granite is transformed to gneiss, sandstone to quartzite, limestone to marble and shale to slate.

DETERIORATION

Stone may be damaged by:

- weathering and eroding agents (sun, wind and rain);
- pollution;
- salt contamination; and
- biological activity.

Igneous stones such as granite are hard, non-porous and fairly stable. Even so, the surface of a granite monument will deteriorate when exposed to weathering agents and pollution. It may become obscured by soot or damaged by biological growth.

Sedimentary stones, such as sandstones and limestones, are relatively soft, porous and have friable surfaces. The matrix, which cements the various particles together, is readily damaged by weathering, pollution or salts. The surface of the stone is weakened and disintegration follows.

The characteristics and durability of *metamorphic* stones are variable. Marble, for example, is of medium hardness, able to be polished and porous. It stains easily and deteriorates when exposed to conditions which promote weathering. Heat, pollutants and acidic conditions are damaging. Slate is a fine-grained, foliated rock that is susceptible to weathering and splitting into thin sheets.

All porous or rough stone surfaces are dirtied by the deposition of airborne particles such as dust and smoke. Moisture condensing on a stone surface will increase the amount of deposition. In addition to disfiguring the stone, accumulated debris can contribute to chemical and biological attack.

Carbon dioxide and sulfur dioxide in the environment is incorporated in falling precipitation and leads to the formation of **acid rain**. Acid rain will dissolve the calcite in limestone, marble and sandstone. On limestone monuments, acidified rainwater slowly dissolves the calcite, leaving whitish patches. In the areas protected from direct rain, the dirt accumulates as a black gypsum powder or crust.

Porous stone in contact with the ground will suffer **salt damage** eventually. The base of the stone absorbs

Slate headstone.
Flaking caused by exposure to the elements.

Limestone headstone.
Showing erosion and discolouration from lichen.

Examples of rocks, minerals, ores and fossils.

Salt crystals forming on limestone wall.

Alabaster vase.

water and soluble salts, which rise by capillary action. A cycle of wetting and drying is established with the pressure exerted by crystallising salts eventually disrupting the stone. Deterioration occurs in the area of stone which experiences fluctuating humidity, not where the stone is constantly wet. Visible damage includes pitting, spalling, crumbling and delaminating and is accompanied by salt efflorescence. Numerous examples of salt damage can be seen on sandstone, marble and slate gravestones and monuments.

Moisture also contributes to the corrosion of metal components on stone monuments. Green, black or brown stains from corroding metal can disfigure stone and corroding iron dowels can cause fracturing.

Biological activity on stone is encouraged by a combination of factors including light, warm temperatures, high humidity levels and the presence of organic matter (from pollution or oils and waxes from previous conservation).

The type of organism likely to thrive on a stone substrate will be determined by the particular conditions associated with the site. Algae, for example, need only light, a few inorganic compounds and a little water to develop. They may be found in relatively dry places. Once established, algal growth is able to trap water and establish an environment conducive to the growth of other organisms such as bacteria, lichens, mosses and ferns. Damage to the stone is both chemical and physical. The growth process releases chemicals, such as acids and chelating substances, which attack the stone. Penetration of the stone surface by the organism exerts pressure which may lead to fracturing of the stone surface.

Moveable objects may be protected from extreme conditions and pollution by moving them indoors. Even then, factors such as heat, humidity, acidity, salt and dust can continue to cause problems. Heat from spotlights and fireplaces, for example, can cause irreversible damage to marble. The calcite crystals of marble have different directional coefficients of thermal expansion. Heating, even to 100°C, causes more expansion of the crystals in one direction than in the other. This distortion causes stresses and cracking on the marble surface, which may develop a white, 'sugary' appearance.

Acidic vapours can build up in timber showcases or storage areas, especially at high temperatures and relative humidity, and damage calcareous stones such as limestone and marble.

Careless handling can result in breakage, staining or scratching of softer stones.

PREVENTIVE CONSERVATION

Environment

Avoid sudden or large changes in temperature and relative humidity for stone on display or in storage. Preferred environmental conditions are temperatures of less than 20°C and relative humidity levels in the range 45-50%.

Do not expose marble or limestone to direct heating from strong lights, sunlight, radiators and the like.

Handling

Potential problems associated with handling of stone objects include:

- scratching the surface of highly polished or soft stones (talc, soapstone, marble);
- the absorption of dirt, oil and salts from hands by porous materials (marble, alabaster, limestone); and
- breakage when handling or moving objects.

To minimise the risk of damage, wear cotton gloves when handling unpolished stone. Wear clean disposable latex gloves to reduce the risk of dropping highly polished stone objects.

When moving stone objects, adopt the following practices:

- check the attachment between an object and its pedestal or base before moving;
- move large objects one at a time. Rest them on thick, soft padding. High density polyethylene foam is suitable;
- use padding such as soft tissue paper, dacron or polyethylene bubblewrap both on the tray and between small objects being moved; and
- pack around protruding parts and distribute the weight evenly.

Storage

When storing stone objects, the following guidelines are useful:

- store small, lightweight objects in acid-free cardboard boxes. These must have a rigid base;
- place padding under and around objects; Clean cottonwool, acid-free tissue or polyethylene bubblewrap are suitable for padding. Do not compromise the stability of the object by this padding;
- large, heavier objects can be placed on open shelves, with curtains to minimise dust problems, or in closed cupboards;

- storage on painted metal trays or shelves is recommended over storage in or on wooden furniture;
- place the largest objects on the lowest shelves; and
- line the shelves with layers of acid-free blotting paper or cotton towels.

If wood or wood-based composite materials are used for storage, seal them correctly (see the chapter, Preventive Conservation).

Stone monuments

Control salt contamination, biological attack and weathering of outdoor stone monuments by isolating the stone from water sources. Achieve this by adopting the following strategies:

- construct a shelter for protection from rainwater. Direct the run-off away from the base; and
- isolate the stone monument from the ground or any cement (which also contains soluble salts). Place an impermeable layer such as lead sheet under the stone.

Chemical methods for creating an impermeable layer have also been investigated. Seek the advice of a conservator so that the most appropriate isolation method is used.

Avoid applying protective coatings such as oils, waxes or acrylic resins as these will degrade over time. Although many water-repellent coatings have been developed, review their use carefully before application as these materials have the potential to trap water behind the treated surface layer. In the longer term this may cause surface spalling.

TREATMENTS

Examination

Thoroughly examine and document the condition of stone objects before beginning any treatment. Record this information through a combination of notes, diagrams or photographs.

Describe any deterioration, usually indicated by changes to the surface or structure of the stone. Such visible effects may include:

- staining and other discolouration;
- salt efflorescence;
- encrustation; and
- pitting, crumbling, spalling, erosion, delamination and breakage.

Take samples of any salt efflorescence as future analysis may be required.

Note any previous repairs and marks which provide information about the history of the object.

Cleaning

Cleaning methods aim to remove unwanted substances without leaving behind any soluble salts or chemical residues and without abrading the stone surface.

Both dry and wet cleaning methods may be applied to stone objects. As dry methods involve the least intervention and pose the least risk to stone objects, try these methods first. Follow the guidelines below when **dry cleaning** stone objects:

- use a low suction vacuum cleaner with the end covered with clean, soft muslin, and a soft brush;
- dusting with a cloth is not recommended as this tends to force dirt particles into the stone;
- a soft brush or soft wooden splint may help to dislodge accretions; and
- take care that the surfaces of soft stones such as alabaster, soapstone or marble are not scratched.

If required, **wet cleaning** may be attempted after dry cleaning. The following guidelines should be noted:

- avoid solvent cleaning with damaged or friable stone;
- always test solvents on an inconspicuous part before cleaning;
- as most stones are fairly porous, avoid using large quantities of water;
- use cotton swabs, dampened with distilled water or a mixture of 50% water and 50% methylated spirits to remove dirt and grime from marble and other smooth stone surfaces;
- roll the swabs over the stone surface and discard them as soon as they become dirty; and
- do not scrub the swabs back and forth as this forces dirt into the stone pores.

If dirt persists, add a small quantity of soap solution to the water or water and methylated spirits mixture. The soap solution is prepared and applied in the following way:

- dissolve one gram or about one teaspoon of pure soap flakes in a little hot water;
- add enough cold water to make one litre of solution. Add 100 ml of this soap solution to 100 ml of water or water and methylated spirits;
- apply the soap solution with cotton swabs in the manner described above;

- use a cotton swab soaked with distilled water to rinse the soap from the stone surface; and
- do not use brushes on soft or porous stone as this will scratch or force dirt into the surface.

For cleaning more porous or rough stone surfaces, use a **poultice**. The steps in preparing and applying a poultice have been outlined previously (see the chapter, Ceramics).

Poultices are also useful for removing soluble salts from objects, where immersion in water is not practical or advisable. If **salt contamination** is suspected, for stone recovered from a marine or burial site or on the basis of a previous treatment, consult a conservator for advice on identification and removal techniques.

Stain removal

Removing stains usually requires some form of chemical treatment and as such is fraught with difficulties. Note the following points before attempting any form of stain removal:

- some stones such as marble acquire a patina as they age. This is an intrinsic part of the stone and should not be removed;
- exercise care if strong acids or alkalis (caustic soda, ammonia) are used as they will destroy patinas (and some stones);
- indiscriminant use of chemicals on stone may result in salts forming, disintegration of the stone or changes in colour;
- it is often difficult to remove chemicals completely after treatment;
- iron and copper stains require specialist conservation treatments;
- do not treat iron-stained stones composed of calcium and magnesium minerals with chelating agents (such as disodium EDTA). In addition to iron, these chelating agents tend to remove calcium and magnesium;
- hydrochloric acid reacts with marble and limestone;
- acids cause brown stains on sandstone with a high iron content;
- alkali cleaners used on porous stone lead to salt efflorescence; and
- stains often penetrate deeply into stone and may become insoluble with age.

For these reasons, consult a conservator before any stain removal is attempted.

Cleaning oil and grease stains poses less risk to the stone matrix. Hydrocarbon solvents, such as white spirits or X-4 solvent, are more successful at dissolving oils and greases than water-soluble solvents like acetone and methylated spirits. Steps in the removal of oil and grease stains include:

- initial testing to determine the most effective solvent;
- testing to ensure that the stain does not spread further;
- using a cotton swab, cottonwool strip or paper poultice to apply the chosen solvent; and
- if applying a poultice, slow the evaporation of the solvent by either placing the object in a sealed container or covering the poultice with polyethylene film.

Cleaning stone monuments

In some cases it is appropriate to clean outdoor stone monuments by *nebulisation* (the application of a very fine water mist). In this process small nozzles, such as those used in greenhouses, spray water **near** the stone surface. Only the mist contacts the monument, not the direct water spray. In this process the water particles slowly deposit onto the stone, giving a mild cleaning action. The small size of the water droplets results in a greater wetting and cleaning effect for the small quantity of water used. Collect the run-off water from the base of the monument.

Neutral chemical poultices can be used to treat stains and encrustations on advice from a conservator.

Before cleaning biological growths such as lichen, algae and moss from stone, first kill the growth by applying an appropriate biocide. Choose a biocide that will have no chemical action on the stone, is non-polluting and is safe to the user. The best time for treatment of outdoor stone is at the beginning of vegetative development (either spring or autumn). The dead biological crust can be removed by the use of a poultice, by low suction vacuuming or by gentle brushing.

Ask a conservator's advice on the most suitable cleaning products, biocides and procedures.

Repair

There are many adhesives available that may be used on stone objects and research is continuing into the best materials and techniques for repair of these objects. It would be prudent therefore, to consult a conservator before attempting any repairs to stone objects.

Small and medium sized stone objects can be repaired with Paraloid B-72 and UHU All Purpose Adhesive (see the chapter, Ceramics). These adhesives, which can be removed or diluted with acetone, meet the required conservation standards.

Steps involved in the repair of stone objects are outlined below:

- prime porous stone fragments before joining. Dilute the adhesive with an appropriate solvent by mixing one part adhesive to four parts solvent;
- brush the dilute solution (primer) over all surfaces to be joined and allow it to dry completely;
- for a multiple repair, and to avoid 'locking out', practise the order of joining the pieces before applying any adhesive;
- use a shallow container filled with clean, dry sand to support fragments;
- begin joining at the base of the object where appropriate;
- select two fragments to be joined and apply adhesive along the centre of **one** broken surface. Fit the two fragments together, pull slightly apart, to allow some evaporation of solvent and to check distribution of adhesive and then push firmly together again;
- place the joined pieces in the sand tray for support while the adhesive sets. Balance the top fragment carefully and ensure the weight of the stone pushes down onto the join. This will help to tighten the join; and
- remove excess adhesive with a cotton bud, dampened in solvent, or by careful trimming with a scalpel after the adhesive has set.

If a large or very heavy stone needs to be repaired, then dowels may be needed to strengthen the join. Although most epoxy resins yellow with age and are difficult to reverse, it may be necessary to use such an adhesive if high cohesive strength is required.

Seek help from a conservator if there is any doubt about the materials or techniques required for stone repairs.

GEOLOGICAL COLLECTIONS

INTRODUCTION

Rocks and minerals may be collected for either research, education or aesthetic reasons. The colours and crystalline forms of many minerals make them particularly attractive to collectors.

General rock types, their modes of formation, factors affecting deterioration and conservation were described at the beginning of this chapter. Whereas the materials described earlier were considered stable, being used for monuments and similar structures, the many and varied samples that make up geological collections are not necessarily so.

Expressions such as 'solid as a rock' give the wrong impression of the stability and fragility of many materials that make up geological collections. It has been estimated, for instance, that about 10% of all minerals are unstable (Howie 1992) and prone to deterioration unless adequately cared for.

One of the purposes of this section is to alert readers to the need to care for rocks and minerals. Because of the perceived stability of these materials, they are often overlooked and consequently neglected.

DETERIORATION

The usual environmental factors, light, heat, dust, relative humidity and pollutants affect rocks and minerals in similar ways to which they affect materials considered to be more sensitive. Certain minerals, realgar (AsS) and pyrargite (Ag_3SbS_3) for example, are so sensitive to light that they only retain their true colours if they are stored in the dark.

In addition to light-induced damage, deterioration mechanisms for rocks and minerals include:

- physical damage of fragile specimens due to abrasion and poor handling;
- dissolution of specimens by absorption of water from the environment;
- loss of water to the environment and subsequent changes in chemical composition and properties;
- corrosion of components;
- fracturing or volatilisation of crystals by exposure to heat or cycles of hot and cold;
- chemical attack by acidic pollutants released by certain wood types, such as oak, birch and chipboard used in storage cabinets and attack by

agents used in cleaning and other cosmetic treatments;
- biological attack and chemical degradation under conditions of high relative humidity; and
- deterioration by radioactive decay.

Dust is potentially very damaging to minerals and rocks. In addition to disfiguring surfaces, dust encourages corrosion and other reactions by providing nucleation sites for the absorption of water and pollutants from the air.

One of the problems associated with collections of rocks and minerals is the presence of impurities in some specimens. It has been suggested that the presence of impurities may account for the different behaviours of supposedly identical minerals exposed to the same conditions. Some brown topaz specimens, for example, fade in light while others are stable (Nassau 1992). Thus, although guidelines can be given for the care of rock and mineral collections, these may be compromised by impurities which lead to the deterioration of some specimens.

Note that while some deterioration processes are rapid, others may only become evident after many years.

PREVENTIVE CONSERVATION

Unlike materials made from leather, paper or a particular metal, it is not possible to recommend generalised storage and display conditions which will satisfy the conservation requirements of all rock and mineral samples. This is because of the potentially differing conditions needed to preserve the range of chemical types that may comprise such a collection.

Unfortunately in a publication of this size it is also not possible to specify all mineral types and their particular conservation requirements. As conditions for storage and display may have to be tailor made to cater for the differing sensitivities of materials in a collection, custodians of collections will need to refer to specialised publications and contact experts in the field for more specific information.

It is obviously very important to identify the minerals and rocks that make up a collection. Unless materials are correctly identified their needs cannot be adequately catered for. Consult experts and textbooks to ensure that correct identifications of specimens in a collection are made.

General information can be provided, which will act as a guide for the care of these types of collections. Protect materials against:

- physical damage by abrasion or shock;
- unfavourable environments;
- inappropriate chemical treatments; and
- poor handling.

Environment

It is generally accepted that rocks and minerals are best stored in clean, dustproof surroundings in which conditions of low light and stable, moderate temperatures and relative humidity levels prevail.

Ideal conditions have been described as 50% relative humidity at 15-20°C (Price 1992). Apply strategies previously described to minimise damage from overexposure to light or inappropriate conditions of temperature and relative humidity (see the chapter, Preventive Conservation).

Of these factors, relative humidity control is the most critical as inappropriate relative humidity conditions can lead to corrosion, gain or loss of water from crystal structures, changes from one crystal phase to another and fracturing of crystals by mechanical stresses induced by cycles of moisture gain and loss.

Store specimens prone to corrosion at relative humidity levels between 30 and 60%. Stability being enhanced at the lower level. Pyrite is one example of a mineral that will oxidise unless the relative humidity is strictly controlled.

Handling

Begin care and conservation of rocks and minerals at their point of collection. From this time ensure that:

- poor handling does not lead to physical damage;
- specimens are not 'over-cleaned'; and
- environmental fluctuations are taken into account in transporting the specimens from the point of recovery to their new environment.

Some samples, fluorite, wulfenite, apatites and fibrous zeolites, for example, are susceptible to physical damage. When handling these objects, follow the usual guidelines (see the chapter, Preventive Conservation). If samples of this type are to be packaged for transport, take additional care, as outlined below:

- to minimise physical damage, wrap specimens in acid-free tissue and place in labelled, washed cotton or linen bags; and
- further sealing in a polythene bag will buffer against environmental changes that may occur in transit.

For transporting particularly vulnerable specimens such as wulfenite and zeolites, "open tissue-lined trays and transport by hand is perhaps the only practical method" (King 1992a).

Storage and display

When designing storage conditions, take into account the needs of the specimens and of the people that care for them. For example, store mercury in sealed containers to prevent loss through evaporation and poisoning by inhalation of toxic vapours. Take similar care when storing radioactive materials. The degree and type of radioactive emission will determine the type of storage facility required.

Any materials likely to come into contact with the specimens should be of archival quality so that the chemical stabilities of the specimens are not jeopardised.

Materials used in the construction of the storage building and in storage or display areas may affect specimens. The alkaline nature of concrete, for example, is likely to affect metals, sulfides and silicates. A comprehensive list of common construction materials, their likely effects on mineral specimens and recommended actions is provided in Howie (Appendix I, 1992).

Storage options for particularly sensitive specimens include:

- sealing in glass ampoules or tubes;
- refrigerated containers or environments; and
- buffered microenvironments (silica gel, zeolites).

In all cases the chemical stabilities and sensitivities of specimens must be known before undertaking a particular type of storage. Transparent containers are recommended so that the condition of samples can be monitored easily.

TREATMENTS

General guidelines for the cleaning, 'development' and repair or consolidation of rocks and minerals are provided by King (1992b). Some of the key points made by King and others in the same publication are outlined below.

Cleaning

Only undertake any treatment if the mineral type and its properties are well known. Irreparable damage may occur if inappropriate treatments are applied.

Restrict cleaning of rocks and minerals to the removal of dust, dirt, clay and similar materials.

If it is necessary to immerse rocks during cleaning then ensure the liquid and the rocks are at the same temperature before immersion. This will reduce the risk of thermal shock.

Water will affect some minerals. Rock samples are generally more tolerant of water-based cleaning than are mineral specimens. Ethanol and propan-2-ol have been used to remove clay from water-soluble minerals. Some wet cleaning methods which may be useful for water-resistant samples are described earlier in the Stone section.

Dry cleaning techniques, including gentle brushing, vacuuming with a soft brush attachment, air-blowing with a photographer's hand blower and 'airbrasive' methods, may achieve the desired result without involving potentially damaging liquids. Airbrasive methods involve the use of fine cork or powdered walnut as abrasives.

Development

Chemicals have been used to etch surfaces, to improve the appearance of coloured crystals and to remove unwanted mineral species. Such treatments are not generally recommended and if necessary, as preparation for scientific examination for example, should only be carried out by specialists. The potential loss of information and the risk of long-term damage to the specimen outweigh the usually sought after benefits of these processes.

Repair and consolidation

The nature of the sample and the reason for the repair will determine the type of repair technique and the adhesive used. Do **not** use very strong adhesives such as polyesters, cyanoacrylates ('superglues') and epoxy resins to repair minerals (King 1992c).

Repair techniques and suitable adhesives for the repair and consolidation of stone are described earlier in this chapter. A summary of commonly used adhesives, their constituents and features of their application is provided elsewhere (King 1992c).

SUMMARY

- Store or display stone in an environment with temperatures below 20°C and a relative humidity in the range 45-50%. Do not expose marble and limestone to direct heating.
- Use cotton gloves for handling most stone objects and disposable latex gloves when handling highly polished stone.

- If wooden storage or display cabinets are used they must be properly sealed to protect calcareous stone objects from acidic vapours.
- Isolate outdoor stone monuments from water sources to avoid or control salt contamination, biological attack and weathering.
- Examine and fully document objects before any treatment.
- Use dry cleaning methods before any solvent cleaning is undertaken. Take care to avoid abrasion of surfaces.
- Test treatments on an inconspicuous part of the object before any large-scale application.
- As most stones are porous, use a minimum amount of water or solvent for cleaning.
- Use easily removable adhesives that have good ageing characteristics to repair stone. Large or heavy stone repairs may require dowels and stronger adhesives.
- Mild cleaning techniques, such as nebulisation, may be suitable for some stone monuments.
- Apply a suitable biocide to biological growths on stone monuments before removing them by mechanical cleaning.
- Maintain geological collections (ideally) with temperatures and a relative humidity level of 15-20°C and 50% respectively.
- Protect specimens from dust, handle only wearing disposable latex gloves and store in enamel-coated metal cupboards.

BIBLIOGRAPHY

Booth, B., 1993, *Rocks and Minerals*, Quintet Publishing, London.

Howie, F.M. (Ed.), 1992, *The Care and Conservation of Geological Material: Minerals, Rocks, Meteorites and Lunar Finds*, Butterworth-Heinemann, Oxford.

King, B., 1992a, Appendix II: Collecting rocks and minerals, *ibid*, p. 127.

King, B., 1992b, Appendix III: Cleaning minerals, *ibid*, pp. 128-132.

King, B., 1992c, Appendix IV: Repair and consolidation of minerals and rocks, *ibid*, pp. 133-134.

Nassau, K., 1992, Conserving light sensitive minerals and gems, *ibid*, pp. 11-24.

Price, M., 1992, The stability of minerals, *ibid*, pp. 1-10.

Wheeler, G.S., 1992, Stone objects, in *Caring For Your Collections*, National Committee to Save America's Cultural Collections, Arthur W. Schultz (Chairman), Harry N. Abrams Inc. New York, pp. 122-127.

METALS

INTRODUCTION

The significance of metals to human society is so great that two of the major eras of prehistory are described in terms of the bronze age and the subsequent iron age. The earliest metallic artefacts were beaten from native copper metal and date back to more than 4000 BC.

The development of western and eastern societies have been linked with the working of metals. These materials have been used, either in pure form or when combined with other metals, to produce an enormous variety of objects including weapons, tools and decorative art objects. Consequently, metal objects make up a large part of many collections kept in museums, historical societies and private households.

Alloys

Properties of metals, such as appearance, strength, malleability and chemical reactivity, can be altered by alloying with other metals or by the presence of other impurities. Iron, for example, may be alloyed with carbon to form cast iron or with chromium and nickel to form stainless steel. Copper is often combined with zinc to form brass and with tin to form bronze.

Distinctive colours were often prized and as a result the compositions of metals were manipulated to obtain the desired effect. Chinese bronzes and Japanese sword guards are examples of objects where colour is an integral part of the object.

Patina

The patina is a film of metal corrosion products which forms on the surface of an object, either as a result of exposure to the elements or because of deliberate artistic intervention.

Before any decision is made to remove the patina from an object the nature of the object and its history must be considered very carefully. For instance, under no circumstances should the patina be removed from an ancient bronze sculpture. On the other hand, as Victorian era silver candelabra were usually kept in a highly polished state, accumulated tarnish would be removed.

Do not confuse the patina with a lumpy, pustular or uneven corrosion mound that may lie above the original surface of an object. If in any doubt, avoid any treatments that will remove these minerals until professional advice has been obtained.

Corrosion

The tarnishing, or corrosion, of metals is the major issue of concern confronting those responsible for the care of metal items.

Gold, silver, platinum, mercury and copper are the only metals stable enough to be found in their natural metallic state, with only small amounts of the latter four materials being found. All other metals are more stable when combined with other elements to form oxides, sulfides, chlorides, carbonates or mixtures of these.

There is, therefore, a natural tendency for most refined metals to return to their more stable, 'corroded' states. As a consequence, metal objects need to be protected from environmental conditions and pollutants which encourage corrosion.

In some cases, as the metal corrodes, the oxide film that forms acts as an 'insulating' barrier, slowing the rate of corrosion to an acceptable level. Copper and aluminium are two such metals in which oxide coatings form protective, passivating layers. When iron corrodes however, it does not form a protective film. The corrosion of iron continues until no metal is left unless some other coating is applied to protect it from the elements.

DETERIORATION

The main causes of deterioration of metals include:

- exposure to conditions of high relative humidity;
- the presence of oxygen;
- exposure to salty conditions;
- reaction with pollutants;
- contact with other metals;
- stresses induced during manufacturing processes; and
- careless handling.

Moisture and **oxygen** are required for corrosion (oxidation) of metals to occur.

Chloride ions, present in common salt (sodium chloride), may originate from human or animal contact or from airborne sea salts. They can speed up the corrosion rate and are capable of penetrating protective oxide layers on metals such as copper and aluminium, to form metal chlorides. These latter materials do not form a coherent surface layer, effectively removing the corrosion resistance of the metal.

Any agent that affects protective films on metals may enhance corrosion of the underlying metal. **Physical**

damage to painted or coated surfaces, or the uneven application of oil coatings, for example, will alter the access of oxygen to the metal surfaces. This usually causes one part of the object to corrode at the expense of another.

Oils and sweat from people's hands are potential agents of decay, with the organic acids and chloride ions transferred upon contact between skin and metal, causing significant attack on metallic surfaces.

Normally unreactive metals, such as copper and silver, can suffer significant corrosion if sulfide-containing species are in the same environment as the metal. These sulfide **pollutants** are usually associated with the breakdown of plant matter and the decomposition of sulfur-containing proteins such as wool. Common pollutants include hydrogen sulfide and carbonyl sulfide.

Inorganic acids such as hydrochloric acid, derived from the decay of plastics such as polyvinyl chloride, and nitric and sulfuric acids, formed from air pollutants and moisture, will cause significant chemical attack on metals in the same storage environment or in the open air. Outdoor monuments and sculptures are particularly vulnerable to this type of attack.

Corrosion may be increased by stresses imparted to metals during their manufacture. Changes in the microstructure of metals, produced by processes such as hammering, drawing and rolling, usually encourage corrosion and in doing so reduce the service life of affected metals.

Corrosion also will occur if dissimilar alloys and metals come into contact with each other. This type of corrosion is known as **galvanic corrosion**. In this situation, the more reactive metal or alloy corrodes while the less reactive metal is protected. If, for example, iron and copper were in direct physical contact, then in the presence of moisture and oxygen, the iron would corrode selectively while simultaneously protecting the copper from these agents of corrosion. A galvanic series, which lists metals in increasing order of reactivity is provided in Appendix 8.

Many problems associated with galvanic corrosion can be overcome by avoiding direct contact between dissimilar metals.

It is important to remember these basic issues when examining corroded artefacts or when assessing storage environments. Removing chloride salts, restoring oxide coatings, repatinating metals with aesthetically pleasing patinas and coating metals with protective materials, such as lacquers and paints, are all effective tools in the conservation battle against corrosion.

PREVENTIVE CONSERVATION

Environment

Keep relative humidity levels in storage and display areas at no more than 45 per cent and light levels below 300 lux. Techniques to control the relative humidity and light levels are described earlier (see the chapter, Preventive Conservation).

Storage and display

Since the major forces of deterioration for metals are oxygen, water and airborne pollutants, any storage system which minimises the effects of these agents will extend the life of a metal.

Simple steps such as storing objects wrapped in acid-free tissue, in acid-free boxes, on painted, preferably baked enamel, metal shelving will increase their longevity. Steps such as these will help avoid both environmental attack and galvanic corrosion.

Avoid storage in or near cabinets made of chipboard or wood. These materials give off formaldehyde gas and organic acids which can accelerate corrosion. If there is no option but to store metal objects in cabinets made of these materials, take the following steps:

- coat wood with a water-based polyurethane finish to seal the wood; and
- paint chipboard with a solution of urea (400 grams) in water (one litre) and then seal with a water-based polyurethane finish.

Do not seal objects in plastic bags which may trap moisture and increase corrosion. Avoid polyvinyl chloride (PVC) bags in particular as they can give off hydrogen chloride, an acidic gas which will affect most metals.

When handling metal objects wear white cotton gloves. This will prevent the transfer of sweat and fats from the skin to the metal object, minimising potential corrosion problems.

SILVER

The lustrous appearance, relatively low natural abundance, corrosion resistance and ability to be easily worked has ensured that silver has always been a prized metal, often being used for coinage and jewellery.

Most silver objects in collections of former British colonial countries will be sterling silver or plated silver.

Sterling silver is the standard alloy used in jewellery and cutlery and is made up of silver (92.5%) and copper (7.5%). The addition of copper to silver increases the hardness of the alloy without any significant loss of lustre or colour.

There are two common forms of plated silver, Sheffield Plate and silver plate or electroplate.

Silver plate or electroplate is formed when a thin layer of pure or sterling silver is deposited electrolytically on the surface of a base metal. Common base metals include copper, brass, nickel silver (an alloy of copper, zinc and nickel) and Britannia metal (a tin alloy with 5-10% antimony).

Electroplated materials are often stamped EPNS or EPBM for electroplated nickel silver or electroplated Britannia metal respectively. As commercial electroplating was developed in the 1840s it is likely that many artefacts in Australian collections will be made of silver plate.

Sheffield plate is a duplex alloy where sterling silver has been fusion bonded ('sweated') to both sides of a copper sheet. It is subsequently worked to produce the desired object.

Deterioration

Unless kept polished, silver artefacts usually will tarnish, forming a layer of black silver sulfide. Artefacts excavated from underground or from the sea may be coated with grey silver chloride and blue-green copper corrosion products.

With age and polishing, silver may be removed from the high spots of plated silver, exposing the base metal which often looks duller than the silver layer.

Even if the most gentle polishing techniques are used, all electroplated silver ultimately will show pinpricks of corrosion as the plating wears thin. Once the plating has been perforated the underlying metal is prone to pitting corrosion and gradually the surface will become covered with a blotchy black and green-blue corrosion matrix.

Preventive conservation

Apply the guidelines for safely storing and displaying metals described in the general introduction to this chapter to silver objects.

If there is no option but to place an object in a display case previously shown to be corrosive towards silver, add acid-free blotter impregnated with either zinc oxide or zinc carbonate, to the base of the case. This will help absorb acidic and sulfurous compounds and minimise tarnishing.

Zinc carbonate-impregnated blotting paper can be prepared as follows:

- in a flat tray, prepare a solution which contains a soluble zinc salt such as zinc sulfate, by dissolving 10 g of the salt in 1 L of water;
- immerse a sheet of the acid-free blotting paper in the solution;
- once the blotter is wet, pour a solution of sodium carbonate (20 g in 1 L of water) into the bath, producing a white cloudy solution of zinc carbonate; and
- remove the blotter from the bath and allow it to dry out under glass to prevent puckering.

When dry, place the blotter underneath textile coverings in the base of a display or storage cabinet, or rolled up and placed in a support underneath a raised platform within a display cabinet. This is a very effective means of minimising corrosion.

Alternatives to blotting paper are commercially available sintered zinc oxide pellets or sachets of multi-metal vapour phase corrosion inhibitors.

Treatments

Cleaning

Only clean silver when absolutely necessary and not as a routine treatment, as any cleaning will remove minute amounts of silver.

If a piece is in good condition, maintain it in that condition rather than continually cleaning it and wearing down the silver coating. Wiping with a silver cloth, followed by storage and display under low relative humidity conditions will provide the simplest method of protection.

Take care to differentiate between tarnish and decorative treatments which are an intricate part of the object and which would be destroyed by cleaning. An example of such a decorative treatment that should not be removed is niello, a black silver sulfide deliberately used to highlight incised sections of silver jewellery and silver ornaments.

As a general rule, avoid abrasive cleaners as they can cause fine scratching of the surface and will remove small amounts of silver.

Many commercially available '**silver dip**' solutions readily remove tarnish. These are usually made up of thiourea and acid mixtures. Only use silver dips when the object is badly disfigured and apply them with care. Never use silver dip on objects with decorative treatments such as niello.

If using a silver dip, only apply or dip the solution for as long as it takes to remove the tarnish. Rinse the object in hot water to remove residues and then dry it with a lintless cloth. After drying, impart a thin layer of corrosion inhibitors to the surface of the silver by using a silver cloth.

Any kind of cleaning may expose areas of fire scale (copper oxide), sometimes formed during manufacture. These marks can discolour the surface and are very difficult to remove.

If **Sheffield plate** is in reasonable condition, just wipe it with a silver cloth and display or store it under conditions of low relative humidity. Do not replate the object as it completely devalues it by removing the technological evidence of its manufacture.

Electroplate or silverplate objects in good condition, but on which the silver has been worn away to reveal underlying metal, can be restored by using commercially available solutions which gradually deposit small amounts of silver on worn areas. This is a better way to rejuvenate the surface than is standard electroplating. The latter process is a lot more costly and is not always successful.

Electroplate which shows signs of blotchy black and blue-green pitting corrosion usually will not respond to treatment with silver polishing cloths, silver dips and cleaning foams. If confronted with materials of this type, remove the gross corrosion by using a solution made up of thiourea and citric acid. This treatment will remove much of the silver corrosion since thiourea is a very strong complexing agent that also dissolves silver sulfides. Steps in this treatment include:

- prepare a solution which contains thiourea (10 g) and citric acid (50 g) in 1 L of water;
- immerse the object in the solution, gently brushing the corrosion areas with a soft brush;
- after cleaning, place the object in a bath which contains sodium carbonate (10 g) in 1 L of water. Leave the object to soak for about one hour to remove any citric acid from beneath the electroplate; and
- remove any residual sodium carbonate by a final wash in deionised or distilled water.

If the corrosion damage is not too severe then touch up the underlying metal with one of the silver solutions that gradually redeposit small amounts of silver. Only use this treatment for electroplate or silverplate after carefully considering the history of the object. Polishing with a silver cloth is the final step in this cleaning process.

Coatings

There are commercially available lacquers for coating silver objects. These can slow tarnishing processes significantly. On the downside, these lacquers can be troublesome to remove if they break down. In addition, unless an even coating is applied, a patchy and blotchy tarnish may develop on the surface.

NICKEL SILVER

Most 19th and 20th century nickel silver objects will be found either as the unchanged copper-nickel-zinc alloy or with a thin film of electrodeposited silver on the surface. A simple spot test may be used to distinguish these materials (see Appendix 9).

One very easy way to recognise the presence of nickel, either as nickel plating or its presence in an alloy, is to look for the bright lemon-green corrosion products which characterise nickel (II) compounds. The colour is a much more lemon-yellow-green than the characteristic blue-green of copper.

In Australia only coins minted before the introduction of decimal coinage (1966) will contain any significant amounts of silver. To remove tarnish from imperial (pre-1966) coins, follow the procedures outlined above for silver.

For decimal coinage and other nickel silver objects, treat corrosion products according to the methods outlined below for copper and its alloys in the form of brass and bronze.

To treat electroplated nickel silver, follow the guidelines for silver objects.

COPPER AND ALLOYS

Copper, a lustrous red-brown metal is regarded as the first metal commonly used by man. It is commonly combined with other elements to produce a range of alloys with different mechanical and corrosion resistances. Materials made from copper and its alloys are used in almost every facet of life and human activity.

The two main categories of alloys are those created when copper (Cu) combines with zinc (Zn), to form **brasses**, and those with tin (Sn) which are known as **bronzes**.

Some typical **brass** compositions are:

Yellow brass	65% Cu 35% Zn
Red brass	85% Cu 15% Zn
Muntz metal	60% Cu 40% Zn
Gilding metal	95% Cu 5% Zn

Horse-drawn vehicle spring. Severe rusting is forcing the leaves apart.

Bronze Buddha head - showing patina and gold-leaf additions.

Above and right: Lead sculpture showing selective corrosion of the lead-rich phase of the lead-antimony alloy. *Inset*: detail of corrosion pattern.
Photographs by Ian MacLeod

Silver knife handle with high copper content (green corrosion) and evidence of rusting iron shaft beneath ivory.

Although the primary components of bronzes are copper and tin (Sn), secondary elements such as lead (Pb), nickel (Ni), zinc and even silver (Ag) and gold (Au) have been incorporated into these materials.

Some typical **bronze** compositions are:

Bell bronze	75-80%	Cu
	25-20%	Sn
Lead bronze	80%	Cu
	10%	Sn
	10%	Pb
China silver	65%	Cu
	20%	Sn
	13%	Ni
	2%	Ag
Statuary bronze	65-85%	Cu
	10-30%	Zn
	2.5-5%	Sn

Spelter bronzes, popular from the 1850s to the early 1900s, are not bronze at all but a white, zinc-based metal to which various coatings have been applied to give the effect of patinated bronze. Any attempt to clean these chemically renders them worthless.

Deterioration

Constant high humidity, pollutants such as sulfide gases, acids and careless handling causing physical damage can all result in the deterioration of copper-based objects.

Heating and acidic cleaning solutions can etch the zinc out of brasses, leaving a copper-red discolouration on the surface.

Objects may have special surface coatings, such as lacquers, which can be damaged easily by scratching or improper cleaning.

The types of corrosion products formed on copper and its alloys depend on the environment and the metal composition. The most common corrosion products are copper oxides, basic copper sulfates and basic copper carbonates. These are generally stable and protect the underlying metal from further corrosion. The corrosion products are sometimes produced artificially to provide the attractive green-brown patina seen on outdoor bronze statues.

As noted in the general discussion on metal corrosion, the passivating layers of copper corrosion products tend to break down in the presence of chlorides. Whether the chlorides are derived from the sea or from ground water the overall impact, accelerated corrosion, is the same.

In a humid environment the presence of chlorides in copper alloys may lead to the development of the cyclic corrosion phenomenon known as **bronze disease.** Copper and copper alloys which have been buried or recovered from a wet site may suffer from this effect. Bronze disease corrosion is characterised by the presence of a light blue-green, crumbly outgrowth on the surface. If this is brushed away a pit will be evident on the surface. The tests for and treatment of metals affected by bronze disease are described later in this chapter.

It is important to note the difference between bronze disease and a natural patina. Many bronzes are formulated specifically to obtain a certain coloured patina. If you are not sure, consult a conservator before attempting any treatment. This is especially important for Chinese and Japanese bronzes and for bronzes from the Renaissance period onwards as the patinas of these objects are intrinsic to the objects and should **not** be removed.

Preventive conservation

The preventive conservation guidelines described in the general introduction to this chapter are applicable to copper-based objects.

Treatments

Cleaning

Copper-based items in good condition only need wiping with a dry cloth. Use ethanol to remove greasy stains but **only** after spot testing to ensure there are no surface coatings that may be affected by this solvent.

If a badly tarnished copper alloy has to be cleaned, immerse it in a solution made up of citric acid and thiourea. The thiourea is an inhibitor which prevents chemical attack on the metal itself. If thiourea is not used in the treatment solution dissolved copper will be redeposited on the surface of the object, leaving a salmon pink blush on the surface. This then has to be removed by polishing.

Wear rubber gloves when cleaning and coating copper objects so that no marks are left on the surface of the metal.

A typical treatment regime is as follows:

- prepare a solution containing citric acid (50 g) and thiourea (10 g) in water (1 L);
- place the object in the solution and leave it until it is clean. This can take from several minutes to several hours depending on the condition of the object. Brushing with a soft bristle brush, such as a toothbrush, will speed up the process;

- to remove all traces of acid, wash the object thoroughly. Immersion in baths of clean water (preferably distilled) or under running water will usually suffice; and
- if the object has been soaked for a prolonged period, or is porous, immerse it in a bath containing sodium carbonate (5 g) in water (1 L) and then rinse it with clean water.

Ideally the pH of the metal surface and that of the wash water should be checked to ensure that the washing has been effective. Washing can be considered to be complete when the pH of the wash solution is unchanged after washing and when the pH of the metal surface is neutral.

Note that this cleaning procedure will not produce a bright, shiny surface finish on the metal. If this is required, a proprietary metal polish can be used. Avoid repeated polishing, however, as it tends to wear the metal surface.

If the above solution is not effective in removing tarnish then the amounts of citric acid and thiourea can be increased (up to twice the strength). A fine pumice powder can be used as a mild abrasive if necessary.

After washing and before any protective coating is applied the metal surface must be dry and free from grease and dirt. Wear gloves so that fingerprints do not get on the object between the cleaning and coating stages. Any such contamination will otherwise show up later in the form of corrosion areas.

If oven drying at 100°C is not appropriate, dewater the object by 'painting' it liberally with acetone. The acetone dissolves water in crevices and cracks, ensuring that the metal is dry. The metal is considered dry when there is no longer any smell of acetone. This treatment must be carried out in a well ventilated area.

Bronze disease

To determine if an object is affected by bronze disease, expose it to conditions of high humidity (greater than 85%) for a period of about two weeks. For smaller objects this may be achieved by placing the object in a large, clear plastic bag with about 100 ml of water. Do not let the object come into contact with the water. Seal the bag and inspect it after the two-week period. If droplets of green solution are observed on the surface of the metal or if new fluffy outgrowths of pustular green corrosion products are found then bronze disease is indicated.

If the object is too large, or too valuable for the above procedure, then take samples from the suspected bronze disease areas and test them (using X-ray diffraction) to determine the nature of the corrosion products. The presence of basic copper (II) chloride (atacamite or paratacamite) is indicative of bronze disease.

The main aim of the treatment is to remove the majority of the chlorides from affected objects. This is done most simply by immersing the object in a solution of sodium sesquicarbonate. The preparation of this solution and its application are described below.

- remove any protective coating (wax, lacquer, resin) from the surface of the object before treatment;
- dissolve sodium carbonate (10 g) and sodium bicarbonate (10 g) in 1 L of water;
- allow the object to soak in the solution for two to four months;
- prepare a fresh solution and immerse the object for a further four to six months;
- remove residual chemicals by immersing the object in baths of clean water;
- dewater the object using either acetone or methylated spirits; and
- paint or spray the object with benzotriazole (3 g) dissolved in methylated spirits.

If the object originally had a bright metal surface this treatment will produce a green-brown patina. This patina is quite attractive and stable. If a clean metal surface is desired, remove the patina after treatment using the citric acid stripping process described earlier in this chapter.

This method will be effective for all cases of bronze disease but treatment times will vary greatly from object to object. The treatment times given above are sufficient for most cases. If an object subsequently shows signs of renewed bronze disease, repeat the process.

As artefacts made of essentially pure copper normally do not contain significant amounts of chloride ions, one long wash of about six months is usually sufficient to stabilise them. Brass and bronze objects, however, need at least two washes and possibly a third one if they are extensively corroded.

One potential problem associated with sesquicarbonate washing of artefacts which had been previously stripped of corrosion products in a thiourea-inhibited, citric acid solution, is that roseate blue crystals can form on the surface of the objects. These crystals can be removed by soaking the artefacts in an alkaline Rochelle salt solution (20 g sodium hydroxide and 50 g sodium potassium tartrate in 1 L of water).

If desalination is not practical, stabilise artefacts by maintaining the relative humidity below 25%. This tends to slow the corrosion rate to an acceptably low level. Other treatment options include excavation of pits and the application of corrosion-inhibiting chemicals such as silver oxide paste. Wax must then be applied to seal out moisture.

Mineralised and heavily corroded copper-based objects may need to be impregnated with wax to consolidate them. Consult a conservator if this is thought necessary.

Coating

To maintain a clean, unpatinated (shiny) surface on copper-based objects, apply a protective coating. Lacquers and waxes are used for this purpose. On the other hand, the patinas (except bronze disease) which form on bronze and copper objects are attractive and stable and do not need any form of protective coating unless they are in a harsh environment. In the latter case, consult a conservator for advice.

Microcrystalline-polyethylene wax mixtures can be used as protective coatings. A recipe that has been found to be useful is comprised of:

microcrystalline wax	100 g
polyethylene wax	25 g
white spirits	250 ml

Prepare the paste as follows:

- melt the wax components together and stir well to ensure thorough mixing; and
- quickly pour the mixture into white spirits (250 ml) and stir constantly while it cools to produce a smooth white paste.

Note that the sheen of the resultant wax film can be altered by varying either the grades or the proportions of the waxes used.

When it is dry the wax can be either polished, for a shiny finish, or left untouched for a matt finish. If subsequent bronze disease treatment is found to be necessary this wax can be removed with white spirit.

An alternative coating is an acrylic lacquer containing a corrosion inhibitor. This has proved most satisfactory in preventing retarnishing of bronze and copper. A commercially available lacquer, Incralac, can be obtained either in a spray can or as a brush-on paint. If necessary this product can be removed with acetone.

IRON AND ALLOYS

Iron is the most useful and abundant of metals and would probably be the most common metal type to be found in collections. It has been known from prehistoric times and in its various forms, such as cast iron, wrought iron and various steels, is the element upon which our present industrialised civilisation has been built.

Deterioration

Iron and steel (except some stainless steels) are readily attacked by oxygen, in the presence of moisture, to form rust. Rust is a term used to describe non-specific corrosion products which form on the surface of degraded iron. It is a mixture of ferrous and ferric hydroxides and hydrated ferric oxide. In the presence of aggressive salts such as sea water, iron chlorides are formed.

Unlike copper, the surface layers of iron corrosion products are not protective and tend to accelerate corrosion of the metal by forming localised corrosion cells.

When an object is first acquired, examine it to determine the extent of deterioration and to ascertain whether the corrosion is still active. If the surface is covered with brown droplets, active corrosion is still occurring and the presence of salt is indicated. This necessitates a specialised conservation treatment which involves the removal of chloride ions.

Preventive conservation

Although the general guidelines, outlined in the introductory section of this chapter, also apply to iron and its alloys a few additional points need to be made.

As iron is one of the most reactive of the commonly used metals, effective control of the storage environment is essential to ensure objects made from iron do not continue to deteriorate. To minimise corrosion, the preferred relative humidity for storage and display is less than 45%. Details of methods used to control relative humidity are described elsewhere (see the chapter, Preventive Conservation).

Once an object has been treated and coated, correct storage or display conditions and careful monitoring will maintain its stability.

House **large objects** such as machinery and vehicles (horse-drawn and motor), if not in controlled environments, with at least some protection from the elements. This protection may be in the form of a shed, a verandah or even a lean-to. Unless some protection is provided moisture and dust accumulation will soon initiate deterioration processes.

If an object is displayed in the open, raise and support it above ground level, monitor it regularly for signs of deterioration and treat as necessary.

Clean and re-oil metal components of **firearms** frequently and, if possible, keep them in a protective environment (see the chapter, Case Studies).

Highly polished metal surfaces, if not protected by a clear lacquer, can be coated with a light machine oil or a periodic spray of CRC or similar. As long as they are stored in a dust-free environment this is a simple and effective means of preventing deterioration.

Treatments

Many objects are covered with thick scales of rust but there is often sound metal underneath. Do not clean an object that has very little metal remaining, but instead store it in a plastic bag containing silica gel (desiccant) to keep it dry. Note the following points:

- self-indicating silica gel is blue when active, changing to pink when no longer acting as a desiccant;
- replace the desiccant when pink;
- regenerate the activity of the silica gel by heating it in an oven until the blue colour returns; and
- before storage, totally dry out the object. This may be done by placing the object in an oven at 110°C for three to four hours. By removing moisture from fissures deep within the metal the effectiveness of the silica gel is improved.

The future role of the object, either display or storage, will affect the choice of treatment method. If we wish to display an object in its working mode perhaps no treatment may be necessary other than keeping it in a dry environment or coating it with an appropriate protective layer.

As with every metal type there is a range of treatment options available, with the final decision depending on the balance between aesthetics, economics and the proposed way in which the object will be used (for example, static display or as a functioning component).

Surface cleaning

Dirt, grease and loose or flaking rust must be removed before protective coatings can be applied to iron objects. Such deposits can be removed by either chemical or mechanical techniques.

Chemical cleaning techniques include:

- using soapy solutions to dissolve grease and remove surface dirt;
- immersing the object in an aqueous alkaline solution (caustic soda) to remove grease and paint. Concentrations in the range of 20-40 g sodium hydroxide/L of water are normally used for this purpose; and
- stripping corrosion products by immersion in a solution of citric acid (50 g/L of water). Do not use hydrochloric and phosphoric acids as they attack the underlying metal.

As the effect of some *mechanical cleaning* techniques can be severe, be careful when using this option, especially with small or fragile objects. Techniques which may be applied include:

- wire brushing;
- sandblasting; and
- flame cleaning.

Wire brushing is often very effective in removing loose or flaking rust. As wire brushes are available in a range of bristle materials (steel or brass) and grades (coarse to fine), select the one appropriate for a particular object. **Never** use a brass brush on an iron object as shedding of bristles will increase the risk of galvanic corrosion.

Sandblasting, which uses a high speed jet of sand, may be applied to either small or large iron and steel objects. It is especially suited to large objects, such as agricultural machinery. This method is quick and provides an excellent surface for long-life coatings. Owing to the associated dust problem it requires approval from local authorities.

An alternative form of sandblasting, *wet sandblasting*, uses a suspension of sand in water, combined with a corrosion inhibitor. This method causes less pollution and is more acceptable to local authorities. In both cases the work should be done by commercial operators with conservators close at hand to provide advice. To prevent flash rusting, apply a protective coating immediately following sandblasting.

Flame cleaning involves the use of a blowtorch or an oxyacetylene flame to remove paint and rust quickly and effectively. Apply this technique very carefully as thin section metal is likely to distort rapidly and spring steel will lose its 'temper' and 'spring', if overheated. Wear eye protection as there is a risk of injury as rust particles fly off rapidly with this method.

All of the techniques described can be used in conjunction with each other.

A *typical cleaning scenario* involving a steel object may proceed as follows:

- use a wire brush to remove as much loose or flaking paint as possible;
- immerse the object in a caustic soda solution to remove grease, old paint and dirt. This may require immersion for some hours. Occasionally remove the object, wash it with water, scrub it and replace it in the solution;

- rinse the object under running water;
- transfer the object to a tub containing citric acid. Dissolution of rust may take several hours. Periodically remove and brush the object;
- fully immerse the object in the citric solution to prevent the development of 'tide lines' on the object. These are difficult to remove, requiring extensive polishing;
- when the rust has dissolved, place the object in a caustic soda solution for a few minutes. This neutralises excess citric acid which would otherwise cause further rusting;
- thoroughly rinse the object with water and then **immediately** rinse it with acetone or dewatering fluid to prevent further rusting. Brush these liquids onto the surface and allow the object to dry; and
- the artefact is then ready for surface coating.

While citric acid is relatively safe on most objects, do not leave cast iron, cast steel and spring steel, or combinations of these unattended for long periods in a citric acid bath as these metals will corrode. Bubbles rising to the surface of the bath indicate the surfaces of these iron materials are corroding. In the case of harder alloys, this can lead to hydrogen embrittlement and result in pitted, weakened or destroyed objects.

If in doubt regarding the type of iron or the duration of acid treatment, spend more time removing corrosion products by mechanical means. Once the worst deposits are removed, a short treatment in citric acid should clean the object with reduced risk of damage. Some rust leaves spots on the object, which cannot be removed by citric acid. These can be picked off mechanically.

Large steel objects

In many cases it is impossible to find containers or tubs large enough to immerse an object for caustic or citric treatment. In such situations the acid or alkaline stripping solution can be applied to the surface by using a bentonite paste. Higher concentrations of chemicals are needed when a paste is used.

Bentonite paste is prepared and applied in the following way:

- prepare solutions of caustic soda (80 g/L of water) and citric acid (100 g/L of water);
- sprinkle and mix enough bentonite powder into each of the prepared solutions to make a spreadable paste;
- apply the paste directly to the area to be treated;
- if the surface is not smooth, place a water-dampened tissue over the treatment area first and then apply the paste. This will minimise 'clogging' of surface indentations;
- if possible cover the poultice of paste with plastic to prevent it drying out. Repeated applications of the paste may be required; and
- remove the paste by hosing the surface with water and scrubbing with a bristle brush. Dry the object as described previously.

Composite materials

Composite objects, which are made up of different metals or metal and organic components, require specialised treatments. For instance, if an object is made up of iron and aluminium or iron and zinc, do not clean it in caustic as it will react with the aluminium and the zinc.

Likewise treatment of a composite of iron and brass in a citric acid solution will result in the copper from the brass corrosion products 'plating' out on the iron. This will accelerate the iron corrosion. Suspension of the iron only in the citric bath, or the use of bentonite paste (see above), may allow such a problem to be overcome.

Bentonite paste treatment is recommended if solder joints or related fastenings are present as these also are attacked readily by citric acid.

Consult a conservator for advice before treatment.

Plated iron

Iron may be plated with zinc (galvanised iron), tin, copper, chromium or nickel. These coatings protect the base iron sheet from corroding and also provide a bright surface finish. Corrosion usually occurs when the surface plate breaks down. This exposes the iron which, in turn, begins to rust.

To remove rust, a citric acid solution containing an inhibitor can be used. The inhibitor is included to prevent any attack on the plating metal. Before the solution described below is used, test it on an inconspicuous area of the object or on a scrap piece of the same material. Prepare and apply the solution as follows:

- dissolve citric acid (50 g) and thiourea (10 g) in one litre of water;
- periodically remove the immersed object from the solution and brush it gently with a soft bristled brush;
- when the rust has been removed rinse the object thoroughly with fresh water followed by immediate rinses with either acetone or dewatering fluid; and

- clean the plating metal with methylated spirits or, if there are rust stains present, with a mild abrasive such as pumice powder in methylated spirits.

After a final cleaning, if a bright surface finish is required, apply a proprietary metal cleaner as a once-only polish. The artefact can then be coated with a clear lacquer.

Finishing techniques

There are many methods available to give the object the 'right' colour and protective coating. The type of finish chosen will depend on the intended role of the finished object, with the final decision being a balance between aesthetic, practical and personal considerations.

The most commonly used techniques include:

- tannic acid-based rust converters;
- fish oil;
- oil quenching;
- 'blueing';
- painting;
- clear lacquers;
- microcrystalline wax;
- flame colouring; and
- natural patina.

Tannic acid-based rust converters are commercial products which can be applied to an object that has been cleaned either chemically, mechanically or which still has light rusting present on its surface. This product turns the object 'light black'. Subsequent applications further darken the object. This coating system results in the formation of stable iron tannates which passivate the metal and protect it from further corrosion. Do not use this treatment on iron objects which will be displayed outdoors unless some additional protective coating is applied.

A mixture of 80 parts white spirit to 20 parts *fish oil* can be applied to freshly cleaned iron objects with great effect. Thinning of the mixture with white spirit allows it to soak into the steel. It usually dries within minutes. Several coats can be applied and when dry the object can be painted if required. This mixture does not change the metal colour and gives effective protection.

Oil quenching is an old blacksmith's method which provides effective protection from rust. The end result is a deep blue-black object. This method works best on low carbon steel as flaking occurs in small patches on high carbon or alloy steels. Wear protective clothing and eye protection to avoid injury. Steps in this method include:

- heat the iron object to a dull red colour by either oxyacetylene torch or forge and then plunge into old, dirty engine oil (the dirtier the oil, the blacker the final colour);
- agitate the object for 30-60 seconds (depending on size), remove from the oil and then wipe with a rag; and
- repeated applications of this method will darken the object further.

'Blueing' is a method that has been applied to many types of firearms, especially their barrels, to produce a lustrous dark blue finish. Although this is usually done by commercial gunsmiths, a 'blueing' paste is available commercially (from gunsmiths) and is easily applied. Take care when handling 'blued' objects as acids from skin contact etch these surfaces.

There are numerous *paints* available, both enamel and water-based, that protect and beautify metal surfaces. A range of primers, undercoats and topcoats may be used. If applied correctly to properly prepared and cleaned surfaces adequate protection should be maintained for many years. For iron objects displayed outdoors, particularly in aggressive marine environments, use an inorganic zinc primer, a high build epoxy top coat and a final clear polyurethane coating, with a UV-absorbing reagent in the paint, to provide protection.

Clear lacquers are available in spray cans or can be applied by brush. Obtain the desired surface finish and colour before applying the lacquer according to the instructions on the product. Provided the entire object is coated this finish gives a lasting protection against oxide build-up. If air or moisture penetrate beneath this layer, lifting will occur and oxidation will recommence.

Microcrystalline wax provides both thorough protection and an attractive finish to iron objects. Its preparation and application are described below:

- mix the wax with white spirit until it forms a smooth paste;
- apply using a soft rag; and
- allow to harden and then gently buff to the desired finish.

Microcrystalline waxes are available commercially for a range of metals and timbers, each formulated for a particular use. Use white spirit to remove the wax at any time.

Flame colouring involves alteration of the colour of iron and steel by applying direct heat from a forge or an oxyacetylene flame. After cleaning and derusting, apply a gentle flame to the object. The colour will change from light straw through to deep blue. When the object has attained the desired colour, plunge it into water. Note that this method can change the molecular structure of the steel depending on the grade and its carbon content. As the temper or spring will be lost if flame coloured, do **not** use this method on spring steel.

If an iron object is in a stable condition, with only a lightly rusted surface, it may be that this *natural patina* is the type of finish you require to demonstrate the history and past use of the object. Such finishes can be maintained if the storage and display conditions are controlled to prevent further deterioration.

LEAD AND PEWTER

Lead is a soft grey metal used mainly in combination with tin to form pewter. Due to toxicity problems associated with the use of pewter food vessels the lead in pewter was replaced in the 18th century with antimony and some copper. Usually modern 'leadless pewters' are alloyed tin such as Britannia metal.

Deterioration

Lead and pewter are prone to attack from acetic acid and other organic acid vapours given off by poor quality papers, some fabrics and various woods.

The main corrosion product formed on lead and pewter is white-grey, basic lead carbonate. This provides a deep, protective patina to the metal surface which should not be removed.

If pewter and lead have been in a low oxygen environment and exposed to sulfide compounds, a rich lustrous grey-black patina of metal sulfides forms on the surface. These minerals are stable and should not be removed.

Both pewter and lead are very soft and susceptible to denting and scratching.

Preventive conservation

As lead and pewter objects are particularly susceptible to attack by acids emanating from certain woods, storage or display in enamelled metal cupboards is very important.

Adhere to the general guidelines described in the introduction to this chapter.

Treatments

Cleaning

Do not remove the stable patinas that form on lead and its alloys, the white-grey lead carbonate and the dark lead sulfide, as they form a protective layer that prevents further corrosion. Other corrosion products may require treatment.

Carry out general cleaning in the following way:

- wash with warm water and a pure soap;
- rinse the object with fresh water;
- wipe with methylated spirits;
- polish with a soft cloth; and
- apply a protective surface coating of microcrystalline wax if necessary.

As it is difficult to obtain very mild abrasives, their use is not generally recommended on soft metals. However if the white bloom on the surface of these metals (lead or tin acetate) is thin, and one micron grade alumina powder is available, use a slurry polish of this alumina in water to remove the deposit from the surface.

If the white acetate layer is pustular or thick it is best removed by either electrochemical or chemical reduction. These specialised techniques require the skills of a conservator.

Thin layers of corrosion products can be removed by soaking the objects in a solution of disodium ethylenediamine tetraacetic acid (50 g/L of water). Avoid prolonged soaking as the dissolved oxygen will accelerate corrosion.

TIN

Tin is a soft white metal found in essentially pure form in some objects such as plates, but more often as an alloy with lead, in the form of pewter.

In the 19th and 20th centuries tin was combined with a number of other elements to produce a range of alloys used principally for utensils and ornamental ware. An example of Britannia metal is 93% tin, 5% antimony, 2% copper.

Britannia metal was developed in England during the mid-1700s in response to the threat to the pewter utensil industry from cheap porcelain. Old pewter was dull and because of its lead content, undesirable as a food container. Although the new alloy was brighter and stronger it eventually lost favour as a metal for the production of household utensils.

Deterioration

Although it is normally quite stable, tin reacts slowly with the atmosphere to form grey stannous oxide and finally stable white stannic oxide.

Many objects made of tin or its alloys are found covered with a dull grey coating of corrosion products.

These form a protective patina. Unless very pronounced or unsightly, retain this patina where possible.

Preventive conservation

Observe the general guidelines mentioned at the beginning of this chapter.

Treatments

Cleaning

Although tin objects are quite strong, careless handling will still damage their surfaces.

If an object has to be cleaned, try the following regime:

- use a pure soap in warm water to remove dirt and grime;
- rinse with fresh water;
- wipe with methylated spirits; and
- polish with a soft cloth.

For badly deteriorated objects, seek the advice of a conservator.

ALUMINIUM

Most aluminium objects found in museum collections will be alloys containing copper as a minor component. The addition of only 3% (by weight) of copper trebles the mechanical strength of the parent metal.

As aluminium corrodes, the oxide layer that forms protects the surface against further corrosion. Under normal environmental conditions the metal does not corrode to any great extent.

Deterioration

If allowed to come into contact with metals such as copper and iron, or in the presence of chloride ions (such as found in sea water), aluminium and its alloys corrode appreciably.

Do not allow aluminium to come into contact with mercury as mercury prevents formation of the protective oxide patina, promoting rapid corrosion of the aluminium.

Preventive conservation

Apply the guidelines described in the general introduction to this chapter to aluminium and its alloys.

Treatments

Cleaning

To remove dirt, clean aluminium with methylated spirits or a soft brush. Do not use any abrasives on aluminium as these may remove the protective oxide layer.

Never use caustic soda to remove grease or paint from aluminium objects as it reacts vigorously with aluminium. Remove heavy deposits of oil, grease and petroleum products, commonly encountered on vintage car parts, with kerosene or similar products.

If the metal is heavily stained or corroded, apply a solution of phosphoric acid (1%). This will produce a mild uniform etch on the metal surface which, after thorough washing and drying, should be left for a day to enable the film to reform through contact with the air.

Coatings

After cleaning, aluminium surfaces may be coated with a protective clear lacquer. Usually this form of protection is not needed unless the aluminium is likely to be affected by salt such as found at a seaside location.

GOLD

Gold has been used from the earliest times. It is yellow, lustrous and the most malleable and ductile of the metals. As a rare metal, it has been used for jewellery and coinage.

Gold is often applied as a decorative surface coating in the form of gold leaf for manuscript illumination, as a top layer on prepared gesso and as gold amalgam for gilding copper and silver. It is also alloyed with copper and silver to improve its mechanical properties.

Treatment

As gold is resistant to corrosion it will usually only require polishing with a soft cloth.

No coating is required on pure gold but if it is alloyed with copper or silver, a clear acrylic or nitrocellulose lacquer will provide protection against tarnishing.

SUMMARY

- Identify the type of metal before attempting any cleaning.
- Only remove a patina after ascertaining that it is not as originally intended.
- Wear gloves when handling highly polished artefacts.
- Keep relative humidity low (45%) to reduce corrosion and tarnishing.
- Observe maximum light levels of 300 lux for composite objects.

- Where possible, store in enamelled, metal cupboards or acid-free boxes.
- Do not carry out any treatment if unsure. Contact a conservator for advice.
- Contact a conservator for advice regarding the treatment of composite objects.

BIBLIOGRAPHY

Canadian Conservation Institute, 1988, The cleaning, polishing and protective waxing of brass and copper objects, *CCI Notes 9/3*, Ottawa, Canada.

Department of Materials Conservation, Western Australian Museum, 1981, Metals, in *Conservation and Restoration for Small Museums*, 2nd Edition, Western Australian Museum, Perth, pp. 35-48.

Drayman-Weisser, T., 1992, Metal objects, in *Caring for Your Collections*, National Committee to Save America's Cultural Collections, Arthur W. Schultz (Chairman), Harry N. Abrams Inc., New York, pp. 108-121.

Untracht, O., 1975, *Metal Techniques for Craftsmen*, Doubleday, Garden City, New York.

MODERN ORGANIC MATERIALS

INTRODUCTION

Plastics and rubbers have played important roles in human endeavours since the beginning of the 20th century. This prominence suggests that objects composed of these types of materials will make up an increasing proportion of museum and private collections in the future.

Plastics and rubbers belong to a group of substances known as polymers. Polymers may be described as chemical compounds made up of smaller units (monomers), linked together to form a larger structure.

Some polymers tend to form links which result in long chains with very little cross-linkage between the individual chains. These substances, known as **thermoplastic resins**, do not undergo any change during moulding other than a change of shape. They will soften if the temperature is raised, form a rigid solid when the temperature is lowered and tend to be soluble in organic solvents.

Other polymers form cross-links between long chains, an arrangement which usually leads to the production of a much harder and less soluble polymer than the purely chain-like equivalent. These polymer types, known as **thermosetting resins**, undergo a chemical change (curing), due either to the effect of heat or a catalyst, which makes them infusible. They do not soften again, even if exposed to heat and tend to be insoluble in organic solvents.

The chemical nature of the polymer itself and the presence of additives such as plasticisers, fillers, stabilisers and colorants all affect the properties of the polymer in question.

The first polymers developed were those that involved the chemical modification of natural polymers. Cellulose nitrate was first prepared in 1833 and rubber was vulcanised in 1839. In this latter process sulfur atoms were used to form cross-links between the natural rubber chains, allowing a new moulding material to be produced.

Other important milestones included the preparation of a type of thermosetting plastic used in the production of 'union' cases in 1853 (see the chapter, Photographs), the production of mouldable cellulose nitrate in the 1860s, its subsequent plasticising with camphor in the mid-1860s, the preparation of cellulose acetate in the 1890s and that of casein plastic in 1900.

The first fully synthetic polymer was produced by reacting formaldehyde with phenol. This polymer, developed by J.L. Baekeland in 1909, produced a substance which was dark in colour, hard and brittle ('Bakelite'). This material dominated the domestic market until the 1950s, and was used for items as diverse as toasters, clocks, radios, ash-trays, toilet seats, electrical fittings, car components and even coffins.

The subsequent development of urea-formaldehyde and combined urea and thiourea-formaldehyde resins provided an unlimited colour range to complement the rather dark, sombre tones of the phenol-formaldehyde range.

In the 1930s the 'poly' age began. Thermoplastic resins began to make an impact with the development of polyvinyl chloride (PVC) and polystyrene. Polymethyl methacrylate ('Perspex') was first produced commercially in 1933. Its shatter-resistant properties were soon in demand. The development of polyethylene ('polythene') soon followed in the 1940s.

The commercial development of polyesters, silicones, polyamides such as nylon 6,6 and polyurethanes all occurred about this time.

Although the speed and number of developments in the history of polymers preclude any further discussion here, texts are available which document these developments (Kaufman 1963, Kroschwitz 1987).

Since these times there has been a tremendous amount of research and development into the manufacture of plastics. The next generation of plastics is being produced by combining resins, both together and with fillers, and reinforcing agents. Advances in electronic and automotive engineering depend heavily on plastics. This, combined with the increasing use of plastics in household appliances, sporting goods, electronic devices and a myriad of other areas will ensure that these objects will be collected, forming the basis of historical and technological collections.

Identification

A few simple tests have been described which may allow the more common plastics to be identified (Braun 1982). Generally, the identification of plastics is not easy.

In some cases it may be possible to use visual clues such as design, colour and trademarks to identify polymers in a collection. Function, touch, smell (particularly if in a state of degradation), date of manufacture and even flotation tests may allow a tentative identification to be made.

Where a doubt exists as to the identity of a plastic it may be necessary to use analytical techniques such as infra-red (IR) spectroscopy to allow a conclusive identification to be made. IR spectroscopy will be able to identify at least the major organic component (the polymer) of a plastic. Often it is not possible to determine a polymer's complete formulation due to the complex assortment of plasticisers, stabilisers, dyes, pigments and fillers which make up these substances.

DETERIORATION

As plastics not only form part of collections, but are often used to store and conserve artefacts, it is important to be aware of the agents that contribute to the deterioration of these materials. Deterioration of plastics may be due to chemical, physical or biological activity.

As with most organic materials, polymeric objects will be affected by such elements as temperature, moisture, oxygen, light and pollutants.

Heat and light can provide sufficient energy to break weak bonds in a polymer chain. Generally, the higher the temperature, the faster the rate of degradation.

In addition, oxidation reactions are enhanced by the presence of heat, light and metal ions. Light, and UV radiation in particular, may also cause colour changes via either alteration of the polymer itself or of the pigments and dyes present in the matrix.

Certain atmospheric **pollutants**, such as oxides of nitrogen and sulfur, are acidic and under conditions of high relative humidity may cause considerable damage to plastics. Ozone is particularly damaging to rubber.

Physical stress and the use of **solvents** can also have an effect on the rates of change. Areas of physical stress are more prone to chemical attack and bond-breaking. Solvents may not only dissolve a plastic but may also leach out plasticisers or cause the plastic to swell, thereby making the object more susceptible to chemical attack. These latter effects of solvent damage are often not immediately visible, with changes only becoming evident over a prolonged period.

Biological attack may occur, but this mode of deterioration is usually confined to those semi-synthetic polymers derived from natural sources such as cellulose and casein. This type of attack is favoured by conditions of high relative humidity.

Physical ageing is a less well known phenomenon in which polymeric materials (thermoplastics) continue to alter for long periods after their manufacture. Physical ageing is due to changes in the arrangement of the polymer chains with respect to one another. These changes are reflected in changes in properties such as brittleness, stiffness, solubility and optical characteristics. The effects of physical ageing would be reversible were it not for the complications introduced by associated chemical degradation.

It is rare for only one mechanism of degradation to operate on a polymeric material.

Usually changes in the chemical make-up of polymeric materials are reflected in corresponding changes in properties and appearance. For instance, evaporation or migration of plasticisers from a plastic will produce a material with reduced flexibility and increased brittleness.

Chemical attack on the polymer chain or on the cross-links between chains is likely to produce a weaker material with an altered resilience and changed stress relaxation. On the other hand, chemical changes which introduce cross-links into a plastic will produce a material with a reduced ability to stretch, a reduced tear resistance and with an increased chance of suffering fatigue cracking. These sort of changes may be brought about by heat and oxidising conditions.

It is difficult to predict the precise behaviour of a particular object to a set of conditions. The formulations of many of the early polymers varied considerably, even for materials which were meant to be the same. The use of impure materials in manufacturing processes also contributed to the variation in properties of these early polymers. Thus with age, rubber may become hard, brittle and cracked or it may soften, becoming sticky and even liquid. Plastics may shrink as they age and the surfaces of rubbers and plastics may craze or become chalky.

It is likely that recently produced polymers will have a greater resistance to deterioration due to the use of improved stabilisers and purer starting materials.

PREVENTIVE CONSERVATION

Environment

Conditions which slow the rate of deterioration of plastics include:

- low temperatures;
- relative humidity levels of less than 50 per cent;
- low oxygen levels; and
- low light levels.

Storing plastics and rubbers at low temperatures and low relative humidity (less than 50%) will retard the rate of chemical deterioration. The use of frost-free deep freezers or cold rooms have been recommended in the past, but caution is still needed as some plastics may undergo stress cracking at low temperatures.

Self-indicating silica gel may be used to maintain a dry environment. As for all artefacts, it is wise to maintain stable conditions to minimise problems associated with adjustment to a different environment.

Oxygen exclusion also will enhance the longevity of plastic and rubber artefacts. Achieve this by using an inert storage atmosphere (nitrogen or argon) or a chemical oxygen scavenger such as 'Ageless'. There are obvious practical difficulties associated with building and maintaining a large, oxygen-free storage area. It would appear to be more practical to seal sensitive artefacts with Ageless in transparent, oxygen-impermeable envelopes.

Transparency is an important feature of storage media as it allows objects to be monitored without having to open them. To absorb degradation and other potentially damaging products in sealed containers, incorporate materials such as activated carbon, potassium permanganate pellets and buffered tissue paper in storage envelopes.

To minimise photochemical degradation, maintain light levels at 50 lux with a maximum UV exposure of 75 μwatts/lumen.

Storage and display

Regardless of the storage medium it is essential to monitor the condition of plastic artefacts closely, especially when they are stored in closed environments. In these situations, if degradation continues, deterioration may be accelerated by the build-up of a harmful microenvironment in the closed system. The deterioration of cellulose acetate, for example, is usually accompanied by the release of acetic acid vapours. These would build up in a closed system and increase the rate of degradation of an already degrading object.

Isolate deteriorating plastics from other materials to prevent damage to unaffected objects. Do not store deteriorating objects in a closed environment; instead, store them in open metal cupboards, protected from dust and light by muslin (or similar) curtains. This arrangement will permit maximum ventilation. Use buffered acid-free paper to scavenge free acids and acid-free card to line the metal shelving.

Make replicas of particularly valuable objects and use these for display. Store the originals under the best conditions possible (cold, dark and with both low relative humidity and oxygen levels).

Fully support flexible objects, such as rubber-based materials, at all times. As rubber degrades and plasticisers are lost from plastic objects, artefacts made from these materials may harden over time. Support these objects in their correct shape using polyethylene foam or tightly crumpled acid-free tissue paper.

Do not allow objects which contain a high proportion of plasticisers, such as those made from cellulose acetates and polyvinyl chloride, to come into contact with each other or with other plastics. This will avoid the possibility of migration of plasticiser from one object to another, a process which could lead to either the softening of objects or of their 'welding' together.

Special mention needs to be made of objects composed of **cellulose nitrate**. As these types of objects degrade there is an increased risk of fire. In addition, the release of acidic or oxidising gases by degrading cellulose nitrate objects increases the risk of damage occurring to metal and other objects that may be stored in close proximity.

Ideally cellulose nitrate objects should be isolated from other objects in any collection, preferably in a fire-proof, but well ventilated area. Do not circulate vented air to other areas of the collection. Obviously isolation from heat and ignition sources is also essential.

Careful monitoring is critical in these cases. Stages of degradation include progressive yellowing, the formation of bubbles or foam, embrittlement and shrinkage. Store these artefacts at 10°C and at a relative humidity of between 40 and 50%.

TREATMENTS

Approach the treatment of plastic materials with utmost caution. Before undertaking any treatment, determine the type of plastic in the object. Because of the sensitive nature of many plastics and the difficulty involved in identifying them, contact a conservation professional for advice.

Cleaning

Reasons for cleaning plastic objects include the removal of surface degradation products and the improvement of unsightly appearances. Few reports have been made about cleaning and stabilising degraded plastic and rubber because of their delicate nature, susceptibility to further damage and relative impermeability.

Most plastics may be safely washed with warm water containing a few drops of a non-ionic detergent (for example, Lissapol, Teric N9, Arkopal N090) and a soft cloth or brush. Dry washed objects immediately with either a soft cloth or tissue to avoid the possibility of swelling.

It is not recomended to use water on:

- vulcanite (hard rubber) that is beginning to degrade;
- surface-dyed casein;
- degrading cellulose nitrate or cellulose acetate where the surface is cracked or crazed; and
- objects which contain metal components which may corrode.

(Morgan 1992)

Stabilising deteriorating objects

There have only been a few descriptions of attempts to stabilise deteriorating polymeric objects.

Despite the reservations expressed above (Morgan 1992) deteriorating cellulose nitrate beads were washed in water to remove acid and then soaked in very dilute sodium carbonate solution to neutralise any remaining acid and to buffer any future acid formation. This approach was successful in stabilising these objects. It would be unlikely to be effective in the treatment of large objects due to the lack of porosity of cellulose nitrate (Green and Bradley, 1988).

The consolidation and repair of a pair of severely degraded rubber bathing shoes has also been described (Maltby 1988). The shoes had areas of differing degradation, soft and slightly tacky in some areas, hard and brittle in other areas and supple and undegraded elsewhere. Specialised techniques were used to reshape the shoes, fill lost areas and strengthen fragile areas. A fitted padded support, made from ethafoam, was constructed and a specially designed display mount was prepared. As the shoes were extremely fragile and could not be strapped in place, a tin plate insole was inserted in each shoe and magnets fixed under the acid-free mount. Removal of the magnets allowed the shoes to be 'freed'. To enhance the longevity of the shoes they were stored in a nitrogen atmosphere.

Repairs and inpainting

Before embarking on the repair or treatment of plastics there is a number of factors that must be considered. These include the basic nature of the plastic, the plastic's state of deterioration, the solvent and plastic interaction, the flexibility of adhesives used to join different materials and the relative flexibility of any conservation materials compared with that of the substrate.

To repair or even inpaint a plastic object effectively, it is necessary for a bond to form between the applied adhesive or inpainting medium and the substrate. If this is not the case then there will be no effect. The adhesive will not hold and the paint will fall off. Implicit in this process is the use of a solvent which will not affect the plastic in some way.

Water-based systems appear to be the most appropriate to use, but extensive studies are still needed in order to understand their full impact. Contact a conservator for detailed advice. For more information concerning these aspects of plastics' conservation, consult a paper written by Sharon Blank (1988).

SUMMARY

- Store plastic and rubber materials at low temperatures and maintain relative humidity levels below 50%.
- Maintain low oxygen environments and low light levels to enhance stability of plastics.
- Monitor the condition of plastics carefully to prevent damage to nearby artefacts.
- Support flexible objects in their desired shapes.

BIBLIOGRAPHY

Blank, S., 1988, Practical answers to plastic problems, in *Modern Organic Materials*, Preprints of the Meeting, Edinburgh, 1988, Scottish Society for Conservation & Restoration, Edinburgh, pp. 115-122.

Braun, M.D., 1982, *Simple Methods for the Identification of Plastics*, Carl Hanser Verlag, Munich/Vienna.

Green, L. and Bradley, S., 1988, An investigation into the deterioration and stabilisation of nitrocellulose in museum collections, in *Modern Organic Materials*, Preprints of the Meeting, Edinburgh, 1988, Scottish Society for Conservation & Restoration, Edinburgh, pp. 81-96.

Kaufman, M., 1963, *The First Century of Plastics - Celluloid and its Sequel*, Plastics and Rubber Institute, London.

Kroschwitz, J.I., (Ed.), 1987, The history of polymer science, in *Encyclopedia of Polymer Science and Engineering*, vol. 7, Wiley-Interscience, New York.

Maltby, S.L., 1988, Rubber: the problem that becomes a solution, in *Modern Organic Materials*, Preprints of the Meeting, Edinburgh, 1988, Scottish Society for the Conservation & Restoration, Edinburgh, pp. 151-157.

Morgan, J., 1992, The cleaning and care of plastic artifacts, *Polymer Preprints*, vol. 33, pp. 643-644.

ETHNOGRAPHIC MATERIAL

INTRODUCTION

The care of ethnographic objects, probably more than any other type of collective material, presents a tremendous challenge to conservators and collectors alike. This is because they can be constructed from almost any type or mixture of materials.

It is worth listing some of these materials to highlight the extra care needed in handling, documenting and treating these artefacts. They include textiles, metals, plant material, stone, ceramics, skins, leather, furs, glass, feathers, shells, ochres, pigments and ivory, coupled with dyes, resins, oils, paints, blood and so on. Each of the above material types can be further subdivided to give an even more imposing list of possible components which make up the class of collectables known as ethnographic objects; plant material, for instance, can include wood, gourds, bark, paper, linen, cloth, reeds, leaves and vines.

Documenting, handling, storing and treating these objects requires the highest degree of sensitivity and skill.

Note that some traditional societies have introduced modern materials into their objects. A background knowledge of the recent history of an artefact is pertinent. It is also very important that the social and cultural backgrounds associated with objects are understood so that no offence is caused, for example, by having a particular object on display.

In order to preserve ethnographic material it is essential to identify both the material components and the agents of deterioration.

DETERIORATION AND HANDLING

Deterioration

Because of their complex nature many ethnographic objects are extremely susceptible to damage from the usual agents of decay (relative humidity, light, temperature, pollutants, dust and insects).

Materials such as wood, leather, furs, paper and animal sinew react at different rates to changes in relative humidity. Stresses will develop in composite objects if they are exposed to rapid changes in relative humidity. Painted or pigmented material, for example, may become detached or powdery due to changes in either relative humidity or extremes of temperature.

Potential damage to the patina of metals, to low-fired clays, problems of salt incorporation in objects recovered from buried or wet sites and the effects of high temperatures on resins and waxes all complicate the already difficult situation of caring for these material types.

Objects that are moved from one climatic zone to another need special attention. Cellulose-based material moved from the tropics, for example, should be slowly acclimatised to its new environment if drying stresses are to be avoided. Packing, handling and acclimatisation of sensitive materials are described earlier (see the chapter, Preventive Conservation).

Documentation and handling

Always wear cotton or rubber gloves when handling ethnographic objects. As ethnographic objects often have been treated with toxic chemicals, this will protect both the artefact and the handler.

Thoroughly examine the object and make notes on its condition, history (if known), the materials from which it is composed and the presence of any previous repairs or alterations. Record all components even if positive identification of the material type is not possible (for example, a specific resin type).

Photographs and sketches are extremely important components of the overall documentation.

As these objects are often susceptible to insect infestation and fungal attack it is wise to have an inspection area away from any other objects that may be affected by cross-contamination.

Note that as some materials may be poisonous by intent, arrow tips or material in gourds for example, take great care during the examination process.

As the range of ethnographic materials is too diverse to cover in this book, the following section on bark paintings has been included to illustrate a general approach to the care of ethnographic material. A recent publication by Coote (1998) discusses protection, preservation and preventive measures that can be adopted for Aboriginal and Torres Strait Islander keeping places and cultural centres.

Aboriginal bark painting. Ochre paint flaking due to bark curling.

This parang shows a range of materials that can be found within one object.

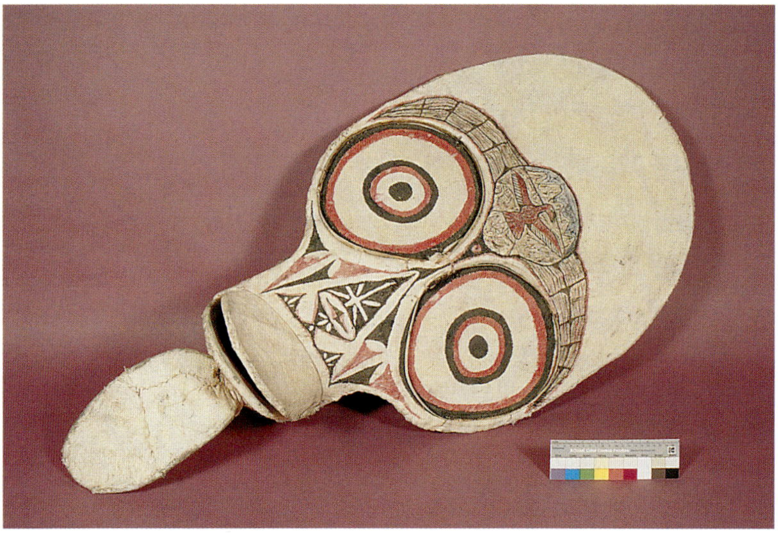

Decorated bark from New Britain.
Cloth mask needs a support made before going into storage.

BARK PAINTINGS

Introduction

Bark paintings produced by Australian Aborigines are usually made from sections of the outer bark cut from eucalyptus trees. The bark is heated and weighted to obtain a flat surface, scraped and then sometimes treated with natural resins before painting takes place.

Traditionally natural ochres, clays, minerals and charcoal were used for pigments. These were sometimes mixed with natural binders such as plant gums or blood. More recently PVA emulsion has been used to bind pigments. For the past 20 years, commercial acrylic paints also have been used.

Deterioration

Most conservation problems associated with bark paintings are associated with relative humidity. High relative humidity levels encourage mould and fungal attack on binders and can cause bark fibres to relax and return to their original curved form. Some of the traditional pigments, clays in particular, are able to absorb moisture from the air. This may eventually cause them to break up (for example, flaking, blistering, cracking).

In addition, fluctuations in relative humidity cause bark to expand and contract, usually across the grain. Pigments, because of their different composition, generally react to fluctuations in relative humidity to a lesser degree than, or differently from, the bark. This causes tension at the pigment-bark interface which, if left unchecked, will separate the two.

Initially, pigmented areas crack, then 'tent' and finally spall off. White pigment, perhaps due to its relatively coarser grain, appears to be more sensitive than other colours. Problems with changes in relative humidity are common due to the fact that many bark paintings may be produced in a humid area for example, but end up in a drier area. Low humidity can cause shrinking in bark fibres and splitting and flaking of paint.

Physical damage also may be caused by insect attack of the bark itself.

Preventive conservation

Store and display bark paintings at relative humidity levels of 45-60 per cent. A stable environment is most important as twisting and warping may occur otherwise. Maintain temperatures in the range 15-25°C.

Store bark paintings flat and covered with acid-free tissue or in archival quality cardboard boxes to prevent dust accumulation. Support any curved areas with dacron or polystyrene beads in washed cotton or linen. Keep the storage area clean.

Control light levels to a maximum illuminance of 50 lux, so that dyes and natural pigments do not fade.

As bark paintings respond to changes in their environment they will be damaged if they are attached to rigid supports which restrict these responses. It is important to allow the painting some flexibility. Recently, fibreglass backings have been applied to the paintings, with foam inserts which permit movement. Unfortunately, the fibreglass backing technique is time consuming, involves the use of toxic chemicals and is very expensive. More practical methods using aluminium strips and polyethylene foam have been developed (Coote 1995). As the backing procedure is highly specialised, consult a qualified conservator for advice.

Inspect paintings regularly to guard against insect attack.

Treatments

Cleaning

Cleaning bark paintings which contain traditional pigments may be difficult because these pigments often become powdery as they age.

If consolidation of the pigments is needed, and dust is found on the painting, remove the dust to prevent staining of the pigment during consolidation. Use a very soft brush, preferably sable, with a very light action. Due to the sensitivity required, ask a conservator to carry out this work.

Although it is possible to clean acrylic painted areas in good condition with cotton swabs that have been slightly moistened with water, avoid using water and organic solvents to clean bark paintings. If moistened cotton swabs are used, do not contact the bark and dry cleaned areas immediately. Use dry cotton swabs or something similar for this latter task.

Consolidation

Traditional pigments used in bark paintings often require consolidation. The main risk associated with consolidation is staining or darkening of the pigments by the consolidant. As results vary from painting to painting, test a range of possible consolidants before full-scale treatment begins. Consolidation is a specialist task, requiring the skills of a conservator.

Although cellulose-based consolidants have less cohesive and adhesive strength than their synthetic counterparts, their use is generally recommended. Synthetic resins are not in keeping with the natural materials used in bark paintings and may produce a surface which is both glossy and prone to yellowing.

Carboxymethyl cellulose (CMC, five grams in 100 millilitres of water) is a widely used consolidant that usually produces minimal staining of pigments. As CMC may affect any water-soluble pigments present in a painting, test it before application.

If flakes are lifting, introduce consolidant beneath flakes, with the flakes then gently laid down with the aid of silicon-release paper and weights.

Powdery areas may require application of the consolidant over the pigment surface. Do this by wetting out the pigment with ethanol (after testing for staining) and then manually applying the consolidant. The ethanol helps to draw the consolidant into the pigment and in some cases helps to reduce staining.

Occasionally, consolidants are sprayed over the bark surface. Although time-efficient, this procedure may not provide the thoroughness or penetration of consolidant, which can be achieved by working manually.

Other adhesives, which can be used include ethulose, potato starch, Klucel G and Klucel EF. Although the Klucel products (cellulose ethers) do not give a particularly strong bond, they have the advantage of being soluble in ethanol. Klucel EF is especially useful as it has a lower molecular weight than Klucel G and a more concentrated solution can be achieved without the viscosity which makes application difficult.

Note that cellulose-based consolidants are prone to mould attack. Display and store paintings treated with these materials in a stable environment with a relative humidity in the range of 45-60%.

Insect attack

Consult a conservation specialist if insect attack is a problem.

Oxygen deprivation is the most appropriate technique for insect control in bark paintings. Details of this technique are provided elsewhere (see the chapter, Mould and Insect Attack in Collections). This approach is the least likely to damage the pigments.

Chemical fumigants and freezing techniques are not recommended as both will have deleterious effects on pigments in bark paintings.

SUMMARY

- Identify all materials within the object.
- Obtain as much background detail or history before starting any treatments.
- Handle only with cotton or rubber gloves.
- Maintain temperatures and relative humidities in the ranges 15-25°C and 45-60% respectively.
- Avoid direct sunlight and control display lighting.
- Consult a conservator before treating ethnographic materials for insect attack.

BIBLIOGRAPHY

Coote, K., 1995, Mounting Aboriginal bark paintings, *SSCR Journal*, vol. 6, pp. 7-9.

Coote, K. (Ed.), 1998, *Care of Collections. Conservation for Aboriginal and Torres Strait Islander Keeping Places and Cultural Centres*, Australian Museum, Sydney.

WET MATERIALS

INTRODUCTION

Materials isolated from marine, freshwater or wet terrestrial sites pose quite different conservation problems from those of dry materials. Both the extent and the type of deterioration that occur in wet environments differ from those that take place under dry conditions.

Factors which will affect the extent of deterioration in a wet environment include the following:

- temperature;
- degree of oxygenation;
- presence of bacteria, fungi and other organisms;
- light;
- acidity or alkalinity of the burial environment;
- period of immersion or burial;
- nature of the material surroundings (for example, sacrificial metals, toxic metals);
- extent of burial/exposure cycles; and
- development of encrusting concretions.

In general warm, moist conditions increase degradation whereas cool, dry conditions will be less damaging. Damp surroundings encourage breakdown of materials through chemical and biological processes.

Water is essential for many chemical reactions, the corrosion of iron and the hydrolytic degradation of the cellulose fibres of wood and textiles being examples of two such reactions. Moisture also encourages attack on materials by fungi and bacteria.

The type of aqueous environment from which an object was recovered will give an indication of the type and degree of degradation to which the material has been subjected. Preservation chances improve under conditions of low temperature and low levels of dissolved oxygen and light.

Wood buried in low oxygen surroundings, for instance, has been known to survive in marine environments for thousands of years. On the other hand, timbers exposed on the seabed will be broken down rapidly by marine borers, microorganisms, chemical attack and the abrasive action of waterborne particles.

For objects found in wet land sites additional factors, such as soil acidity and the chemical characteristics of the ground water, influence the state of degradation.

Some objects are fortunate enough to have been afforded protection from their surroundings by being buried, encapsulated in concretion or by being under the protective influence of a neighbouring object. The process of removing an object from these surroundings upsets this relatively stable state. Unless appropriate steps are taken, accelerated degradation will result.

Although the emphasis in this section will be on materials recovered from marine sites, the same principles can be applied to objects recovered from freshwater and wet terrestrial sites. Differences may be expected to be seen in materials from these different environments with respect to both the nature and extent of degradation and obviously the degree of salt incorporation.

In this chapter discussion will be centre on organic materials and metals, wet ceramics and wet glass having been discussed in separate chapters dealing with those particular material types. Materials that contain at least an organic component include wood, leather, bone, ivory, horn, textiles and any materials made from natural fibres (such as rope and matting). Organic materials may be found as discrete objects or in conjunction with other materials, such as metals or ceramics, as part of a composite object.

Identification

It is essential to identify the materials from which an artefact is made. This information, combined with knowledge of the environmental conditions to which it has been subjected, will assist in determining an artefact's likely condition before handling and treatment. Once identified, specific recommendations can be made regarding storage and treatment procedures.

Often the type of object is a reliable initial indicator of the likely material of manufacture as are the types of corrosion products found on metallic objects.

The colours of corrosion products are often useful, providing information about both the material type and the burial conditions to which the object has been subjected. In aerobic conditions, for example, iron corrodes to produce characteristic orange-brown rust colours whereas copper corrosion under similar conditions produces distinctive blue-green corrosion products. If the site is anaerobic, however, black metal sulfide corrosion products predominate.

Experience in dealing with these types of materials is useful as even the general appearance, the effects of exposure of the object to light and the odour derived from metal breakdown may provide a guide to the metal type. Note that a magnet can be used to detect the presence of residual iron or magnetite.

On-site storage considerations

Following excavation, an artefact is exposed to a set of conditions quite different from those of its former environment. It will be vulnerable to both physical damage and chemical changes. For example, a corroded iron object recovered from a reducing, anaerobic environment usually will exhibit black or grey corrosion products. Exposure to aerobic conditions results in a transformation to orange rust. With time, expansive oxidation processes will cause destruction.

It is important to provide stabilising conditions as soon as possible following excavation and to be prompt when recording information about recovered objects. If documentation is prolonged then keep artefacts wet with a fine water spray.

The extent of material alteration of recovered artefacts is not always immediately apparent. Handle objects with great care to minimise further damage. Label all artefacts and storage containers.

As there are too many possible scenarios, only basic guidelines can be given.

Metals

The guidelines listed below afford recovered metal objects some protection:

- if in doubt about the metal composition store the metal wet (freshwater is preferable to salt water);
- only store like metals in the same container;
- retain adherent concretions;
- if possible, remove the majority of marine organisms and plants;
- use common sense if putting more than one object in a container (smaller, lighter objects on top); and
- do not store metals in the same container as organic materials unless they are part of an inseparable, composite object.

Further details are provided for individual metal types later in this chapter.

Organic materials

Adhere to the following guidelines for organic materials:

- keep the object wet;
- support large or fragile objects;
- wrap fibrous objects;
- retain concretions;
- do not store objects that are contaminated with iron corrosion products in the same container as uncontaminated objects;
- do not expose objects to direct sunlight;
- store objects at low temperatures (4-5 °C) and in the dark where possible;
- change the water if biological growth is observed;
- use fungicides in solutions if storage is prolonged and biological growth is a problem. Do **not** add any fungicides to a storage solution if the object is to be used for subsequent analyses such as radiocarbon dating; and
- begin treatment as soon as possible after recovery.

Upon recovery, do not allow organic materials to dry out. In most cases irreversible damage will be done if this occurs. Wood, for example, is prone to shrinking, cracking and warping upon drying. Many objects recovered from buried wet sites appear black and it is sometimes difficult to identify the material of which the object is composed. **If unsure of the nature of the object, then keep it wet.**

When lifting large objects, such as wood, or fragile materials, such as leather and rope, ensure they are:

- supported on planks, netting or similar materials. Place cushioning between large objects and the support;
- lifted by gripping the supports, not the object; and
- protected against accidental damage by cushioning any fastenings or protuberances.

To prevent fibre loss and water movement damage when storing fibrous materials (such as rope and textiles), ensure:

- they are wrapped in materials such as tulle which will not snag the fibres; and
- they are stored in containers completely filled with water to minimise damaging 'slopping' movements.

Alternatively, wrap the objects in tulle and then wrap them again in water-saturated paper towel or cloth, which is then placed in a sealed polyethylene bag or container.

Store small objects in polythene bags or containers. Initially water from which the object was recovered may be used to keep the object wet. Placing one bag inside another provides additional protection against both drying out and physical damage.

Use freshwater for longer term storage, in conjunction with an appropriate fungicide if biological growth is a problem. A range of fungicides is available, including Panacide (used as a 0.2 per cent solution), Shirlan Plus (1%), Dowicide (1%), Densil P (0.3%) and thymol crystals (excess in tap water). The choice of fungicide depends on the nature of the material in storage. Dowicide and Panacide, for instance, are not suitable for use with textiles or leather due to their alkaline character (Pearson 1987).

Begin treating wet materials as soon as possible after their recovery. Long-term storage is not recommended as often deterioration not only continues but is accelerated during such storage.

If long-term storage is necessary, attempt to maintain conditions which minimise deterioration. Keep temperature, light and oxygen levels of the storage environment as low as possible. The latter two factors may be assisted by the use of narrow, deep storage tanks. Use refrigeration to minimise biological degradation and to reduce the need for biocides. Do not expose objects to direct sunlight (Keene 1977).

Where possible, retain adherent concretions until treatment begins.

If polythene bags, tanks and other containers are not available, wrap materials in dampened, water-absorbent material such as cotton cloth or hessian, and then wrap them again in plastic. Inspect the wrapped materials regularly to check the object is still moist and that there have been no outbreaks of mould.

Packing and transportation

As for on-site storage, care and common sense are needed when packing wet materials for transportation to a treatment laboratory. Find a balance between the maintenance of an appropriate storage environment, support for the object and possibly even the weight of the object and its storage medium. An overview of packing and transportation is provided by Leskard (1987).

Containers used for wet packing must be waterproof with lids that form tight seals. Plastic containers, liners and bags, although still susceptible to physical damage by puncturing or fracturing, are preferred to glass containers for transportation.

Avoid problems of excess weight or the possibility of damage being caused to an object by water movement by using damp wrapping and padding materials.

Do not use packing materials that will contribute to the further deterioration of the object or that are difficult to remove when the object is unpacked. If suitable padding materials, such as bubblewrap, are not be readily available, improvise. Use materials such as the original supporting matrix (for example, soil, concretion), sawdust, seaweed, undyed fabrics and even moss to maintain a damp, supportive environment (Lucas 1982, Rice and Murdock 1982).

Do not expose objects to extreme conditions such as direct sunlight during transport. Use insulating materials around supportive packaging to avoid this problem.

METALS

When wet, metals are generally much more reactive than when they are dry.

Of the factors that affect the deterioration rate of wet materials three are probably more significant for metals than they are for other materials. These are the:

- development of a layer of encrusting material;
- concentration of dissolved oxygen available to the metal surface; and
- position and relationship to other materials.

Some metal compositions encourage biological growth. Iron objects in particular enhance the formation of coral-like concretions which eventually encase the object. By providing a diffusion barrier to dissolved oxygen, concretions serve to slow destructive corrosion processes. They also provide protection against physical damage that may be caused by moving sand and wave action. Copper and its alloys, on the other hand, tend to be toxic to marine organisms and encrustation is much less on objects made from these materials.

If factors which affect the dissolved oxygen concentration at a metal surface, such as salinity, temperature and depth of burial in the sediments, are similar, the depth of the water at an archaeological site becomes significant. As water movement and turbulence are greater in shallower sites more oxygen is supplied to the metal surfaces, increasing corrosion rates.

The least reactive of two metals in contact or close proximity can be protected by the other. In this process the most reactive metal or alloy corrodes while protecting the least reactive metal at the same time. If, for example, copper and iron were in contact, the iron would preferentially corrode and the copper would be protected.

A beneficial example of this process is demonstrated by the use of sacrificial anodes attached to the hull of ships. Similar protection can exist with the metal of an artefact. Unfortunately it will frequently mean that another part of the artefact, or a connected artefact, must suffer more severe corrosion to provide this protection.

Metals and their alloys most commonly recovered from wet sites include gold, silver, copper, lead, tin, pewter, iron and aluminium. Of these gold is the most stable and aluminium the most reactive (see Appendix 8).

The following sections contain information on the identification, handling and stabilisation of these more commonly recovered metals.

Gold

Identification

The appearance of gold and its use in jewellery manufacture usually allow this material to be identified. It is possible, however, that corrosion products from the commonly alloyed metals (copper and silver) will disguise the gold appearance. Alternatively, selective corrosion of these metals can cause surface enrichment of the gold component giving an impression that the artefact is very pure.

Handling

As pure gold is soft, mishandling can damage the surface of gold artefacts. Alloyed copper and silver impart strength to uncorroded gold artefacts but selective corrosion of these metals causes structural weakening.

Initial stabilisation

- rinse pure or uncorroded gold in fresh water and store dry;
- store wet any gold which shows signs of copper corrosion, preferably in a solution of benzotriazole (BTA, 10 grams in one litre of water); and
- store wet any gold exhibiting silver corrosion so that any surface details contained within the corrosion products will be retained.

Silver

Identification

Silver corrosion products are usually grey or black. Silver salts react in the presence of light and in some instances blackening of freshly exposed silver corrosion products has been observed in strong light.

Blue-green copper corrosion products also may be present on alloyed silver artefacts recovered from aerobic sites.

Handling

Silver artefacts from freshwater sites are more likely to retain structural strength. As more extensive corrosion is expected in artefacts recovered from salt water sites, handle these materials carefully.

Retaining corrosion product layers is important as archaeological information can be preserved and recovered from them.

Initial stabilisation

To stabilise silver recovered from a wet site, observe the following guidelines:

- if the metal is sound and clean, rinse the artefact with fresh water and allow it to dry;
- if the artefact is mineralised or possesses corrosion product layers, keep it wet; and
- use a solution of BTA (10 g in 1 L of water) to store silver-copper alloys.

Copper and its alloys

Identification

In aerobic and particularly alkaline (high levels of carbonate) conditions, often the presence of copper is indicated by green-blue corrosion products (copper hydroxycarbonates) which frequently stain the surrounding burial material. Under anaerobic conditions, protective layers of black copper sulfide are formed instead.

Due to the toxicity of copper compounds towards marine organisms copper objects usually possess little encrustation.

Selective corrosion in copper alloys can result in the formation of a surface corrosion layer derived from the alloying metal. This complicates identification. For example, under low oxygen conditions the galvanic corrosion of bronze produces a grey-coloured, tin-rich corrosion layer. Weight loss, diminished strength and an increase in porosity result. Corroded bronze objects can appear to be made solely of copper if there is extensive destannification. Dezincification of brass has a similar result.

Handling

Although artefacts made of copper and its alloys frequently are recovered in very good condition, support will be needed if extensive corrosion of sheet metal has occurred. Handle cast brass and bronze objects with caution as sometimes they will have soft and weakened surfaces due to selective corrosion of the more reactive component metals of the alloys.

Initial stabilisation

To stabilise copper artefacts, follow the procedure outlined below:

- in the short term store dry recently recovered and structurally sound copper objects;
- immerse badly corroded and structurally unsound copper objects in a solution of sodium sesquicarbonate (10 g of sodium carbonate and 10 g of sodium bicarbonate in 1 L of water). This washes out the chlorides and stabilises the object.

Iron and its alloys

Identification

The following features indicate the presence of iron:

- a large, concreted mass; and
- typical orange-brown, rust colours.

Iron found in a wet site is usually weakened, with the degree of strength loss being related directly to the extent of corrosion. It is important to distinguish between cast and wrought iron as the effect of the corrosion processes is different.

Carbon, some in the form of graphite, is a constituent of *cast iron*. This inert substance does not corrode and often will help retain the physical shape of the object even though the iron content is reduced.

Corrosion is associated with weight loss and diminished structural strength. Concretion protects structurally weakened surfaces and reinforces corroded cast iron artefacts.

The corrosion pattern of *wrought iron* is determined by its manufacturing process. Since the metal is forged, beaten and folded into shape, the object acquires inclusions of impurities and different qualities of metal are laid down.

In addition, manufacture sometimes imparts stresses to the metal, which become a focus for corrosion activity. Consequently corrosion processes produce a furrowed surface not unlike the weathered grain of wood. The amount of uncorroded residual metal and the extent of the connection with the remaining structure usually determine how well an object survives.

Handling

Handle all concretions carefully as the encapsulating medium, although providing protection for the encased materials, may contain fragile materials in addition to the original iron artefact(s).

Provide support and do not lift concretions by protuberances.

Initial stabilisation

To stabilise iron objects recovered from wet sites:

- store them initially in either the water from which they were excavated or in fresh water which contains an alkaline agent such as sodium carbonate (washing soda);
- for long-term storage, keep iron in a solution of sodium hydroxide (caustic soda, 20 g in 1 L of water) or sodium carbonate (50 g in 1 L of water);
- store iron from freshwater sites initially in distilled or deionised water; and
- in the short term, place small iron objects in an airtight container with a desiccant such as self-indicating silica gel.

Note that on safety grounds it is generally inadvisable to transport artefacts in caustic solutions, water only being preferred.

Alkaline solutions will attack composite iron objects such as tinned wares, enamelled wares and any associated organic materials and should **not** be used to store composite objects which contain these components.

Lead

Identification

Indicators that an object may be made of lead include:

- a high weight-to-size ratio;
- grey appearance;
- cream-white encrustation (aerobic conditions); and
- areas of black corrosion products (anaerobic conditions).

In wet alkaline environments a combined layer of lead sulfate and calcium carbonate may form. This cream-white layer may have surrounding debris attached.

Under anaerobic conditions an inert layer of grey-black lead sulfide will form. Aerobic conditions can transform this layer to lead sulfate. Passivation of lead in aerobic and anaerobic conditions protects it from further rapid corrosion.

Lead is, however, susceptible to attack by organic acids such as those found in peat and clay deposits and those formed when organic matter decays.

Handling

As lead and its corrosion products are toxic, handle lead artefacts with gloves. Wear a dust mask to avoid inhalation of corrosion products.

The passivating nature of lead corrosion products usually ensures that these objects are often found intact. The innate softness of lead means, however, that it is highly susceptible to physical damage. Lead objects are often found deformed, torn, or abraded.

Handle lead objects carefully to prevent further damage to the surface of the lead or to its shape. Large objects, especially those made of sheet lead, will need support to prevent bending under their own weight. Corrosion products impart little reinforcement and easily fracture and detach if bending occurs.

Initial stabilisation

To stabilise lead objects:

- store dry;
- remove any marine growth to prevent attack from organic acids produced during the decay of these organisms; and
- store away from potential sources of organic acid vapours (acetate adhesives and unsealed wood,

ıding composite wood products such as ıpboard).

Do not place lead in distilled, deionised or soft tap water as it will speed up corrosion.

Sometimes dry storage does make later removal of concretion more difficult. An alternative is to store the object in seawater or freshwater containing sodium sulfate (1 g in 1 L of water).

Pewter

Identification

Depending on environmental conditions, pewter recovered from the sea can be found in excellent condition. Pewter surfaces are usually grey to dark grey in colour. Cracks and damaged surfaces will sometimes be defined by contrasting lighter corrosion products.

Surfaces may exhibit an even-sized, blistered appearance with occasional large, sporadically distributed blisters.

Handling

Pewter is a relatively soft alloy susceptible to physical damage. Handle it carefully. Do not force distorted pewter artefacts back into shape as the metal may have become brittle.

Initial stabilisation

To stabilise pewter artefacts recovered from wet sites:

- remove any marine growth to avoid potential corrosion problems associated with their decay; and
- store in freshwater containing sodium sulfate (1 g in 1 L of water) and BTA (10 g in 1 L of water).

As for lead, avoid storing pewter in deionised water and soft tap water as it increases corrosion rates.

Tin

Identification

The shape of an object (ingot, food tin) may give an indication of the material used in its construction.

Aerobic tin corrosion products are usually crumbly and whitish in colour.

Handling

Handle carefully objects made from either tin or coated with tin plate so that the corroded surfaces are not damaged and the intact metal is not subject to additional stresses. Support thin objects.

Initial stabilisation

To stabilise tin artefacts, rinse objects in fresh water and allow them to dry.

Aluminium

Identification

Aluminium has a light grey, naturally oxidised surface.

Handling

Aluminium objects need support when perforated.

Avoid exposing aluminium to alkaline and acidic substances and solutions.

Initial stabilisation

To stabilise aluminium, rinse the object with fresh water and allow to dry.

TREATMENTS

The treatment of wet metals is a specialised area and one in which research is ongoing, particularly in the area of composite objects. Consult a conservator before attempting any treatment of wet metals to obtain the most up-to-date advice on particular techniques and treatments.

STORAGE AND DISPLAY

For preservation it is important that artefacts are kept in a suitable environment following treatment. The optimum is not always possible as museum standards are difficult to achieve. An awareness of the best environmental conditions for an artefact will, however, allow collectors to assess their own particular environments and strive for the best possible conditions.

It is generally easier to establish a suitable environment when artefacts are placed in storage than when they are on display.

Principles for storing and displaying stabilised metals are described in the introductory part of the general Metals chapter of this book. Specific details pertaining to particular metals may be found in the relevant sections of that chapter.

In some cases formerly wet metals that have been stabilised will be more susceptible to damage by the environment and to materials used in storage and display areas than will their historic counterparts.

ORGANIC MATERIALS

Wood

Identification

In some cases, as in the recovery of a blackened object from an anaerobic site, it is not always easy to identify the material type from which the object was made. The fibrous nature of wood usually allows it to be easily identified.

If it is important to identify the wood species from which an object has been made, consult timber specialists. By examining either a polished end-grain surface, or by preparing a microscope slide of this surface, the identity of a wood sample usually can be determined. This type of analysis is necessarily destructive.

Handling

The condition of recovered wet wood can vary from solid to mushy. Handle it accordingly, especially as the surface is usually soft. It is important to ascertain the condition of wet wood before it is handled as its appearance can be deceptive. Being bulked by water, a wooden object can appear quite robust when in reality it is highly degraded and in need of support.

Follow the general guidelines described in the Introduction to this chapter (On-site Storage Considerations) for wooden artefacts.

Initial stabilisation

To stabilise wood recovered from wet sites:

- keep it wet;
- store objects at low temperatures and in the dark if possible;
- change the water if biological growth is observed;
- use freshwater with a fungicide if biological growths are persistent and storage is prolonged; and
- store metal-contaminated wooden objects separately from uncontaminated objects.

When recovered, wet wood must be kept wet. Irreversible damage will occur if it is allowed to dry before treatment. Use baths, plastic bags or containers, tubs or even wet cloths covered with plastic to keep artefacts wet.

Initially store the object in water from its recovery site. Use freshwater for objects from a marine environment so that desalination can begin. Incorporate a fungicide such as Densil P (3 g in 1 L of water) in the solution if biological growth cannot be controlled by refrigeration or other means of low temperature storage.

Leather

Identification

How easy leather is to identify is directly related to its condition. Highly degraded wet leather may appear as nothing more than mush or just as a mass of fibres held together by corrosion products. Often, however, wet leather retains its shape and its characteristic appearance, making its identification relatively easy.

If an object is thought to be leather, but there is some doubt, confirm its composition by infra-red spectroscopic analysis. This is a specialised technique which only needs a pin-head sized sample for the analysis.

Handling

When handling leather objects:

- use supports; and
- wrap in gauze or similar and sew the edges together.

If wet leather is in thin sheets or is in a fragile condition, handle it extremely carefully as it is prone to tearing while wet. Place it on a support and use the support, **not** the leather, when lifting the object.

Wrapping leather objects in soft gauze (for example, tulle) and sewing the edges together to make handling easier also ensures all parts of the object will be retained.

Initial stabilisation

To stabilise leather from a wet site:

- store wet;
- store at low temperatures and in the dark if possible;
- change the water if biological growth is observed;
- store in freshwater containing an appropriate fungicide if biological growths persist; and
- store metal-contaminated objects separately from uncontaminated objects.

Do not allow wet leather to dry out before it has been treated. For marine objects, seawater is acceptable for short-term storage before transferring them to a freshwater solution. If a fungicide is needed only use pH neutral or slightly acidic fungicides such as Densil 'P'. Alkaline fungicides contribute to leather breakdown. If possible store wet leather in a refrigerator or similarly cool environment.

Do not store wet leather for long periods as deterioration processes continue. Although research results are preliminary it appears that PEG stabilises collagen, the major component of leather. In addition, PEG solutions allow some iron corrosion products to be removed while in storage. It may be useful therefore to store wet leather in a refrigerator, in a solution containing PEG 400 (200 g in 1 L of water) and Densil P (3 g in 1 L of water). As research is on-going consult a conservator for the latest information on this subject.

Examples of bronze astrolabes.
One protected by concretior the other exposed to changing conditions on the sea bed.

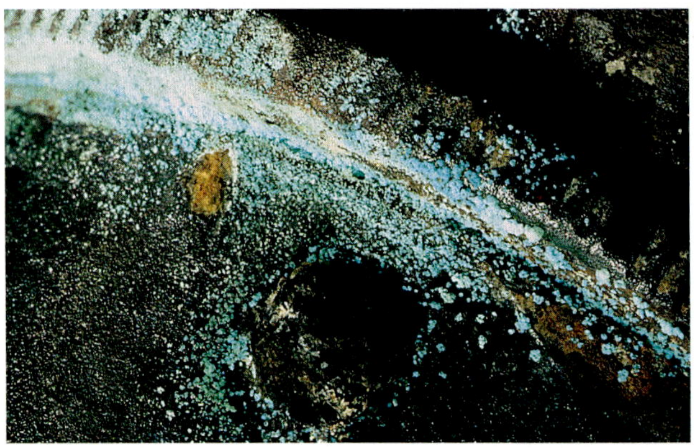

Close up of bronze disease.

Treated wood fragment from the wreck of the *Rapid* (1811), after drying.
Red outline showing wet dimensions.
Inset: untreated wood after drying. Red outline showing wet dimensions.

Tusk fragment from the *Vergulde Draeck* (1656) shipwreck showing contamination with iron corrosion products.

Inset: cross-section of fragment showing different areas of deterioration.

Before and after treatment of bell from the *Cambridgeshire* (1875).

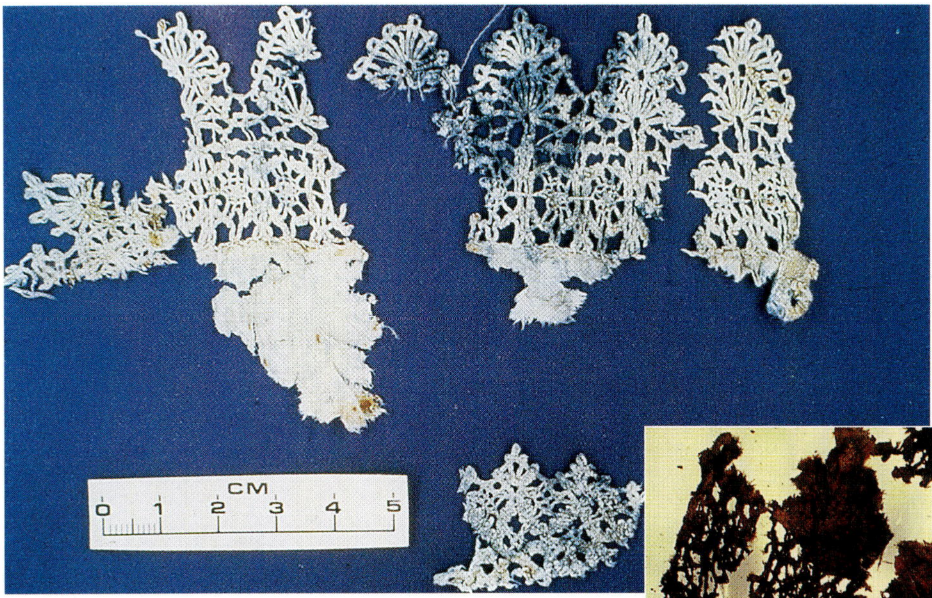

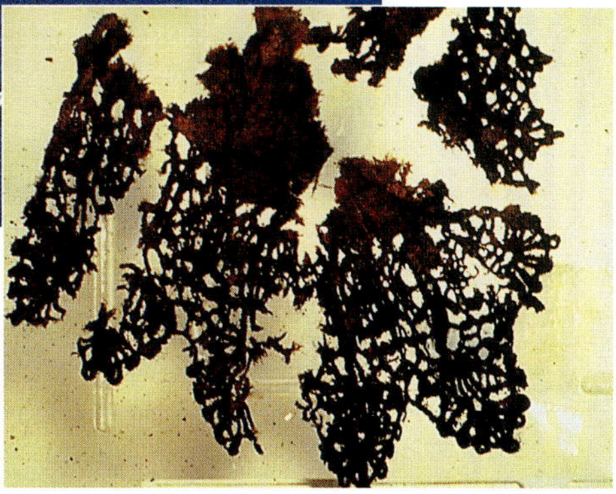

Lace from the *Batavia* (1629) shipwreck, before and after treatment to remove iron corrosion products.

Bone, ivory and horn

Identification

Identifying bone and related materials is often complicated by their dark colouration (due to burial in predominantly anaerobic conditions) or staining by corrosion products. As a consequence, these materials have been mistaken for materials such as wood, ceramics and even vegetable nuts.

If these objects are incorrectly identified, they may be treated inappropriately. Use microscopic examination to distinguish these materials (Penniman 1952).

If microscopic identification is inconclusive, use infra-red spectroscopic analysis. IR analysis will allow bone and ivory to be identified but cannot easily differentiate between these two material types.

Handling

Bone, ivory and horn are fragile objects which require careful handling.

If these objects have been closely associated with iron objects they are often heavily contaminated with iron corrosion products. These often create a hardened exterior finish which can hide a multitude of problems, including a highly degraded core. As these protective outer layers can be quite brittle, take care not to dislodge them. Wrap these materials in bubblewrap or similar for protection.

Initial stabilisation

To stabilise bone, ivory or horn materials recovered from wet sites:

- store wet;
- use water from the excavation environment or freshwater;
- store at low temperatures if possible (not freezing); and
- store metal-contaminated objects separately from uncontaminated objects.

Ensure these objects remain wet as the laminated structures of ivory and horn are usually coherent while wet; upon drying they tend to delaminate.

Short-term storage in the water from which the objects were recovered is acceptable.

After initial storage, place the items in freshwater at low temperatures (about 5°C) to begin desalination, thus avoiding the need to incorporate a fungicide. This is important as the complex nature of these material types (inorganic and organic components with different pH tolerances) means that the choice of an appropriate fungicide is very difficult.

Textiles

Textiles include materials made up of cellulosic fibres, such as cotton, flax, hemp, jute and sisal, and proteinaceous fibres, such as wool and silk.

Fabrics, rope and matting have all been recovered from wet sites. Usually textile materials will survive in a wet environment only if the site is anaerobic or if they have been protected from their surroundings by encapsulating concretions.

Identification

Identifying fibres usually requires a high quality microscope and access to an appropriate reference which highlights the features of different fibre types (see the chapter, Textiles).

In most cases wet textile fibres are highly degraded, so choose the best fibres for examination, otherwise characteristic features may not be evident.

Handling

When handling wet textiles:

- support them so they do not carry their own weight;
- use flat supports for flat textiles; and
- use sewn netting for three-dimensional objects.

Of the organic materials wet textiles are often the most difficult to handle because of their fragility and inability to maintain their own shape when removed from their aqueous environment. At all stages of treatment most textiles need some sort of support to maintain their structural integrity.

Support flat textiles on a glass plate or similar, separated from the support by interleaving with synthetic papers or screening material.

Three-dimensional materials, such as rope, usually need to have a support sewn around them. Gauze screening (for example, tulle) is preferred as it allows easy access for cleaning and offers little resistance to both the outward diffusion of dirt, salts and corrosion products and to the inward movement of consolidants and other treatment chemicals.

Initial stabilisation

To stabilise wet textiles:

- store wet, using either the water from which the textile was recovered or freshwater;
- support and wrap fibrous textiles while in the wet state;
- store at low temperatures and in the dark if possible; and
- consult a conservator for advice on incorporating appropriate biocides if longer term storage is likely.

TREATMENTS

Research into wet organic treatments is on-going. As many of the current treatments require access to specialised equipment (analytical and technical), an overview of the treatment process is described rather than specific treatments. Contact a conservator to obtain the most up-to-date information on particular treatments.

Generally, treatment of wet organic materials involves four distinct stages:

- cleaning - physical and chemical;
- desalination;
- consolidation; and
- drying.

Physical cleaning

Before chemically treating waterlogged organic objects, clean their surfaces. This allows the material type to be determined, improves the rate of outward diffusion of any absorbed salts or corrosion products, and improves both the object's appearance and its permeability to stabilising consolidants.

During cleaning take care not to damage an artefact's surface as it is important not to remove or disfigure potentially useful archaeological information.

Depending on the nature and condition of the object in question, remove soil and similar materials by careful brushing in water and, if available, ultrasonic agitation. To ensure the surface of small, valuable items are not damaged, carry out the cleaning process while monitoring the removal of detritus through a microscope.

To minimise the damage to the surface of soft materials like wood, bone and leather, use wooden and plastic scrapers rather than metal ones to remove more stubborn encrustations from the surface.

Remove adherent concretion with dental tools or by gentle percussion. Wash off or carefully scrape debris from the surface while keeping the object wet at all times.

The fragility of wet textiles, including rope and matting, complicates their cleaning. When cleaning, support these materials on either glass, perspex sheets or netting. As brushing inevitably will lead to fibre damage, use a fine spray of water or careful immersion (still on a support) to clean the object. Carefully applied ultrasonic techniques have cleaned these fragile materials successfully.

Chemical cleaning

Many organic materials excavated from wet sites have absorbed substantial amounts of salts from their surroundings. For shipwreck objects the most commonly incorporated materials, apart from the ubiquitous salt, are metal corrosion products which originate from nearby corroding copper and iron artefacts.

In many cases incorporated corrosion products are not only disfiguring but chemically damaging to objects. In conditions of elevated relative humidity the presence of iron corrosion products in wood, for example, leads to acidic regions developing. Cellulose breakdown follows. Other cellulosic materials, such as rope and many textiles, are also at risk in the presence of iron corrosion products.

Treatments are aimed at removing these incorporated minerals from organic objects. This is achieved by using chelating or complexing agents to remove the intrusive corrosion products. The chemistry associated with these processes is not simple. Monitor treatments regularly to determine the rate at which corrosion products are removed.

Desalination

Desalinate wet organic objects before any impregnation or consolidation treatment. Apply the procedures outlined earlier in this book (see the chapter, Ceramics). Note that the more porous nature of organic materials means that desalination times will be less than for metals and glass.

Incorporate a fungicide in the desalination solution to protect objects while salts are being removed.

Consolidation treatments

As organic materials deteriorate in a wet environment, soluble degradation products leach into the surroundings. In many cases the object is bulked by water which takes the place of the degraded chemical constituents. This helps to maintain the shape of the object while it is in its wet state. Unfortunately, as drying takes place supporting structures are lost and cell collapse, shrinkage and warping result.

The aim of consolidation treatments is to prevent this damage by progressively replacing the water in organic objects with chemicals which will bond with the residual chemical constituents. These provide objects with some structural integrity when they are dried.

If an organic artefact needs to be analysed, sample it before any extraneous chemicals such as fungicides or consolidating agents are used to treat it.

Drying

During the drying process damage to wet objects becomes obvious. Wood may warp, crack or shrink, ivory delaminate and leather shrink. For objects like wood, bone and ivory, drying damage is irreversible. Although leather can be retreated, as shrinkage is reversible, this is to be avoided if possible.

The key to success in drying is to ensure that drying stresses are minimised. To dry objects such as wood, rope and textiles, freeze-drying is the best method, giving a much better end product than air drying. This is because the freeze-drying process allows moisture to be removed as vapour from ice (sublimation). Drying stresses induced by the strong surface tension forces of water are avoided when the liquid state is bypassed in this way.

Although vacuum freeze-drying is the most efficient technique, it requires the use of sophisticated, expensive, equipment. It is used primarily for drying small objects. A frost-free freezer is also very effective at slowly drying PEG-treated objects.

Usually controlled air drying is needed for larger objects. Controlled dehumidification over a prolonged period is the next best alternative to freeze-drying. This process may involve the use of expensive, electronically controlled dehumidification chambers or improvised materials to construct a chamber in which temperature and relative humidity can be regulated.

One way of slowing the drying process is to place objects under polyethylene sheeting, venting the saturated atmosphere that builds up under the plastic once a week. Alternatively, place small objects in plastic bags that have been pierced with a few pin holes.

As the potential exists for mould formation, monitor the progress of drying operations, especially if objects are placed in, or under, plastic.

PREVENTIVE CONSERVATION

Upon recovery wet organic materials are often incomplete and are generally more degraded than their dry historic counterparts. Extra care is needed when handling, storing and displaying these objects.

Environment

Store and display treated wet organic artefacts under the conditions recommended for the material type in question. These may be obtained by referring to the relevant chapters of this book.

As for all materials, the key to improving the stability of wet organic objects is to maintain appropriate conditions that are as steady as possible. This is particularly important for wet organic materials, as in many cases the proteinaceous or cellulosic components of these materials will be substantially degraded.

Extra care should be taken with:

- cellulosic-containing objects from which contaminants such as iron corrosion products were not removed during treatment; and
- objects for which incorporation of consolidating chemicals was necessary.

In both of these cases special attention may have to be paid to the environmental conditions to prevent continued deterioration of the treated artefact. For instance, under conditions of high relative humidity, oxidation and hydrolysis of incorporated iron corrosion products can lead to increased acidity and subsequent damage to an artefact.

The incorporation of PEG into an artefact will affect its response to its environment as low molecular weight PEGs are hygroscopic. Under high relative humidity conditions, PEG-treated artefacts may take on a sticky, greasy appearance. Mould formation and bacterial attack also are enhanced by the presence of a food source such as PEG and by high relative humidity conditions.

Handling

Many formerly wet archaeological objects are more degraded than their historic counterparts and consequently require more careful handling. For fragile objects, the construction of supports that allow them to be handled without actually contacting the objects themselves is recommended.

Whatever the final choice for a support it should allow the object to be manipulated with minimal risk of damage. A support that is suitable for both storage and display is probably the ideal. Choose the support on the basis of the fragility of the artefact and its future use, be it storage, display or research.

In all cases the media used to construct supports must be of archival quality and compatible with the artefact. Acid-free materials in contact with proteinaceous artefacts such as leather and silk, for example, should not contain alkaline buffering agents as these substances increase protein hydrolysis.

SUMMARY

Metals

- If in doubt about the metal composition, keep wet.
- Retain adherent concretions.

- Separate from organic material.
- Do not store dissimilar metals in the same storage container.
- Consult a conservator for treatment advice.

Organics

- Keep wet.
- Retain concretions until treatment commences.
- Store objects contaminated with metal corrosion products separately from uncontaminated artefacts.
- Support fragile material on planks or netting.
- Lift by the supports, not by the object.
- Place cushioning between objects and the support material.
- Begin treatment as soon as possible after recovery. Seek advice from a conservator.

BIBLIOGRAPHY

Grattan, D.W. and Clarke, R.W., 1987, Conservation of waterlogged wood, in *Conservation of Marine Archaeological Objects*, Ed. C. Pearson, Butterworths, London, pp. 164-206.

Jenssen, V., 1987, Conservation of wet organic artefacts excluding wood, *ibid*, pp. 122-163.

Keene, S., 1977, An approach to the sampling and storage of waterlogged timbers from excavation, *The Conservator*, vol. 1, pp. 8-11.

Leskard, M., 1987, The packing and transportation of marine archaeological objects, in *Conservation of Marine Archaeological Objects*, Ed. C. Pearson, Butterworths, London, pp. 117-121.

Lucas, D.A., 1982, On-site packing and protection for wet and waterlogged wood, in *Proceedings of the ICOM Waterlogged Wood Working Group Conference*, Eds D.W. Grattan and J.C. McCawley, Ottawa, pp. 51-55.

North, N. A., 1987, Conservation of metals, in *Conservation of Marine Archaeological Objects*, Ed. C. Pearson, Butterworths, London, pp. 207-252.

Pearson, C., 1987, On-site storage and conservation, *ibid*, pp. 105-116.

Penniman, T.K., 1952, *Pictures of Ivory and Other Animal Teeth, Bone and Antler*, Occasional Paper on Technology, Pitt Rivers Museum, University of Oxford.

Rice, E.L. and Murdock, L.D., 1982, The use of seaweeds as a packing material for artefacts recovered from a marine environment, unpublished.

CASE STUDIES

The aim of this section is to demonstrate approaches to the treatment of particular objects, rather than to describe procedures themselves. Where specific procedures are referred to, readers are directed to the appropriate chapter of this book for further details.

1. FIREARMS

Introduction

There is an increasing interest being taken in the conservation and restoration of firearms. Firearms have figured prominently in Australia's history and are present in great numbers, particularly in the rural community.

Gun laws are generally strict, even for display purposes. Contact police in your state regarding regulations which apply to the repair and handling of firearms.

Construction and deterioration

Firearms are composite objects usually made up of steel of various grades, wood and rubber inlays. Take care when treating them, especially when components have corroded into a solid rusty mass. This is a common problem as the components of the mechanisms are small and intimately positioned. Dirt and unfavourable environmental conditions can 'fuse' these components together.

Safety

Before work of any kind is attempted on a firearm, check that it is not loaded or cocked. If there is any doubt as to its safety, seek help from an approved agency or person.

Documentation

Before treatment, take full notes, diagrams and photographs of the object's condition.

Treatments

Cleaning

If a weapon is in a good state of repair, following the guidelines below will assist in maintaining that condition:

- wear gloves when handling the firearm to stop oils and acids from the skin etching the metal surface;
- light oiling may be all that is needed to maintain the firearm's steel components. An approved light gun oil is recommended;
- if necessary the firearm may be stripped, cleaned in an approved degreaser, dried, lightly re-oiled and reassembled. A lint-free rag is recommended for this;
- dissolve heavy grease with caustic solution;
- a touch-up 'blueing' solution is available if this finish is applicable. Before this can be applied the metal surface must be free from dirt, oils and grease; and
- clean inlays according to their material type.

If, on the other hand, a firearm is in a badly corroded condition, other treatments may be more appropriate. Such a situation is well illustrated by an examination of the treatment of a .32 calibre Japanese pistol. For this object treatment consisted of:

- stripping the firearm as far as possible;
- immersing the corroded iron components in a solution of caustic soda (20-50 grams) in water (one litre) to remove all dirt, paint, grease and similar materials. **No aluminium or wooden components were immersed**;
- separating other components, using a combination of **gentle** heating, along with a lubricant such as CRC or WD 40, to remove nuts and screws. **No heat was applied to springs**;
- soaking the dismantled components (except the springs) in a solution of citric acid (20-50 g) in water (1 L) and gently brushing to remove rust;
- washing the components with caustic soda solution (see above) to neutralise any residual acid, then with fresh water to remove excess caustic and finally with a dewatering agent such as CRC or WD 40;
- wiping the parts dry and coating them with a solution of fish oil (20 per cent) in white spirit (80%). A light gun oil is an acceptable alternative;
- washing the plastic hand grips in fresh water and physically cleaning them with a soft brush; and
- reassembling the pistol. The mechanism could be activated following assembly.

Wood

Clean polished or waxed stocks and handgrips with a clean soft rag or soft brush.

Gun stock oils are available to refurbish wooden components if desired.

Preventive conservation

After treatment the weapon was wrapped in acid-free tissue and stored in an enamelled metal cabinet.

Check stored firearms every six to twelve months for signs of deterioration.

2. FRUIT TIN LABEL

Condition

The coloured, waxed paper label from the C Tuckey and Co. Peel Inlet Preserving Works was fully adhered to a backing which had been cut from a commercial cardboard box. The label had numerous tears, one of which had separated it into two sections. There were also areas of loss, creases, surface abrasion, dirt and stains present.

Treatment proposal

The proposed treatment of the label was drawn up as follows:

- document the label's condition;
- surface clean the label while still adhered to the cardboard;
- remove the cardboard backing;
- deacidify the label if necessary;
- depending on the condition of the label, strengthen it by applying a Japanese tissue backing; and
- encapsulate the label in mylar.

The cardboard backing was removed because its acidic nature would accelerate deterioration of the label. The methods used to remove backings are determined by the nature of the backing material.

The decision to reinforce the label with Japanese tissue can be made only after determining the fragility of the isolated label. Such decisions should never be taken lightly as they involve the introduction of a new component, thus changing the integrity of the object.

Encapsulation allows the label to be handled without touching the label itself while still allowing air circulation around it.

Tests carried out

The pH of the label was 4.6.

Stabilities of the colours and of the waxed surface were tested in water and calcium hydroxide solution. All appeared to be stable in both media.

Treatment

The surface of the label was dry cleaned using a thin, flexible slice of a high quality, soft eraser.

The cardboard backing was thinned initially by removing it layer by layer with a flat wooden spatula until only one thin layer remained. The remaining layer was moistened section by section with damp cotton wool until it was soft enough to be scraped off with a scalpel.

This type of backing removal is not always possible. If yellow strawboard has been used as a backing, do not introduce moisture as it is likely to stain any attached paper irreversibly.

The label was washed several times in distilled water until the water remained clear, deacidified in a calcium hydroxide solution, buffered to pH 9 for 30 minutes and then air dried on a Reemay support.

Since the object remained fragile and because of the sheer number of tears and creases, it was decided to apply a Japanese tissue backing for added stability. Kozo tissue paper was used. A piece, larger than the label, was pasted to the back of the label using a thin and even layer of wheat starch paste.

The reinforced label was dried between blotting paper lined with Reemay and under a sheet of glass as weight. Blotters were changed as they became damp. Reemay is a spun polyester which prevents adhesion of the object to the blotting paper during the drying process. After drying, the Japanese tissue was trimmed to a size slightly larger than the label.

After a paper object has been exposed to moisture, such as in the procedures described above, it is very important that it is dried thoroughly. The drying process usually takes several days but may take more than a week in some cases.

When dry the label was encapsulated in mylar. Only two sides of the mylar were adhered, with acid-free double-sided tape, to allow free air circulation and easy access should the label have to be removed. A strip of buffered Archive Text paper (pH 8.5) was inserted behind the label to counteract any residual acidity.

A window mount was cut from buffered 100% rag mat board (pH 8.5) and the above described 'parcel' was held in place by four photo corners handmade to size from mylar and double-sided tape. This type of storage supports the object and facilitates handling and display at the same time.

3. HORSE-DRAWN VEHICLES

Introduction

Horse-drawn vehicles are synonymous with Australia's history. From the Cobb & Co Coach, the 'Sydney' sulky or the bullock dray, horse-drawn vehicles have contributed to Australia's advancement. In the past

1. Fruit-tin label - before treatment.

2. Removal of backing using wooden spatula.

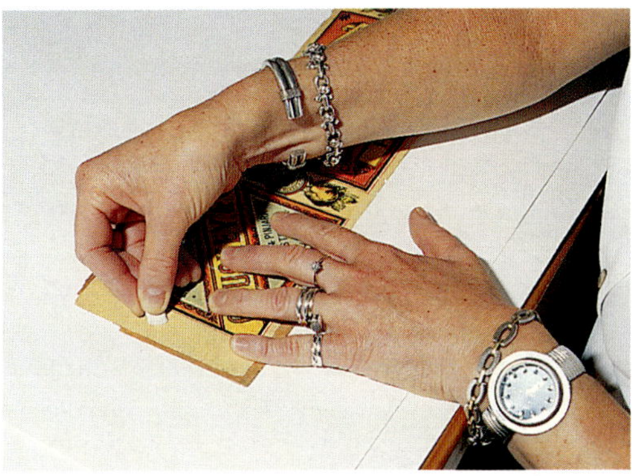

3. Dry-cleaning with sliced flexible eraser.

4. Spot testing for colour fastness using fine brush, water and blotting paper.

5. Application of backing.

6. Completed treatment. Stored in window mat for display, handling and storage.

few years hundreds of these wonderful vehicles have disappeared. Even today there are many vehicles disintegrating in paddocks. With a few simple precautions, these can be saved from further deterioration.

Deterioration and examination

The main materials used in the construction of horse-drawn vehicles are wood (one type or a mixture of woods), steel, paint and leather. All of these materials deteriorate when exposed to the elements. The normal modes and extent of deterioration of these material types is described elsewhere (see the chapters, Wood, Metals and Leather).

If a vehicle is exposed outside, the sun, rain and insects will soon damage spokes, felloes (wheel rims) and joints, eventually immobilising the vehicle.

Carefully examine and record the condition of the vehicle before attempting any work on it. Documentation should include:

- sketches and photographs of the vehicle and its components;
- notes on the condition of components;
- information regarding the original colours used on the vehicle. Scraping back to the original coats is usually necessary. If possible, paint samples should be taken;
- details of any lettering, numbering or patterns present on the vehicle. A stencil should be made of these; and
- any other details that may be of benefit in the conservation and restoration process.

Preventive conservation

Conservation work may not always proceed immediately. If this is the case, move the vehicle under a shelter with the wheels and shafts supported and raised from the ground. These simple steps will prolong the vehicle's life indefinitely. Stopping exposure to sunlight and periodic bouts of wetting and drying will minimise rot in the wood and rusting in metal components.

Make a simple stand to support the shafts and steel stands to support the axles. The latter stands are designed to raise the wheels about 6-12 mm above the ground.

A cover for the vehicle will help to prolong its life by protecting it from dust and the problems associated with the build-up of dirt.

Monitor the condition of the vehicle regularly. For instance, take photographs every 12 months and compare them. Take close-ups of susceptible areas.

Treatments

Conservation or restoration

Conservation of a vehicle involves taking steps that will prevent any further deterioration in its condition. Restoration involves both conservation and additional work designed to restore the vehicle to something approaching its original condition.

As the current condition of a vehicle is a true reflection of its history, display in a 'conserved only' state is often desirable. **Do not look upon complete restoration as a first option.**

Wood consolidation

If the vehicle has been exposed to the elements the wood is usually in a very poor condition. Leaving the vehicle standing on its wheels usually results in split and cracked spokes and felloes.

Use as much of the original wood as possible in any restoration, unless the wood is badly deteriorated or load-bearing. Retain all old wood, no matter how deteriorated, and use as templates for the manufacture of replacement pieces. Keep these pieces in storage when not in use.

For badly cracked pieces still robust enough to use, it may be necessary to split them before consolidation. The wood can then be treated as follows:

- clean out all of the dirt and rotten wood;
- glue the sections with an appropriate wood glue and sawdust mixture and clamp them together. Do not use water-soluble glues if the vehicle is to be displayed outside;
- fill all cracks with a glue and sawdust mixture;
- sand it back to shape when the glue is dry; and
- paint the timber using a primer, an undercoat and a top coat. The top coat should match the original colour sample.

The last three steps outlined above can be used for all pieces of wood from the vehicle.

Wheel repair

Wheels are usually in a very sorry state, especially if termites have made them their home. Rebuilding wheels is a specialist craft – seek expert guidance before disassembling and rebuilding them.

Another common problem is a build-up of rust between the inside of the tyre and the outside of the felloe. This type of problem may necessitate the removal of the tyre for treatment. If the tyre has to be removed, work upon the felloes and spokes becomes much easier. Consult a wheelwright if work of this type is necessary.

Chemical derusting of the tyre can be accomplished as described in the Metals chapter of this book.

If the work required is of a minor nature, splitting the felloe, cleaning as mentioned above and regluing may be all that is needed.

Leather

The treatment of leather objects is described elsewhere (see the chapter, Leather).

The case studies below demonstrate different treatments that can be applied to horse-drawn vehicles, depending on their respective conditions.

Wagon (New Norcia, Western Australia)

New Norcia is a farming community founded by Benedictine monks in the mid-19th century. Like all farming communities there was an abundance of horse-drawn vehicles, ranging from sulkies and buggies to general farm wagons. With the advent of the motor car and truck, these horse-drawn vehicles fell into disrepair and disuse. They were left to rot in paddocks, lost in bushfires or were broken up. Their numbers diminished alarmingly.

This was the case in New Norcia when the local historian realised that of all their horse-drawn vehicles, only one example of a four-wheeled general purpose cart remained.

Condition of the vehicle

This vehicle had been on display at the entrance to the town for many years and was in an advanced state of deterioration. The vehicle was standing on its wheels, which had collapsed under the weight, was infested with black and white ants, had been modified and had dry and wet rot.

Initially it was felt the vehicle was beyond redemption. As it was especially significant to the New Norcia community, being the last of its kind and having been manufactured locally, it was decided to attempt to restore the vehicle.

Research

Research is a critical factor in any restoration project. Relevant information obtained and studied included:

- photographs;
- plans;
- paint samples;
- traces of pin-striping or signage;
- wood identification; and
- condition of the object itself.

Paint samples were taken for colour matching and tracings were made of pin-striping and signage so patterns could be reproduced accurately. This information was needed to ensure that the object would reflect its original state when restored.

Photographs were taken before, during and at the completion of the project. Combined with written records of treatments, repairs and replacements of sections and parts, photographs form an essential part of the object's more recent history.

Treatment regime

Once the research had been completed the following work program was carried out:

- as much of the original timber as possible was used;
- timbers that were to be replaced were used as templates and then placed in storage;
- repairs were made to timber using sawdust and epoxy resin;
- timber was reshaped, primed and undercoated;
- all steelwork was removed and treated. Note that care was taken when treating the springs;
- steelwork was coated with a solution of fish-oil and white spirit to protect the steel components and give a lustrous steel-grey finish. This was painted as required;
- the vehicle was top-coated and pin-striping and signage added as per the original; and
- stands were manufactured to fit under the axles to take the weight from the wheels.

Butcher's cart (Fremantle, WA)

A two-wheeled butcher's cart was used to deliver meats in the Fremantle area.

Condition of the vehicle

As the interior of the vehicle held the meat, it was kept scrupulously clean and well maintained. No treatment was needed for this part of the vehicle. The exterior of the vehicle, however, was ravaged by the elements, with wood rot, deteriorating and flaking paint and rotting leather evident.

Research

As much documentary and physical evidence as possible was collected regarding the original appearance of the vehicle. In addition to the usual research and paint sampling, fabric samples were taken for identification. The sign writing was photographed, noting the colouring and type of shadowing and italics used.

Butcher's Cart - before treatment. Wheels and shafts missing.

Butcher's Cart - after restoration with replacement wheels and shafts. *Inset:* the worn interior of the cart was left in original condition.

Japanese pistol. *Main*: after treatment (refer to text). *Inset*: before treatment.

Time capsule - showing separately packed material.

Above right: This vehicle from New Norcia was so badly damaged full restoration was necessary.

Bottom right: After restoration.

Treatment regime

The wood and steelwork were restored as described for the New Norcia vehicle. The cart was then painted to match its original colours.

Farm wagon (Brookton, WA)

This four-wheeled farm wagon was built in 1903 in the Brookton area. The vehicle was housed in various sheds throughout its life and except for minor repairs carried out during its life, remains a good original example of a horse-drawn vehicle of the period.

Condition

Grease had solidified over the paint on the wheels and the wagon was covered with sand and dust. As sand and dust attract moisture, which begins the corrosion and rotting cycles, these needed to be removed.

Treatment regime

- dust and sand were removed by careful brushing and dusting;
- minor repairs were made to cracking woodwork using an epoxy glue and sawdust mixture;
- solidified grease over the paint on the wheels was removed by careful brushing with soft brushes; and
- some minor surface rusting on the steelwork was treated.

SUMMARY

The vehicles described above are now housed under cover, supported on stands which take their weight. Regular monitoring and cleaning ensures there will be little need for further repairs for many years.

An important factor in the preservation of any object is the environment in which it is stored or displayed. Keep vehicles and machinery clean, dry and undercover. If objects cannot be stored indoors then this cover should be on two or three sides to prevent driving wind and rain from coming into contact with the objects.

4. TIME CAPSULES

Introduction

The most popular notion of a time capsule is something resembling a giant vitamin pill crammed with photographs, coins and assorted memorabilia, which is either buried or placed in the foundations of a building for a period of 100 years. This method, or variations of it, were employed in Victorian times. Unfortunately the use of incompatible or unstable materials and poor packing techniques have meant that little material was recovered in good condition from time capsules of that era.

As time capsules are sealed, deterioration may be enhanced, particularly if unfavourable micro-environments develop in the capsule. Unfavourable conditions may arise if:

- stored materials deteriorate; and
- unstable storage conditions lead to fluctuations in internal temperatures and relative humidity levels.

The lack of air exchange with the surroundings means that if, for example, acidic vapours are released by an object as it ages then the rest of the interred objects will be subjected to an increasingly damaging environment. Some wood, paper and modern materials such as polyvinyl chloride behave in this fashion.

Changes in external conditions also affect the internal environment unless the storage conditions of the capsule are well controlled. A large drop in temperature, for instance, would produce an increase in relative humidity, a condition which may lead to condensation in the capsule. The growth of mould on organic objects and the corrosion of metals would be encouraged under these conditions. Conversely, if the temperature increases too much then the resultant low internal relative humidity may lead to damage such as the embrittlement of paper and wood and crazing or cracking of paint layers. Internally and externally insulating the time capsule will minimise relative humidity fluctuations.

Relative humidity and site selection

The factors affecting relative humidity and strategies that may be used to control it are discussed earlier (see the chapter, Preventive Conservation).

In order to ensure the long-term survival of materials placed in time capsules, pack the capsule when the ambient conditions are such that they allow for storage within the recommended limits of 18-22°C and relative humidity between 45-55%. As long as the capsule is stored in a stable environment then internal fluctuations will be small. If the capsule is packed on a day of very high relative humidity then that moist atmosphere and moisture laden materials will be sealed in the capsule - a recipe for disaster!

In selecting the interment site, consider:

- the temperature range associated with the site; and
- the nature of the material in which the capsule is to be buried.

The burial site may be below ground, in a wall or building or even on the ocean floor! As each site will have its own set of environmental parameters, the nature of the site necessarily dictates the type of construction materials that should be used for the capsule. Chemical features of the soil, depth of the water table and drainage are some of the factors which must be considered for a land site.

If the capsule is to be buried below ground then an appropriate stainless steel container, sealed with an o-ring, would be recommended. This type of container will minimise corrosion and leakage problems. Depending on the size of the capsule such a container could be very expensive. Alternatively if the capsule is to be placed in a crypt within a building then cheaper materials such as polyester powder-coated iron could be used.

Capsule construction

Factors affecting the construction materials and the type of capsule include:

- length of time the capsule is to be buried;
- volume of material to be included in the capsule;
- location and nature of the burial site; and
- available funding.

The capsule should have an o-ring seal on the lid section and be constructed so there is an even pressure exerted on the lid. This may be achieved by having bolts evenly spaced around the lid. An airtight seal is important if moisture, dirt and insects are to be excluded from the capsule.

Silicone sealant can be used externally only as the fumes it gives off could harm the contents of the capsule.

Flushing the capsule with an inert gas such as nitrogen or argon will help to prevent deterioration of the contents by excluding oxygen. To avoid damaging the capsule contents, ensure there are valves at either end and use a long pipe and trickle feed system to introduce the gas. In this way the contents will not be subjected to a sudden drop in temperature and possible condensation. Argon, though more expensive than nitrogen, is preferred as it is heavier and less likely to be lost from the container over time.

Note that if the container is flushed with an inert gas, also flush any materials that are sealed, in polyethylene bags for instance, with the same gas. If this is not done deterioration due to oxidative processes will continue in the sealed bag, defeating the purpose of flushing with the gas.

Insulate the capsule if it is to be interred above ground. The effect required is similar to a thermos flask where the box in a box principle operates. The aim is to minimise changes in internal conditions. This may be achieved, for example, by placing the capsule inside an insulated box which is then stored in the centre of an airconditioned building. If interred below ground to an adequate depth and properly sealed, the surrounding earth provides the insulation.

For burial below ground the following materials are suitable:

- certain grades of stainless steel;
- copper and its alloys; and
- high density polyethylene (HDPE) pipe.

Materials suitable for above ground storage include:

- galvanised metal;
- polyester powder-coated iron; and
- enamelled metal.

HDPE provides a cheaper, though less durable material, for underground burial. This material may be sealed by hot-air welding, avoiding the use of adhesives which would be prone to breakdown in the soil. HDPE is not recommended for above ground use unless it is protected from weathering agents such as the sun and rain.

Do not use iron materials that are not galvanised, enamelled or polyester coated, or polyvinyl chloride piping as they are all prone to deterioration.

Materials for inclusion in the capsule

It is most important to think long and hard about just what is to be included in the time capsule. Factors to consider include:

- significance;
- interest;
- durability of materials;
- quantity and size of objects;
- compatibility of materials; and
- the likely future availability of technology to replay included objects such as audio tapes.

Some materials are more prone to decay than others. Only include them in the capsule if they are of particular significance and if they can be isolated from the other objects in the capsule.

Seek the advice of a conservator regarding objects for inclusion in a time capsule. In this way unsuitable materials may be excluded and any materials that require treatment, to increase their chances of surviving the burial period, can be identified.

Newspapers for example, are notoriously poor in quality and should be double packed to ensure that there is no contamination of other materials. Wrap them in alkaline-buffered paper and encapsulate in polyester to minimise such contamination. As an alternative, photocopies could be used.

Where possible, use archival quality papers. For instance where documents are printed on poor quality papers, copy them onto alkaline-buffered paper for inclusion in the capsule.

Many audiovisual materials, such as video and cassette tapes, are inherently unstable and may not last more than a few decades before suffering serious deterioration. If argon or nitrogen flushing is not possible then vacuum packing or storage of these materials in a sealed container with Ageless oxygen scavenger is recommended. Their inclusion must also be weighed up against the availability of the equipment needed to replay them when the time capsule is opened. Will video technology still be available for playback?

Do not include some synthetics such as PVC, rubber and plasticised materials. Plastics considered safe for use in time capsules include polyesters, polyethylene, polypropylene, polycarbonate and polystyrene. As it is sometimes difficult to differentiate between these synthetic materials, seek advice before making a decision to include them in the capsule.

Photographs are popular inclusions in time capsules. Colour photographs are less stable than their black-and-white counterparts. Cibachrome processing is recommended if colour prints are to be included. Archivally process images to increase their longevity.

Do not stack photographs on top of each other without a sheet of polyester film between them. This will stop the photographs from sticking to each other. Do not use self-adhesive albums. See the chapter Photographs, for more guidelines regarding storage of these materials.

If textiles are included in the capsule, make sure they have been cleaned, are free of insect and microbiological infestation and conditioned to the humidity of the capsule. Wrap them in unbuffered, acid-free tissue.

Packing the capsule

Where possible, individually wrap all items or at least separate into similar materials and wrap as groups. For example, keep paper apart from metals. This can be done most cheaply using either heavy-duty polyethylene bags or polyethylene containers. Heat seal the bags.

As mentioned earlier in this section, packing should be carried out when the temperature and relative humidity are at the most appropriate levels.

Avoid folding objects, as it introduces stresses into them. If materials such as papers and textiles cannot be laid flat then roll them for storage.

Administrative considerations

Label objects included in the capsule and, unless the object is a document or something similar which tells its own story, include some detail relevant to the object in question.

Lodge details concerning the location, contents and future plans for the time capsule with the appropriate authorities (for example, local government agencies, museums, libraries, historical societies). Do not leave information concerning the capsule with just one organisation.

APPENDIX 1:

MEASURING LIGHT LEVELS WITH A CAMERA

Equipment required:

- 35 millimetre camera with a built-in light meter; and
- white cardboard (about 30-40 square centimetres).

Method:

- place the cardboard in the same position and at the same angle as the object or area that is being measured;
- set the camera to 800 ASA and without casting a shadow on the white cardboard, take an f-stop and shutter speed reading with the camera;
- the cardboard should fill the frame in the viewfinder of the camera; and
- use the coordinates obtained to determine the light level using the table shown below (for example, f8 at 1/30 sec = 700 lux).

	Lux	**88**	**175**	**350**	**700**	**1400**	**2800**	**5500**
F-stop	**2.8**	1/30	1/60	1/125	1/250	1/500	1/1000	1/2000
	4	1/15	1/30	1/60	1/125	1/250	1/500	1/1000
	5.6	1/8	1/15	1/30	1/60	1/125	1/250	1/500
	8	1/4	1/8	1/15	1/30	1/60	1/125	1/250
	11	1/2	1/4	1/8	1/15	1/30	1/60	1/125
	16	1	1/2	1/4	1/8	1/15	1/30	1/60
	22	2	1	1/2	1/4	1/8	1/15	1/30
	32	4	2	1	1/2	1/4	1/8	1/15
Shutter speed in seconds								

The values quoted in the table were obtained using a Gossen Lunasix 3 light meter, cross referenced with a range of Nikon cameras. Regard the readings as approximations only.

APPENDIX 2:

HUMIDITY TOLERANCE OF SOME MATERIALS

Material	Upper relative humidity limit	Lower relative humidity limit	Dimensional response	Susceptibility to mould
Paper	65% (critical)	40-45%	Rapid. Loose leaves tolerate moderate dimensional change.	Extreme. For safety 60% RH may be adopted as upper limit.
Stretched paper	65% (critical)	45% (critical)	Paper screens, drawings, pastels stretched on frames will tear due to shrinkage under low RH conditions.	Extreme
Fabric (natural fibres)	65% (critical)	45%	Inverted, as twisted fibres shrink when fibres swell and relax when fibres shrink.	Marked
Parchment, vellum	Steady state near 55%	Steady state near 55%	Extremely rapid. Dryness causes loss of flexibility.	Moderate because of inherent alkalinity.
Leather	65%	45%	Variable according to tanning process.	Variable. Marked for many fine leathers.
Bone, ivory	65%	45%	Very slow, except in thin sheets. Avoid hot lamps in cases for emphasis lighting.	Negligible except at very high RH.
Wood	65%	45% (critical)	Slow, varying with size and moisture barrier coating. Affected by weekly cycles and especially by seasonal cycles.	Negligible except at very high RH
Painted wood	65%	45%	Dryness which causes shrinkage of wood is especially damaging to a class of objects in which wood is the structural support for other materials. Buckling, blistering or flaking may result.	
Metal, ceramic, stone, plaster	Greater than 45% may lead to corrosion of metals such as iron, some steels.		Bronze, stone, ceramic and plaster, long buried, may have been infused with or corroded by salts which behave hygroscopically.	

APPENDIX 3:

CHEMICAL TREATMENTS OF INSECTS

The information contained in this appendix is based on a Technical Bulletin prepared by Dawson (1992).

Only a few representative chemicals are included in this appendix. Inclusion is not a recommendation for use, with a few commonly used pesticides included so that readers will become aware of the potentially damaging effects of these products. Use this information as a guide when considering what action to take in response to insect attack. Always remember to consult a conservator if in doubt about the impact of a particular treatment on objects in a collection.

1. FUMIGANTS

As long as the concentration and exposure times are appropriate, fumigants should be effective against all stages of insect development, from the egg to the adult. Fumigation does not, however, provide any long-term protection. Treated artefacts must be well aired before they are removed from the fumigation chamber. The duration of airing will depend on the type of fumigant used.

Common fumigants include:

Dichlorvos (DDVP, dichlorfos, vapona):

- is the active ingredient in resin pest strips;
- is useful in storage environments and against general household pests;
- lacks penetration and is ineffective against insect eggs;
- reacts with alkaline materials;
- has been found to discolour some textiles, is corrosive to mild steel and black iron and can tarnish copper, silver and brass. It deposits a film on zinc, tin and lead;
- may damage artefacts if they come into contact with them; and
- should be handled carefully as it is toxic to humans (acute oral LD_{50} of 56-80 mg/kg for rats) and is absorbed easily through the skin.

Ethylene oxide:

- has been widely used in the past, but its use is no longer recommended for the treatment of museum objects;
- is effective against major infestations, but is problematic due to its long retention by some materials and its reactions with some material types; and
- is a carcinogen and known to cause mutations.

Methyl bromide:

- is used to fumigate stored materials and soils;
- reacts with materials which contain sulfur;
- should not be used with woollens, viscose, rayons, vinyl, paper (sulfide process), rubber, furs, horse hair, feathers, leather goods and photographic chemicals;
- has no effect on oil paintings on canvas but some powdered pigments are affected;
- is very toxic to humans and is a potential carcinogen; and
- should only be used if there is a major infestation and if there are no other methods available.

Naphthalene (mothballs, white tar):

- is used as a fumigant and a repellent for general and domestic purposes;
- is only effective if used in well-sealed containers with exposure times of two to six weeks at ambient conditions;
- is considered non-corrosive and non-staining, but has discoloured wool and may dissolve fats in biological specimens;
- should not come into direct contact with artefacts because it may damage them; and
- is a risk to the health of users as it is a skin irritant and inhalation of vapour is known to cause nausea, headaches and acute haemolytic anaemia.

Paradichlorobenzene:

- is used as a fumigant and repellent for general and domestic purposes;
- is more volatile than naphthalene and is generally more effective - two weeks at room conditions is sufficient to kill the common clothes moth;
- can affect zinc white, lithopone, scarlet pigments, some cellulose acetate dyes, polystyrene foams,

styrene and cellulose nitrate plastics, paper and ink; and

- is a health risk to users via inhalation, ingestion or eye and skin contact. Signs and symptoms of poisoning include vomiting, headaches, liver cirrhosis and kidney damage.

2. ORGANOCHLORINE INSECTICIDES

Insecticides in this group include aldrin, chlordane, dieldrin, lindane and pentachlorophenol. Due to their damaging effects on artefacts and health considerations they should not be used on museum artefacts or in buildings which contain collections.

3. ORGANOPHOSPHOROUS INSECTICIDES

These compounds are generally more toxic than the organochlorine group but are usually applied at much lower concentrations, reducing the health risks slightly.

Chlorpyrifos:

- is used as a contact insecticide and may be applied in a variety of forms (solution, granules, spray, and so on);
- has a residual action of about thirty days indoors but has poor knockdown and flushing capabilities. It can persist on wood for several years and has a longer residual action on non-porous materials than most insecticides;
- may affect nearby artefacts if they are not covered during its application;
- is corrosive to copper and brass and produces colour changes in some red dyes (acid red and disperse dyes); and
- is moderately toxic to humans via skin absorption, inhalation of dusts and ingestion. Symptoms may be mild (nausea and dizziness) or severe in extreme cases (fever, coma and respiratory failure).

Diazinon:

- is used as a contact insecticide and is available in a variety of forms;
- has a residual activity of about 30 days indoors with a longer life on porous surfaces;
- is moderately to very toxic to fish, birds and bees;
- causes slight to very slight colour changes in acid red and disperse red dyes;
- may affect uncovered artefacts near the application site; and
- is a health risk to users in a similar fashion to that described for chlorpyrifos.

Malathion:

- is a contact insecticide formulated as a wettable powder, a dust or an emulsifiable concentrate;
- is corrosive to iron, steel, tin plate and copper and produces unacceptable colour changes in acid red and disperse red dyes. Malathion's effects on other materials are unknown, so caution is advised in its use; and
- is considered to be the least toxic of the organophosphorous insecticides, but is highly toxic if ingested and may cause foetal abnormalities. Care must be taken when using it.

4. CARBAMATES

These materials are less volatile than organophosphates and consequently pose less of a risk of vapour poisoning.

Bendiocarb (Ficam):

- is a contact insecticide formulated as a dust or wettable powder. It has no fumigant properties;
- has a residual activity for weeks or months, depending on the environmental conditions;
- has no effects on acid red, telon red or disperse red dyes as it is applied as a powder; and
- poses some risk to health via inhalation, skin or eye contact or ingestion, though this is less so than with materials which possess higher vapour pressures.

Carbaryl (Sevin):

- is a contact insecticide available in a variety of formulations; and
- has a moderate residual action (three to four days to several months) depending on conditions;
- is non-corrosive but solvent effects may occur if it is allowed to contact artefacts;
- should not be allowed to come into contact with artefacts due to its residual activity; and
- is moderately toxic to people via inhalation, skin or eye contact or ingestion, toxic to bees, is a carcinogen (in rats), has caused genetic mutations in experiments and foetal abnormalities in many animals.

Propoxur (Baygon):

- is an emulsifiable concentrate which is also available as a pressurised spray and solution;
- has a good flushing action, rapid knockdown and a residual activity of up to forty-five days (indoors);
- appears to have little effect on materials, though excessive wetting of plastics, rubber, asphalt and floor coverings should be avoided. Do not use on any materials prone to staining (carpets, curtains, wallpaper and the like). Avoid direct contact with artefacts; and
- is moderately toxic to humans via inhalation, skin or eye contact or skin absorption. It is also toxic to birds, fish and other wildlife.

5. BOTANICALS

Botanical insecticides are those derived from plants. The pyrethrin class is the most significant of the botanical insecticides. Commercially available synthetic pyrethrins (pyrethroids) have a greater residual activity and higher toxicity than their naturally occurring counterparts.

Pyrethrins:

- act as contact insecticides and are available as pressurised sprays, dusts and oil solutions;
- are unstable and breakdown quickly to produce non-toxic residues;
- have rapid knockdown and flushing capabilities but do not always kill all of the insects knocked down;
- are often combined with other chemicals to increase their effectiveness;
- should not be allowed to come into direct contact with artefacts; and
- are of little danger to mammals but are toxic to fish.

6. INORGANICS

Boric acid:

- is a stomach poison effective against crawling insects. It is relatively slow acting, taking from two to ten days to kill;
- can remain active for up to twelve months, if applied in clean, dry areas;
- should not be applied directly to artefacts or be placed in areas where it will be contacted as no specific information is available regarding its reactivity with materials;
- should be handled carefully despite the relatively low risk of poisoning associated with its use; and
- has been used extensively in natural history collections as a substitute for arsenic.

Diatomaceous earth:

- is a desiccant insecticide often used in combination with pyrethrins;
- should not be allowed to come into direct contact with artefacts or be placed in areas where it is likely to be contacted, as there is no specific information available regarding its reactivity;
- extends the persistence of pyrethrins when these compounds are combined; and
- can be forced into cracks and crevices where liquids would not be effective.

BIBLIOGRAPHY

Dawson, J.E. (revised by T.J.K. Strang), 1992, Solving museum insect problems: Chemical control, *Technical Bulletin No. 15*, Canadian Conservation Institute, Otttawa, pp. 1-26.

APPENDIX 4:

INSECT PESTS

The summary below of common insect pests is based on information provided in a previous Western Australian Museum publication (1981).

Case bearing clothes moth *(Tinea pellimella):*

- the moth lays 100 or more very small eggs on almost any fabric or material of animal origin (wool, feathers, fur and so on) particularly if dusty or dirty;
- the eggs hatch in about one week and the tiny caterpillars (larvae) do the damage through feeding;
- the larvae are creamy-white with dark heads and are about 12.5 mm long when fully grown;
- the larvae spin a cocoon and carry it with them throughout their lives, enlarging them as necessary; and
- when ready to emerge from their cases as moths, the larvae often stray right away from their food materials so that small woven cases containing pupae occasionally may be found suspended from the bare walls or ceiling of a room.

Webbing clothes moth *(Tinea biselliella):*

- the larvae of the webbing clothes moth spins a loose silken web or tunnel on the surface of its food material. Dusty or dirty material is preferred;
- the larval stage may last several months or even years;
- when the larva is ready to emerge a silken cocoon is formed, into which small pieces of wood, grass and similar materials are incorporated; and
- the adult emerges after two to five weeks, after which it spends a brief time mating and laying eggs.

Hide beetle *(family Dermestidae):*

- the adult beetle is a small, ovoid, dark-coloured insect, often with patterns of coloured scales or hairs;
- it is usually found on flowers in the garden;
- the larvae are oval with distinct segments; the body is densely covered with long hairs, some of which may be spear-headed or clubbed;
- the larvae feed on dry animal material of high protein content such as skins, hides, furs, as well as foodstuffs (bacon, cheese); and
- when about to emerge, the larvae leave their food supply and burrow into, and consequently damage, neighbouring material. The adults are often found in materials on which they cannot feed.

Carpet beetle *(Anthrenus sp)*

- one of the most common carpet beetles is *Anthrenus australid*, the Australian carpet beetle;
- the beetle is a small, round, 3 mm long insect, dark in colour with four distinct wavy white bands across its back, giving it a mottled appearance;
- although commonly found in flower beds, the adult lays its eggs indoors, preferably on materials such as wool, feathers, silk or fur. These serve as a food supply for the larvae;
- the eggs hatch after about 14 days and the larvae may be active for several months depending on temperature and humidity; and
- as they grow the larvae shed their skins; the empty hairy skins are one of the characteristic signs of this insect.

Furniture beetle *(Anobium sp):*

- the adult beetle lays white, lemon-shaped eggs in cracks and crevices of wooden furniture and timber, particularly in the end grain;
- the eggs hatch in about four to five weeks and the grub then bores into the timber;
- the larvae attack pine, Australian cedar, European oak, beech or elm, but not eucalypts;
- when fully grown the larva is about 5 mm long, has dark brown jaws, and is covered with short, yellowish hair;
- damage is caused by the burrowing larvae tunnelling into the timber and using the bore dust or 'frass' to pack the tunnel behind it;
- the frass may be used as a diagnostic aid, that being produced by *Anobium* being abundant, loose, gritty and not unlike fine table salt;

- on reaching maturity the larva excavates a small chamber near the wood surface, changes into a pupa and then, in six to eight weeks, into an adult. The adult then bores its way out, leaving an exit hole 1.5 mm in diameter, to fly away and wreak havoc elsewhere; and
- factors which favour attack are high moisture content, warm environment, wide sapwood, low resin content and the presence of fungal decay in the wood.

Silverfish *(family Lepismatidae):*

- the silverfish is the most common pest found in paper and textile collections;
- it is rarely seen because of its preference for dark, quiet and secluded places;
- the insect is silvery-grey in colour and when mature is about 15 mm in length;
- the insects emerge from the eggs as miniature adults and grow through a series of moults;
- the life span of this insect can be up to four years; the eggs hatch in ten to sixty days and sexual maturity is reached in two to three months;
- of most concern to collectors are those silverfish which feed on cellulosic materials such as paper, sizing, glue, cotton materials and rotting wood. If unchecked, these species can seriously damage books, drawings, prints and cotton fabrics; and
- if a silverfish is detected inspection of the whole collection and appropriate treatment is needed.

BIBLIOGRAPHY

Department of Materials Conservation, Western Australian Museum, 1981, Mould and insect attack in museums, in *Conservation and Restoration for Small Museums*, 2nd Edition, Western Australian Museum, Perth, pp. 20-31.

APPENDIX 5:

WOOD FILLERS

The fills mentioned are ones used traditionally by cabinet makers or in the conservation field. This list of fills is an introduction to this broad subject and is not extensive. Experiments often will be needed to determine the best type of fill for a specific object.

Gypsum plaster:

- is mixed with polyvinyl acetate AV 101 and methyl methacrylate AC 135 in proportions of 3:1:1, with 2.5% methyl cellulose; and
- is a strong fill which can be worked and coloured.

Shellac burning-in stick:

- traditionally used to fill cracks on wood where French polish has been applied; and
- skill is needed to apply this material but it is easy to sand and colour.

Two-part filler:

- is an epoxy or polyester resin;
- can be mixed with microballoons, fine sawdust or an epoxy filler to produce hard fills which can be worked as well as coloured with pigments or paint; and
- the fills yellow with age.

Paraloid B-72:

- when applied at 15% in either acetone or ethanol can be mixed with microballoons to produce a fill which can be carved, sanded and coloured with pigments or paints;
- this type of fill can be soft or hard depending on the quantity of microballoons used; and
- it will not yellow with age, unlike epoxy or polyester fills.

Plaster of Paris:

- may be mixed with microballoons to make a lightweight fill;
- can be moulded, carved, sanded, tooled, coloured with pigments, painted, waxed and so on; and
- traditionally, linseed oil was applied over plaster to make a transparent fill. This yellows with age.

Polyfilla:

- is a cellulose derivative;
- may be mixed with sawdust or microballoons to produce a very lightweight material which can be easily worked and coloured; and
- should not be used for fills that will be stressed or strained.

PVA:

- polyvinyl acetate adhesive, or white glue, is best mixed with fine sawdust or microballoons to prevent shrinkage of the fill; and
- it can be easily worked but may be difficult to colour.

Vulcanising silicone resin (RTV):

- the RTV resin (Dow Corning 734 and 738) may be mixed with microballoons (2-3 parts resin to 1 part microballoons) to produce a lightweight fill which can be moulded, carved, sanded and painted; and
- do not use on wooden objects which have metal components to avoid enhancing corrosion.

Wax:

- beeswax, microcrystalline wax and carnauba have been used for fills;
- these waxes may be used individually or as a mixture to obtain different properties, such as hardness;
- they may be purchased coloured or may be coloured with pigments; and
- fills made from wax can be moulded, carved and worked with heat and solvents.

Wax and resin:

- resin of trees such as dammar is often mixed with flakes of shellac into molten wax;
- sawdust and microballoons may be added to make a lightweight fill; and
- this fill is difficult to sand, carve, colour with pigments or paint.

APPENDIX 6:

PAPERS, CARDS AND BOARDS

Listed below are details of some of the papers, cards and boards likely to be encountered by those responsible for the care of collections. Note that not all of these are recommended for conservation purposes.

Acid-free foamcore board:

- contains a polystyrene foam core with alpha cellulose surface paper; and
- is lightweight and rigid

Acid-free tissue paper:

- contains cotton fibres with alpha cellulose;
- all acids, lignin, alum and impurities have been removed; and
- neutral pH of 7.

Alpha cellulose mat:

- contains cellulose derived from cotton;
- all impurities have been removed; and
- high stability and longevity.

Barrier lining paper:

- 100% cellulose;
- all acids, lignin, alum and impurities have been removed;
- buffered with calcium carbonate to a pH of 8.5; and
- used to stop acid migration.

Blotting paper:

- contents vary from 30% up to 100% cotton fibre;
- all acids, lignin, alum and impurities have been removed; and
- usually pH neutral (pH 7), but may be buffered with calcium carbonate to pH 8.5.

Buffered tissue paper:

- contains cotton fibres with alpha cellulose;
- all acids, lignin, alum and impurities have been removed; and
- buffered with calcium carbonate to pH 8.5.

Corrugated (multi-use) board:

- contains purified alpha cellulose pulp;
- all acids, lignin, alum and impurities have been removed;
- may be pH neutral or alkaline (if buffered to 8.5 with calcium carbonate);
- available in single and double wall; and
- suitable for storage boxes.

Glassine paper:

- a smooth, transparent film which is untextured and non-electrostatic;
- is pH neutral; and
- prevents smudging and can be used for interleafing.

Lens tissue:

- is translucent and contains manila and jute fibres;
- is unbuffered and pH neutral; and
- is used for wrapping and interleafing photographs.

Photomount rag board:

- is an untextured, 100% cotton rag;
- is unbuffered (no alkaline reserve); and
- is used for mounting albumen, cyanotype, dye transfer and chromogenic prints where alkaline buffers and textures are not suitable.

100% rag mount:

- contains cotton linters but no groundwood, lignin or alum; and
- may be buffered with calcium carbonate to pH 7.5-8.5.

Renaissance tissue:

- contains 25% cotton fibre, with a 90% alpha cellulose content;
- is unbuffered and untextured; and
- is used for storing albumen, cyanotype, dye transfer and chromogenic prints.

Standard foamcore board:

- contains a polystyrene core with acid-reduced surface paper; and
- is not suitable for conservation purposes.

Strawboard:

- is usually alkaline, but contains harmful impurities;
- the colour runs in the presence of moisture; and
- is not suitable for conservation purposes.

Teton cover:

- contains alkaline buffered (pH 7.5-8.5) purified alpha cellulose pulp; and
- available in 118, 217 and 239 gsm (217 gsm is suitable for storage folders).

Tyvek:

- is water-resistant, inert polypropylene;
- does not tear;
- can be heat sealed; and
- suitable for envelopes, folders, lining and so on.

Virgin groundwood mat

- groundwood paper, buffered with calcium carbonate;
- contains impurities like acid, lignin, alum and glues; and
- is not suitable for conservation purposes.

APPENDIX 7:

PHOTOGRAPHIC PROCESSES

POSITIVE PHOTOGRAPHIC IMAGE

ON METAL

A	Image is on highly polished silver	**Daguerreotype** (1839-1860s)
B	Dull image on black or brown varnished iron	**Ferrotype** or **Tintype** (1852-1940s)
C	Image is on copper, aluminium, zinc. May be sepia, black and white or colour	**Carbon-transfer** (1864-1930s) or **Transferrotype** (1884-1930s)
D	Image is on white enamelled copper plate	**Photo-ceramic** (1860s on)

ON MISCELLANEOUS BASES

A	Synthetic ivory	**Ivortype** (1855-1910) **Eburneum** (1865-1910s)
B	Fabrics - cotton, silk, linen	**Cloth print** (1850 on)
C	Fabrics, oil cloth	**Planotype** (1854-1900) wet collodion positive
D	Fired glaze image on china or porcelain	**Photo-ceramic** (1860s on)
E	Image on wood, stone	**Carbon transfer** (1864-1930s) or **Transferrotype** (1884-1930's)

ON GLASS

A	Dull negative image made positive by viewing against a dark background	**Collodion** positive, also known as **Ambrotype** (1851-1870s)
B	Positive image on opal glass	**Opaltype** (1880-1920)
C	Print on convex glass, translucent, hand tinted	**Crystolleum** (1880s-1930s)
D	Images on 3¼" x 3¼" to 3½" x 4" glass plates - can be collodion, gelatin, carbon, dyed or hand-tinted	**Lantern slides** (1851-1900)

IDENTIFICATION OF PRINTS

(10 x - 30 x magnification)

Image-forming salts embedded in paper

SINGLE LAYER PAPER SUPPORT

A	Uncoated single layer paper. Paper fibres clearly visible. Image is formed in the paper fibres.	Purple to warm sepia highlights, yellow especially at the edges.	**Salted paper print** (1840-1860s)
		Neutral grey or brown image, no fading.	**Platinotype** (1880-1920s)
		Bright blue image.	**Cyanotype** (1840s) Negative image **Cyanotype** (1880-1920) Positive image
		Shows regular pattern.	**Photomechanical process** (1870-on)

Emulsion layer

Paper base

DOUBLE LAYER PAPER SUPPORT

B	Double layer paper fibres may be visible through the binder layer.	Purple to red brown image. Usually yellow in the highlights, cracking of binder layer.	**Albumen print** (1850-1920s)
	Paper fibres visible.	No image fading. Can be any colour. Woodburytype is normally chocolate brown with distinct image relief.	**Carbon print** (1860-1900s) Pigment print or **Woodburytype** (1865-1890s)

Emulsion layer

Barium sulfate layer

Paper base

TRIPLE LAYER PAPER SUPPORT

C1	Fibres visible. Water spot test shows swelling.	Warm purple to red brown image.	**Gelatin printing out paper** (1880-1920)
	Paper fibres invisible. Water spot test shows swelling.	Silver mirroring may be seen in high density areas.	**Gelatin developing out paper** (1880-on)
C2	Paper fibres invisible. Water spot test has no effect.		**Collodion printing out paper** (1880-1920)
	Water spot test has no effect.	No image fading. Neutral image hue.	**Matt collodion POP** with gold and platinum toning (1880-1920s)

NEGATIVE IMAGES

ON PAPER

A	Plain uncoated writing paper	**Calotype** (1840-1860s)
	Translucent waxed paper	**Calotype** (1851-1865) Waxed paper negative
	Oiled paper	**Eastman negative paper** (1884-1895)

ON GLASS

B	Image often creamy	**Wet collodion** (1851-1880s)
		Dry collodion (1854-1885)
		Albumen (1848-1920s)
	Image is black and may be tarnished.	**Gelatin dry plate** (1880-on)

It is difficult to differentiate between the wet collodion, dry collodion and albumen images. An alcohol spot test, which dissolves the collodion, may be necessary

ON FILM

C	There are no easily discernible visual	**Cellulose nitrate** (1889-1950)
	differences between these film types	**Cellulose acetate** and **tri-acetate** (1930-1960s)
		Polyester (1965-on)

These film types can be identified by putting a small sample in a test tube containing trichloroethylene. During a 10-second time test, the cellulose nitrate sinks to the bottom, the acetate hovers about the middle and the polyester floats to the top.

Alternatively, a small sample (pin-head size) can be examined by infra-red spectroscopy. This specialised and somewhat expensive technique will allow unambiguous identification.

APPENDIX 8:

GALVANIC SERIES

The galvanic series shown below was taken from Singley (1988). The most noble (least reactive) metals are shown at the top of the table with the least noble (most reactive) at the bottom. To determine which metal will corrode and which will be protected when two dissimilar metals come into contact, the metals' positions in the series must be noted. The most noble metal (highest in the series) will be protected while the least noble will corrode. For example, if aluminium bronze was in contact with lead, in the presence of moisture and oxygen, then the lead would corrode and the aluminium bronze would be protected.

BIBLIOGRAPHY

Singley, K., 1988, *The Conservation of Archaeological Artifacts from Freshwater Environments*, Lake Michigan Maritime Museum, Michigan, p. 30.

Most noble (least reactive)	platinum
	gold
	graphite
	titanium
	silver
	stainless steel (passive)
	Monel
	nickel (passive)
	leaded tin bronze
	copper nickel (30%)
	silicon bronze
	copper
	red brass
	aluminium bronze
	admiralty brass
	yellow cartridge brass
	nickel (active)
	naval brass
	manganese bronze
	Muntz metal
	tin
	lead
	stainless steel (active)
	lead-tin solder
	high nickel cast iron
	cast iron
	wrought iron
	low carbon steel
	aluminium
	galvanised steel and wrought iron
	zinc
Least noble (most reactive)	magnesium

APPENDIX 9:

SPOT TESTS FOR COMMON METALS

Spot tests may be used to identify metals and to distinguish different metals which make up an alloy. Simple instructions and a list of the tests are provided to facilitate identification of a metal. Note that these tests are only qualitative, providing information regarding the components of a metal but not the proportions in which they are present. These tests follow the procedures described by Laver (1978).

GENERAL ELECTROLYSIS INSTRUCTIONS

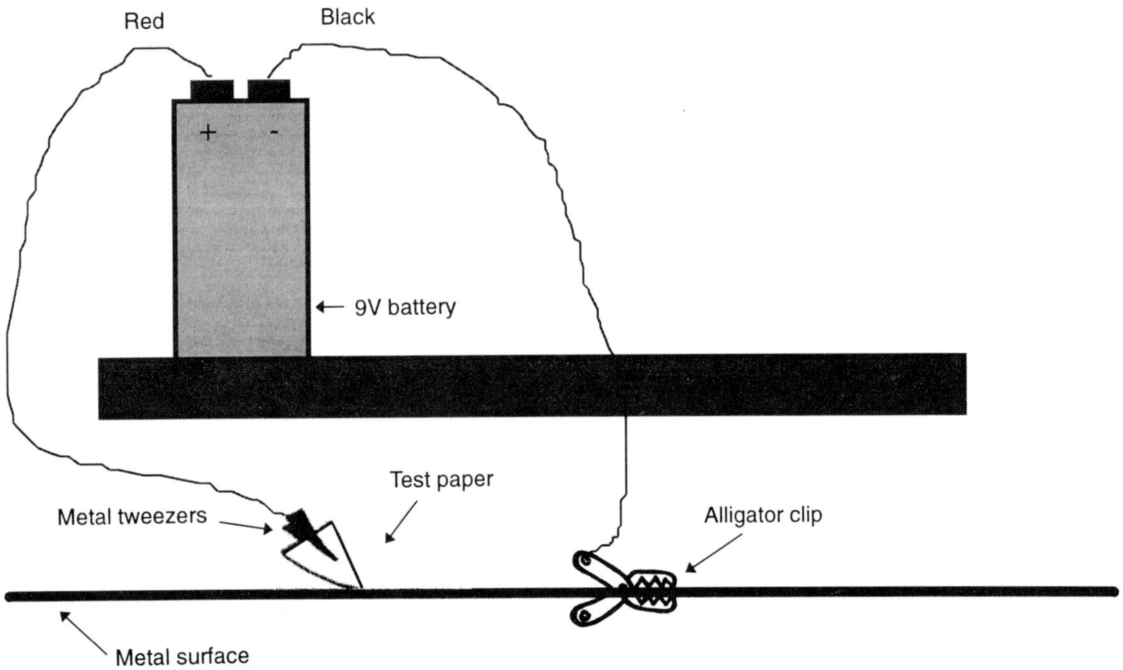

Figure 17: Equipment set-up for metal spot tests (adapted from Laver, 1978)

- tests should be carried out in unobtrusive spots on the artefact, as marks may be left;
- remove protective coatings such as lacquers and waxes from the area to be tested, since no reaction will proceed otherwise;
- the test papers to be used in conjunction with electrolysis are best cut into triangles. When wet with distilled water or salt solution the paper should be shiny-wet, but not soaking;
- the clip needs to be touched firmly to an area of reasonably solid metal;
- touch the test paper in the tweezers to the surface of the object, about one centimetre away from the clip. Do not let the tweezers touch the metal;
- rinse with distilled water and dry wet spots of electrolyte (for example, sodium chloride) or other reagents; and
- disconnect the battery and store it away from the tweezers and clip to avoid accidental discharging if the two should touch.

LIST OF TESTS

Antimony (Sb)

Procedure:

- dip a small piece of antimony test paper in diluted hydrochloric acid (HCl, 2%) and apply to the object.

Results:

- the presence of Sb is indicated by an orange colour;
- the reaction is complete in five seconds on pure Sb using 2% HCl. Surfaces containing trace Sb will be much slower; and
- gold and silver surfaces remain unaffected by the test, lead is slightly darkened, copper and iron corrosion products change colour slightly.

Copper (Cu)

Procedure:

- wet a small piece of commercial test paper (Cuprotesmo) with distilled water and place on the surface of the metal.

Results:

- the copper metal or Cu^+ and Cu^{2+} ions cause the pale yellow paper to turn pink-purple;
- this test works particularly well on corroded or patinated areas and leaves no trace of the test; and
- on highly polished or new surfaces the reaction is much slower, but may be accelerated by briefly applying the electrode to the paper (about five seconds is sufficient).

Gold (Au)

Procedure:

- dip a small triangle of plain filter paper in a solution of sodium chloride (NaCl, saturated solution in water);
- electrolyse for less than 15 seconds. Some darkening will probably be evident if copper is present. Leave the paper on the spot until slightly dried to ensure that gold is on the surface of the paper; and
- dip into a mixture of stannous chloride ($SnCl_2$, 20%) in HCl (15%).

Results:

- the presence of gold causes the paper turn black.

Iron (Fe)

Procedure:

- for corroded objects, dip a small square of dipyridyl test paper in distilled water and place on the surface of the object. This leaves no visible effect on the object;
- for uncorroded objects, dip a long piece of dipyridyl test paper in a NaCl solution (saturated solution) so that the paper is quite wet;
- electrolyse; and
- the paper is long to prevent confusion with any colour reaction which occurs with the steel of the tweezers.

Results:

- for both corroded and uncorroded objects, a red colour will appear on the white test paper after several seconds if iron is present.

Nickel (Ni)

Procedure:

- dip a small piece of nickel test paper into a saturated NaCl solution; and
- electrolyse for about five seconds.

Results:

- on drying, the following colours may be observed - pink-red for nickel, brown for iron, green for copper and yellow for gold.

Silver (Ag)

Procedure:

- wet a filter paper with 10% potassium chromate (K_2CrO_4) and touch the point of the triangle to the metal in as small an area as possible; and
- electrolyse for one second or less.

Results:

- the presence of silver is indicated by the formation of red silver chromate (Ag_2CrO_4) in the spot on the metal; and
- this mark, if small, can be polished off very easily.

Tin (Sn)

Procedure:

- dip a small piece of filter paper in a saturated, aqueous solution of cacotheline (0.6%);
- when the cacotheline dries slightly, dip the filter paper in a saturated solution of NaCl; and
- electrolyse.

Results:

- A purple colour indicates tin; and
- shiny surfaces will become matt and slightly darker after two seconds of electrolysis.

Zinc (Zn)

Procedure:

- dip a small piece of filter paper in sodium hydroxide solution (NaOH, 5-10%);
- apply the paper to the surface of the object for five to ten seconds;
- electrolysis is recommended;
- when the sample has been absorbed in the filter paper, place this paper in the centre of a larger filter paper, making a wet spot; and
- wash this spot with successive drops of dithizone/ carbon tetrachloride*.

Results:

- pink (not orange) around the spot edges denotes zinc;
- any NaOH remaining on the metal of the object should be wiped off immediately. This can be done with the same filter paper on which the dithizone reaction is to be done;
- shiny zinc surfaces may be slightly darkened or dulled after electrolysis;
- there is a small effect on some copper corrosion products; and
- a lead surface tends to develop a shiny spot where the sodium hydroxide droplet was.

* Note that carbon tetrachloride is a known carcinogen and this test must be conducted in a fume cupboard.

BIBLIOGRAPHY

Laver, M., 1978, Spot tests in conservation: metals and alloys, in Preprints, *The International Council of Museums Committee for Conservation, 5th Triennial Meeting, Zagreb, 1978*, vol.3, 78/23/8.

GLOSSARY

Acid Substance which when dissolved in water gives a solution with a pH below 7.

Acid-free Term used to describe a neutral or slightly alkaline pH.

Albumen White of egg. Emulsion layer in most 19th century photo prints.

Alkali Substance which when dissolved in water gives a solution with a pH above 7.

Ambient conditions Natural prevailing conditions within an area or location.

Biocide Substance used to kill plants and/or other organisms.

Bleed Staining normally on paper and textiles when water or solvents are applied to dyes, etc.

Blueing Colouring of iron metal either by chemical means or by heating.

Bronze disease Corrosion of bronzes producing pustules of bright green spots on the surface (not a patina).

Carcinogen Cancer producing substance.

Collagen Protein found in bones and leather.

Collodion A solution of pyroxylin in ether, used in photography and surgery.

Crizzled A condition of some glassware which is usually identifiable as a network of minute fractures. This unstable condition is not always visible to the naked eye.

Delamination Separating of layers of an object or substance (see ***Exfoliation***).

Desiccant A substance which removes moisture from the air and thereby lowers its humidity.

Direct light Light from daylight or artificial light source, which falls directly on an object.

Efflorescence Crystallisation of salts on the surface of an object exposed to air or low humidity.

Ethnographic Material relating to people and/or cultures.

Exfoliation Coming off in scales or layers.

Fibrils Miniature fibres or strands of fibres.

Foxing Red-brown spots that appear on paper, prints, watercolours, etc. No certain cause is known although mould and impurities are the most likely.

Friability The tendency of a material to crumble into a fine sand or powder.

Gelatin Substance derived from animal skins commonly used in cooking and photography.

Gesso A solid coating made with a water binder, either glue, casein, or gelatin solution. The dry ingredient is either whiting, chalk, or slaked plaster of Paris. Used as a painting ground or as a putty or modelling material. In the latter case it is made into a stiffer, plastic paste.

Hygrometer Term used to describe an instrument for measuring humidity.

Hygroscopic material A material which absorbs water vapour from the atmosphere at high humidities and releases it at low humidities.

Hyphae Filaments of fungi; strand-like.

Infra-red (IR) Light having a longer wavelength and lower energy than visible light. It produces a heating effect when it shines on an object. Sometimes referred to as radiant heat.

Inhibitor A substance which slows down the rate at which some specific chemical reaction occurs. In this text it generally refers to substances which slow down the attack of acids on metal.

Keratin Sulfur-containing protein forming the basis of horns, nails, hair, etc.

Microclimate	Climate produced in a small space (such as in plastic bag, display case and like) which may be quite different from the climate in the rest of the room.
Microcrystalline	A substance composed of crystals which are very much smaller than normal.
Miscible	Liquids which are capable of being mixed together; e.g. alcohol and water are miscible but oil and water are immiscible.
Mylar	Clear, stable polyester sheet used for encapsulating documents. Known as mellinex in the UK.
Non-ionic detergent	These detergents do not have a specific electric charge. The hydrophilic or water-soluble portion of the molecule is usually achieved by incorporating a polyethylene oxide group into the molecule.
Oxidation	Chemical change produced by reaction with oxygen; or the same change produced by other means.
Oxidising agent	Any substance which is capable of causing oxidation.
Patina	The skin of corrosion products which forms on the surface of metal artefacts; term is most commonly used in reference to bronze and copper objects.
Photochemical degradation	Damage which is caused or accelerated by light (UV, visible, or IR) falling on an object.
Polymerisation	The joining together of a large number of small molecules (units) to form a few large molecules.
Precipitation	The opposite process to dissolution; the formation of two separate phases from one phase. For example, when air temperatures fall the relative humidity increases until it reaches 100%. If the temperature falls further the air can no longer contain all the water vapour and the excess *precipitates* as droplets of water (dew, snow or rain).
Reagent	Substance used to cause reaction or to detect another substance.
Refractive index	The extent to which light rays are bent when they pass through the material.
Repatination	The formation of a replacement patina on an object. Generally done either to improve appearance and/or to protect metal.
Sherds	Fragments of ceramic which result when a vase or other object is broken.
Silica gel	A crystal used to extract moisture from the air.
Thermohygrograph	Instrument for measuring temperature and relative humidity and recording it on a graph. Normally over seven days or one month periods.
Tulle	Fine net material.
Ultraviolet (UV)	Light which has a shorter wavelength and a higher energy than visible light. Can be very damaging to museum objects and should be eliminated whenever possible.
Vitrify	To heat to the point of glass formation.
White light	Light giving the same appearance to objects as does natural sunlight, but preferably without the ultraviolet and infra-red components of natural light.
W/V	Weight to volume ratio. Used to specify the concentration or strength of a solution.
W/W	Weight to weight ratio. Used to specify the concentration or strength of a solution.
X-ray diffraction	A process in which a beam of X-rays is passed through a substance. The substance scatters the X-rays at various angles and by recording these scattered X-rays the arrangement of atoms within the substance can be determined.

INDEX

A
Acclimatisation 9
Acid-free 167, 177
Acid rain 103
Acids 20, 21, 63, 114, 177
Adhesives 91, 92, 98, 99, 107, 110
Ageless 17, 18, 129, 158
Airconditioning 8
Albumen print 74, 77, 170
Alkalis 20, 21, 177
Alloys 113, 116, 120
Aluminium 125, 140, 149
Ambrotype 73, 74, 77, 79
Archival 65
Argon 157, 158
Artefact treatments **19-21**

B
Bark Paintings 131-134
Bentonite paste 31, 122
Benzotriazole 31, 119, 138
Binders 83, 133
Biocide 136, 137, 177
Biological pests 7, **11-18**, 105
Blueing 123, 149, 177
Boards 167
Bone **47-52,** 144, 145, 160
Books 31, 61, 67, 70, 71
  cradle 68
Bottles 99
Brass 116, 119, 138, 172
Bronze 118-120, 138, 142, 160,172, 177
Bronze disease 118-119, 177
Buckskin 24
Buildings 8, 9

C
Calotype 73, 74, 171
Carboxymethyl cellulose 133
Caustic 121, 122, 125, 139, 149
Celluloid 75
Cellulose acetate 75, 129, 130, 171
Cellulose diacetate 7
Cellulose nitrate 7, 8, 47, 48, 75, 80, 129, 130, 171
Ceramic **87-93**, 160
Chipboard 7, 8
Citric acid 116, 118, 121, 122, 149
Cleaning 69, 86
  aluminium 125
  bark paintings 133
  bottles 100
  ceramics 88-90
  copper alloys 118-119
  firearms 149
  geological collections 110
  glass 98
  iron 121
  ivory/bone 51
  lead/pewter 124
  leather 26
  paintings 86
  paper 69
  plastics 129
  stone 106-107
  textiles 42-46
  tin 125
  wet organics 145
Collagen 24, 141,177
Collodion 74, 75, 169, 170, 171, 177
Colour fastness 44, 45
Colour prints/negatives 78, 80, 81
Composite 122, 149
Concretion 135-137
Condensation 5
Conservation 19, 152
Consolidants 57, 133, 134
Consolidation 51, 57, 110, 133, 145, 152
Copper 116, 118, 138
Corrosion 113, 114
Corrosion inhibitors 115, 116
Crizzling 95,177
Cyanotype 75, 76, 170

D
Daguerreotype 73, 74, 77, 78, 79, 169
Dehumidification 6, 7, 146
Desalination 90, 91, 98, 145
Desiccant 12, 121, 177
Display 8
  books 68
  ceramics 87
  geological collections 110
  glass 96
  ivory/bone 50
  leather 26
  metals 114
  paintings 84
  paper 64
  plastics 129
  textiles 36-37, 39-43
  wet metals 140
  wood 55
Documentation 20, 84, 131
Dry-cleaning 62, 69, 70, 151
Drying 46, 146
Dust 8, 35, 37, 63
Dyes 34

E
Earthenware 87
Electromagnetic spectrum 1
Electroplate 115, 116
Encapsulation 67, 150
Encrustation 98
Environment
  ceramics 87
  geological collections 109
  glass 96
  ivory/bone 50
  leather 25
  metals 114
  paintings 83
  paper 64
  plastics 128
  stamps 69
  stone 105
  textiles 36
  wet organics 146
  wood 55
Epoxy resin 57, 91, 98, 108, 153
Ethnographic **131-134**, 177
Examination
  ceramics 88
  glass 96
  ivory 51
  stone 106

F
Ferrotype 73, 169
Fibres 33, 46, 170
Fillers (wood) 166
Firearms 121, 149
Fish-oil 123, 153
Flame cleaning 121
Flame colouring 123, 124
Fluorescent light 2
Foxing 63, 177
Formaldehyde 7, 8
Framing 26, 39, 65, 84
Freezing treatment 13, 14, 16
Freeze-drying 146
Fumigation 14, 161
Fungi 12
Fungicide 136, 141, 144
Furniture 57-59

G
Galvanic corrosion 114
Galvanic series 172
Gelatin (prints /negatives) 74, 75, 78, 170, 171, 177
Geological collections 108-110
Glass **95-101**
Glaze 87
Gold 125, 138, 174

H
Handling 9, 146
  books 67
  ceramics 87
  ethnographic 131
  geological collections 109
  glass 96

ivory/bone 50
paintings 84
paper 64
stone 105
wet metals 138-140
wet organics 141-144
wood 55
Hardwood 53
Holding area 9
Horn 48, 144
Humidification 29, 31
Hydrogen peroxide 20, 90
Hygrometer 5, 177
Hygrometric chart 4, 5
Hygroscopic 177

I
Identification
ivory/bone 47
plastics 127
wet materials 135
wet metals 138-140
wet organics 140-144
Igneous 103
Infra-red (IR) 1, 2, 48, 128, 177
Insect Attack **11-18**
ethnographic 134
leather 29
paper 63
textiles 35-37
wood 54
Insect traps 15
Interleafing 70
Insect Pests 164
Iron 120, 138, 139, 160
Ivory **47-52**, 142, 144, 160

L
Lacquers 120, 123
Lantern slides 78, 169
Lead 124, 139
Leather **23-32**, 160
Leather dressings (lubrication) 29-31
Light 1
Light levels 2, 3
measurement 159
Lumen 2
Lux 2

M
Mannequin 42
Metals **113-126**
galvanic series 172
relative humidity 160
spot tests 173-175
wet metals 136-140
Metamorphic 103
Methyl bromide 29, 161
Microcrystalline wax 58, 100, 120, 123, 124, 166
Microwatts/lumen (μw/lumen) 2
Monuments 106, 107
Mould 11-14, 29, 36, 37, 54, 63, 71, 134
Mountboards 167
Mounting 39, 40, 63- 66, 134
Mylar 65- 68, 150, 178

N
Neats-foot oil 30
Nickel silver 116

O
Oil quenching 123
Opaltype 76, 78, 169
Organic materials 127, 135, 136
modern **127-130**
Oxidation 113, 178
Oxygen depletion 16-17, 129

P
Packing 9, 137
Paintings **83-86**
bark 131-134
Paper **61-71**, 160
types 63, 167
Paraloid B-72 51, 92, 99, 107, 166
Parchment 24, 25, 26, 160
Patina 113, 124, 178
Pesticides 15, 17, 161-163
Pewter 124, 140
pH 21
Photo-ceramic 78
Photographic processes 169-171
Photographs 67, **73-82**
Photomechanical (processes) 75, 170
Pigment (prints) 78, 80, 170
Plasticisers 7, 127, 128
Plastics **127-130**, 158
Plated iron 122
Platinum print 75, 80
Pollutants 7, 35, 114, 128
Polycarbonate 7
Polyester 7, 33, 38, 39, 42, 57, 171
Polyethylene 7, 90
Polyethylene glycol (PEG) 141
Polymers 7, **127-130**
Polymethyl methacrylate (perspex) 127
Polypropylene 80, 81, 158, 168
Polystyrene 7, 127
Polyurethane 7, 8, 58, 114
Polyvinyl acetate 57, 92, 99, 166
Polyvinyl alcohol 7, 127
Polyvinyl chloride (PVC) 7, 114, 129
Porcelain 87
Poulticing 88, 90
Preventive Conservation **1-10**
bark paintings 133
bottles 99
ceramics 87
geological collections 109
glass 96
horse-drawn vehicles 152
iron 120
ivory/bone 50
lead/pewter 124
leather 25
metals 114
paintings 83
paper 64
plastics 128
silver 115
stone 105
textiles 36
wet organics 146
wood 55
Protein 24, 33
Psychrometer 5, 7

R
Rawhide 24, 31
Relative humidity (RH) 4-7, 12-13, 35, 53, 54, 156, 178
Repair
ceramics 92
glass 98-99
ivory/bone 51
minerals 110
plastics 130
stone 107-108
wood 57
Restoration 19, 91, 152
Rochelle salt 119
Rubber 48, 127, 128, 129, 130

S
Safety 14, 149
Salted prints 74
Sandblasting 121
Sealing wood 8, 114
Sedimentary 103
Sellotape 70
Sheffield Plate 115, 116
Shellac 58, 166
Silver 114, 138
Silver dip 79, 115
Silverplate 115, 116
Silver prints 79
Sizing 34, 61, 63
Soap solution 88, 106
Sodium sesquicarbonate 119
Sling psychrometer 5
Softwood 53
Spelter bronze 118
Spot tests (metals) 173-175
Stabilisation 19
plastics 130
wet metals 138-140
wet organics 140-144
Stain removal 90, 107
Stamps 68-69
Sterling silver 114
Stone **103-111**, 160
Stoneware 87
Storage 8
books 68
ceramics 87-88

geological collections 110
glass 96
ivory/bone 50
leather 26
metals 114
paintings 84
paper 64
plastics 129
stamps 69
stone 105
textiles 36-37
wet materials 136, 140
wood 55
Storage folder 65, 168

T
Tannic acid 123
Tanning 24
Temperature 4, 35
Terracotta 87
Textiles **33-46**, 144
Thermohygrograph 5, 178
Thermoplastic 127
Thermosetting (resins) 127
Thiourea 116, 118, 122
Time capsule 156-158
Tin 124, 140, 174,
Tintype 73, 74, 77, 79, 169
Toxicity 15, 17
Tracing paper 67
Transportation 9, 50, 137

U
Ultraviolet (UV) 1, 2, 178
Upholstery 59
Urea 8, 114

V
Vacuum cleaning 28, 44
Vegetable ivory 47, 48
Vegetable tanning 24
Vehicles (horse-drawn) 59, 120, 150-156
Visible light 1-2

W
Washing 44-46
Watercolours 3, 67
Wax 58, 120, 123, 166
Weathering 54, 95, 103
Weaves 34
Wet plate 74
Wet materials **135-147**
Window mat support 66
Wood **53-60**
fillers 166
firearms 149
hardwood 53
softwood 53
wet 140-141

Z
Zinc carbonate 115